witness

The Holocaust Centre 10 Years On

Published by Quill Press
an imprint of Aegis Trust

witness

The Holocaust Centre 10 years on

Published in 2005 in Great Britain by Quill Press

The Holocaust Centre, Laxton, Newark,

Nottinghamshire NG22 0PA England

Copyright 2005 Aegis Trust

A Catalogue reference for this book is available from the British Library

ISBN 0954 3001-6-5

Graphic Design: Rock Solid Creative

Commissioned photography: Kay Halliwell-Sutton, www.photographic-images.co.uk

Printed and bound by Polestar Wheatons Ltd
Paper: PhoeniXmotion supplied by GF Smith

contents

Acknowledgements   i

Preface   iii

Introduction   v

History   1

Testimony   31

Memory   81

Education   115

Visits   171

Professional   181

Religion & Ethics   207

Learning   225

Publishing   269

Film   287

Arts   305

Partnerships   327

Aegis   347

In Our Back Yard   417

Ten Years Ahead   431

The Place of Peace   437

Donors   451

acknowledgements

This whole book is an acknowledgement.

It is an acknowledgement of all the hard work, the heartache, the commitment and the sincerity of hundreds of people who have contributed to making The Holocaust Centre, Beth Shalom what it is today.

To all of you who have been a part of it in the last ten years, whether you are profiled in this short summary book or not... a huge thank you!

Thank you for recognising the Centre's merit, thank you for sharing in its vision, thank you for travelling up and down motorways, for giving of your time, your energy, your soul.

Many thanks to those of you who were asked to contribute to this book. Your reflections at this juncture are appreciated immensely and give new and added strength to carry on the work.

We have used quotations from archival letters at times, and wherever possible have sought permission to use the comments you made. If for any reason we were unable to contact you, we trust that the use of your reflection is in line with your wishes.

A volume like this takes many hours of research, writing, selecting, editing, compiling, designing and proofing; many thanks to all those who put those hours in.

Thank you to all those who supported the project financially, thus making this celebration possible.

And special thanks to Trevor Pears of the Pears Foundation, who insisted that we mark our ten years of work in this way.

preface

Not to be a bystander,

To me this is a primary lesson of the Holocaust.

People often talk about 'learning from history' and more specifically from 'the lessons of the Holocaust'.

However, it seems that no matter in which direction you gaze the news is bleak.

Many say 'I care... but what can I do?'

The Smith family are proof that there is much we can do.

They are not bystanders.

It is a privilege to know them.

Trevor Pears
On behalf of the Pears Foundation

introduction

In 1991, my brother James Smith and I visited Yad Vashem for the first time. It was a day to change our lives. We were moved as individuals. We were challenged as people and professionals. Several points emerged with the kind of clarity to help us understand what our response to the Holocaust should be:

We understood that while the Holocaust was a tragedy for the Jewish community, it clearly was not a Jewish problem. The problem of antisemitism was that of those who perpetrated it; those who watched it; those who condoned it.

We understood that mourning and remembrance were a duty the Jewish community needed to fulfil, but that remembrance is also something that everyone who respects the value of human life could share in.

We understood that the responsibility to question how and why the Holocaust occurred should be taken up equally by everyone.

We understood that the amnesia of the Western world was in all likelihood unconscious, but telling nevertheless. The world was not saying, "Let us forget," but it was also not saying, "Let us remember."

We understood for the first time just how successful the Holocaust had been.

We were disappointed that our formal education had never afforded us the opportunity to learn about the Holocaust, to be challenged by its demands, to reflect upon its meaning… or even its meaninglessness.

We left Yad Vashem that day, knowing that we had to do something to bring the issues to our peers and to our country. The absence of memory, the silence, the awkward ignorance which seemed to typify our response, had to change. It was inappropriate, entirely unacceptable, shameful.

It was another four years before the Centre opened in Nottinghamshire in 1995. When it did, the world had already changed. The launch of *Schindler's List*, the introduction of War Crimes legislation in the UK, the 50th anniversary of the end of the Second World War had contributed to a changed perception and increased level of engagement. The Centre was not ready for the level of interest it was to receive.

Ten years on, the Centre holds a diverse palette of activities, with people attending for programmes from all walks of life. Five hundred schoolchildren visit on day programmes each week. Demand exists for more than twice that number.

We called it Beth Shalom, the place of peace. Soon it became a place of education, a place of

memory, a place of testimony, a place of art, a place of academia, and much more besides.

This book introduces our goals, our ethos, our activities. In it you will meet many of the actors who have made it possible. There are thousands of people involved in the life of this extraordinary place; only a few hundred of you are profiled in the book, just simply because that is all that space would allow.

Thank you to all of you who have participated over the last ten years. Everything you have done to make The Holocaust Centre, Beth Shalom what it is today is sincerely appreciated.

Stephen Smith, Founder

v

And we are the last
Day is declining.
The last Solitary Coach is
about to leave.
Let us too get in quietly
And go,
For it will not wait.

history

"Like a wise person, passing on wisdom and knowledge..." Suzanne Cooke, Pupil

the place of history

We decided to create a museum.

We knew from the start that the history of the Holocaust cannot really be told through a museum. It is a history too complex, too extensive, too overwhelming and too painful for museological representation.

Yet still we created a museum.

history

It was not developed to curate the past in order to contain it, to encapsulate it, or force closure upon it. Rather, to begin the story, to inspire learning, to formulate questions and commemorate the victims of the Holocaust.

We described it as a "memorial museum" as it was not driven by archives, collections, topography or a passing need to express a particular narrative. Its goal was more limited – to provide a dignified space to reflect upon the fact that people suffered immeasurably, and to inspire our visitors to formulate their own responses.

The memorial museum is at the heart of the institution. It remembers, reflects and reminds visitors that knowing what happened is the first necessary step to understanding it.

"It bears the hallmark of first-class planning and excellence of execution. So many people throughout the world, many as yet unborn, owe and will owe so much to you in the years ahead."

Sir Sidney C. Hamburger

history

The museum is built around a series of sets, which integrate history and environments, providing visitors with context and content.

It consciously avoids recreating the past, but sensitively steers a path through a series of steps, processes and emotions, intimately portraying otherwise overwhelming information. Faces, photography and personal narratives keep the museum rooted in personal experiences.

It is never comforting. But it makes the demanding historical journey as accessible as possible for a wide range of ages and levels of background knowledge.

5

history

"I have been teaching for 11 years, during which time I have had contact with hundreds of students. Yesterday afternoon, I witnessed and was part of a unique experience. The students were moved in a way I've never seen before. Some of the comments and questions on the return coach were breathtaking. All of us feel privileged to have been a part of it."

Andrew Kilgour, King Edward VII School, Melton Mowbray

"They came to the Centre as somewhat naive students, but went away as extremely moved, respectful young adults."

Garry Clarkson, History Teacher, Rossington High School

Sir Martin Gilbert
Churchill Biographer and Historian of the Holocaust

The teaching of the Holocaust has gained an important dimension in recent years. It has come to be seen as a crucial element in the study and prevention of genocide. It is no longer possible to look at the past in separate parcels of facts and events, each without relevance to the other. Today the evils in any society are front-page news around the world almost as they are being perpetrated.

Ten years ago this was not understood. Teachers of the Holocaust – of whom there were far fewer than today – worked diligently, but saw no necessary links with the teachers of other man-made calamities. The Holocaust Centre, Beth Shalom has been a pioneer in establishing the importance of these links. We can now write about the Holocaust while at the same time recognising its relevance in the wider history, both of the past, and of current events as they thrust themselves upon us.

In my own sphere of interest, eye-witness testimony, The Holocaust Centre has also been a pioneer. Ten years ago the experiences of survivors were, in the main, marginalised. Relatively few memoirs had been published. Few historians made the testimony of survivors an integral part of their narratives. The Holocaust Centre, Beth Shalom has created direct interface between survivors and students. It is also the repository of some 60 unpublished memoirs by survivors of the Holocaust.

The importance of reaching out to young people cannot be over-stressed. Sixty per cent of the visitors to the Centre are under sixteen. This is the generation for whom the events of the Holocaust need now to be taught. The Holocaust Centre, Beth Shalom is at the forefront of this essential effort.

"The Holocaust Centre is truly an oasis in an area of famine. It stands out as a shining example and it illustrates the inhumanity that can be perpetrated by mankind against a people by reason only of their religious belief."

Simon Waingard, Visitor

"*Like every other history department in the country, we teach the
Holocaust, but last year I wanted to move away from the exercise
and textbook adherence to the subject. The pupils were taught the
facts of the Holocaust, but with a different focus in my mind. They
were asked to produce a response to what they had learnt about the
Holocaust, to look at its significance for the present day. It could take
any form; a written account, artwork, a poem, a focus on an
individual or even a song. I was not prepared for the response I
received. The depth of understanding and the reflection in the work
produced was outstanding.*"

Jane Cocker, Sir Thomas Boughey School

United States Holocaust Memorial Museum, opened in 1993

Copyright USHMM

Sara J. Bloomfield

Director, United States Holocaust Memorial Museum

One could say that the 10th anniversary of The Holocaust Centre in this year of many World War II anniversaries is yet another historic milestone. Indeed it is that; but it is more. This anniversary is about the nature of Holocaust memory and how it evolved over the half-century following this catastrophe. For what is most distinctive about The Holocaust Centre is where it exists, why and for whom.

In the decades after the Holocaust, one could have reasonably imagined Holocaust museums in Israel and the United States. But in Nottingham? The land of Robin Hood? On first glance it seems unlikely, but maybe the metaphor of legend is highly appropriate for The Holocaust Centre – a defiant act of social justice! A place where one learns about evil in order to promote good.

This forward-looking vision answers the "why" question. It is significant that unlike most Holocaust museums and memorials, The Holocaust Centre was not created by survivors or Jews. It was a vision – born so poignantly and appropriately during a family trip to Jerusalem – that *all* of humanity owned the responsibility for Holocaust memory. And that memory had to be more than just that. This institution had to be more than a memorial, more than a museum and more than a teaching centre. It also had to be a moral voice – a challenge to each of us to assume responsibility for the lessons of the past and the events of the future. And so it was.

This answers the "for whom" question. It is for everyone – today and tomorrow. Perhaps especially for tomorrow. For our grandchildren and their grandchildren.

The passion and vision, the dedication and imagination of the Smith family have taken Holocaust memory to new levels of meaning. The Holocaust Centre has been an inspiration to, and a partner for, all of us who care deeply about the challenges and opportunities for Holocaust memory in the 21st century.

Robert Crawford
Director-General, Imperial War Museum

I first visited The Holocaust Centre in 1996 shortly after it had opened together with Suzanne Bardgett, Project Director of our own Holocaust Exhibition – at that time just starting to be planned.

We were naturally very interested to see this new venture in Nottinghamshire. We had read glowing accounts of it in the press, and it was clear that the Centre had won the hearts of the many Holocaust survivors who had attended its opening.

It was truly impressive to see the Centre's Holocaust display: how thoughtfully it had been conceived, and I was impressed in particular by the obvious breadth of talents of Stephen Smith, who had taken personal charge of numerous aspects of the project: the historical account, the design, the making of the testimony-carrying audio-visuals – even the landscaping of the garden.

Schools visit the Imperial War Museum from all over the country, but inevitably the journey to London can be prohibitive for those coming from further afield, and it has been reassuring for us to feel that the important work of Holocaust education has been happening in rural Nottinghamshire as well as in inner-city Southwark, and that it is being done responsibly and with the backing of proper historical scholarship.

The Holocaust Centre's work in presenting history has gone from strength to strength and we have been pleased to partner them on a number of initiatives, and we are grateful to the Smith family for the hard work they have applied to this important field.

Imperial War Museum Holocaust Gallery, opened by Her Majesty The Queen in July 2000

"When I was told that we were going to The Holocaust Centre, I really didn't know what to expect. When we arrived, I was pleasantly surprised that it was a country building in the middle of nowhere. I walked in, and it hit me, this was going to be an unforgettable experience."

Simon, age 15, Landau Forte College, Derby

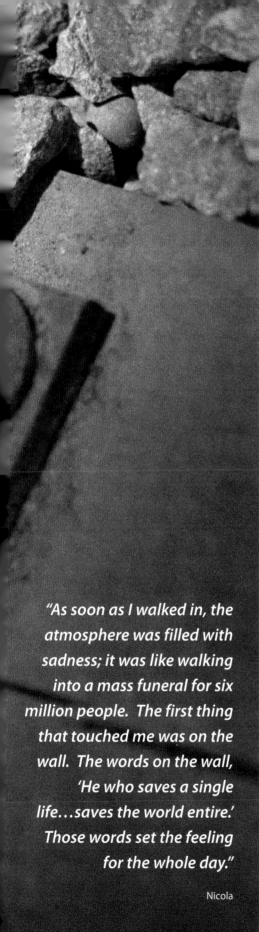

"As soon as I walked in, the atmosphere was filled with sadness; it was like walking into a mass funeral for six million people. The first thing that touched me was on the wall. The words on the wall, 'He who saves a single life…saves the world entire.' Those words set the feeling for the whole day."

Nicola

"It is not often that I am speechless. However, after my visit yesterday I was completely overcome by what I saw. I am fully aware of matters dealing with the Holocaust, but the dedication, care and beauty of what you have created is fantastic."

Victor Huglin, Visitor

An armband found at the Buchenwald Concentration camp. This would have been worn by a Jewish inmate, although it is typical of those worn by Jews in Polish ghettos.

Clothes brush in which Simon Winston's family hid smelted gold. The brush was hacksawed through, chiselled out and gold was melted into the cavity before the brush was nailed back together. *An artefact in The Holocaust Centre's permanent exhibition.*

"I remember sitting working on the text of the exhibition. We had read books on the Warsaw ghetto, we had heard hours of tape, travelled to Poland to visit the ghetto streets, we had hundreds of photos in our possession, tens of life stories. Stephen turned to me and said, 'James, I need everything you know about the Warsaw ghetto in 250 words!' That was when I realised what a challenge we had on our hands."

James M. Smith
Founder

history

history

Developing a deeper understanding of the causes and consequences of the Holocaust is a fundamental principle of the Centre. The research library was installed at the outset with several thousand texts providing a core published collection for students and researchers to access.

The Centre has engaged in commissioning and facilitating academics to bring their latest work to the Centre. Each year two academic lectures, in April and September, provide an opportunity for scholars' recent work to be heard. We aim to ensure that the latest developments in the field impress themselves within the life and thinking of the Centre.

As well as scholars coming to the Centre, the relationship with research organisations such as Yad Vashem, the United States Holocaust Memorial Museum, The Wiener Library,

Lohamei Haghetaot, The Jewish Historical Institute, The Auschwitz-Birkenau State Museum and other archives, ensured that original material of the highest quality informed the integrity of the historical material at the Centre.

15

history

Artefacts in the museum's collection including SS ring (left), donated by Joan Arnold, whose father found it while on military duty immediately after World War II

Tom L. Freudenheim

Former Assistant Secretary for Museums at the Smithsonian Institution, Washington; former Director of the Gilbert Collection, London

I've always been a bit sceptical of those who use expressions such as "the lessons of the Holocaust" to describe reactions to contemporary events. Mass murder is hardly a useful learning experience. And certainly the "never again" mantra hasn't proved true in relation to post-1945 genocides. As a museum worker, I have tended to doubt the efficacy of exhibitions which describe, sometimes with leering proto-pornographic intensity, the multiple ways in which human beings manage to deny their humanity. Some matters are simply too important to be left to museums.

Which explains my admiration for The Holocaust Centre. By eschewing the passive museum-based experience that tends to make even the most sophisticated Holocaust museums into entertainment, The Holocaust Centre makes clear that active engagement presents the only possibility for changing the way in which we see the world and ourselves in it. From the outset, this place was conceived as a learning centre, of which the exhibition was only a part. Yes, it is important to have a place in which, through well-labelled photos and objects, one might learn something about the Holocaust. But this had to be accompanied by classes,

lectures, books, recordings, as well as meetings with survivors and historians.

That, in turn, explains why the exhibition space at The Holocaust Centre is so effective. Smaller than even most of the smaller Holocaust museums, it is nevertheless concise in its editing and use of documentary materials. Lacking the spit and polish of its staggeringly costly sister institutions all over the world, The Holocaust Centre's exhibition is no less powerful. Indeed, it may be a lesson that substance can (and should) triumph over design! This is an important reminder for those of us who spend our lives working in the exhibition field: i.e. the limits that are automatically imposed by virtually all museum formats.

We have learned a lot from these past ten years. Because the exhibition at The Holocaust Centre is part of a seamless whole, there is no pretence that the voyeurism of museum-going suffices. That is why the exhibition combines with the other Holocaust Centre experiences to make certain we take responsibility, not just for a past that may not be ours, but for the present, which is.

Czech scroll confiscated by the Nazis in Prague. One of the Czech Scroll Collection on permanent loan to The Holocaust Centre.

Teresa Swiebocka
Senior Curator and Head of the Auschwitz Museum's Publication and Information Department

The thing about anniversaries is that they evoke memories, facts, people, events and at the same time they provoke reflection on times and what they brought along.

As a long-standing member of the Auschwitz-Birkenau State Museum staff, I am particularly sensitive, on the one hand, to commemorating the victims of mass murder, and on the other hand, to the moral lesson and educational message that can be drawn from such places as our institution and all those others that deal with the Holocaust and genocide.

In the year 2000, I was invited by The Holocaust Centre to a very interesting conference, held in its Centre, about the past, present and future of memorial sites and museums. It was my first visit to this institution. I have to admit that I was very impressed by both the organization of the Centre, its exhibition and activities, as well as the atmosphere that prevailed there. It is worth emphasizing the cooperation between those who survived and the young generations and teachers.

The foundation and activities of The Holocaust Centre bring clearly to our attention that not everything depends on government or political decisions and we should not always wait for the initiatives of others.

The involvement of one family, a non-Jewish family, who recognized that the Holocaust is not only a Jewish issue, but one for all of us, the whole of humanity, brought the results that are visible in The Holocaust Centre's activities.

Due to its sense of responsibility, involvement and passion, The Holocaust Centre has become a very important international Centre to commemorate Holocaust victims and to educate future generations. All the more, it is worth emphasizing that when it was established and developed, there was not a similar centre in Great Britain.

The mission and importance of the Centre has not diminished as time goes by. Fear and crime are widespread in our century. Despite ostensible peace, we constantly meet with racism, fierce nationalism and fanaticism of various kinds – terrorism as well as ethnic cleansing and genocide crimes. However, we believe that only the memory of the past can protect humanity from the atrocities and tragedies experienced by millions of people during the Second World War, that, unfortunately, they still experience now.

I would like to express my sincere thanks and wish further success to all those who created the Centre and through their everyday work fulfil this special mission.

Auschwitz-Birkenau

Photograph by Richard Kolker

The Holocaust Centre library

Reflections

"The library resource which you have built up is indeed impressive, and I was able to use it effectively... The section devoted to Christian-Jewish relations was extremely valuable."
Chris Green, formerly of All Saints' Church, Clipstone

"Without your help, to myself especially, we would not have been able to find such a wide variety of texts in your excellent library... Wherever we can, we recommend it to A-Level historians."
David Cockayne, Queen Elizabeth's Grammar School, Ashbourne, Derbyshire

"Not only did I gain much valuable information for my MA dissertation, but I found the visit a moving and spiritual experience."
Scott Clouder

"Of the reference library, one can only congratulate you for bringing together under one roof such a marvellous collection of books covering such a very tragic time in this century for Jewish and many other peoples. Researchers from all over the world will be ever grateful for this collection."
Phin Levy

18

history

making
history

Holocaust Studies produces volumes of new historical material every month. One of our aims at The Holocaust Centre is to convert new material into accessible resources for the benefit of a general audience. As new views emerge on perpetrators or bystanders, on British responses to the Holocaust, on war criminals or restitution, so the Centre develops its delivery.

The relationship between historical research and activity at the Centre is a dynamic one. Seminars, conferences, lectures, educational resources, films and posters produced by the Centre take the latest scholarship and publications into consideration in the planning process.

As new debates emerge, sixth-formers will be discussing them on their agenda at their next conference. As new books are published, authors will be invited to bring their findings to the Centre. As new sources emerge, they are incorporated into the next poster edition or student guide.

Professor Aubrey Newman

Founding Director and Honorary Associate Director of the Stanley Burton Centre for Holocaust Studies, University of Leicester; Member of the teaching team at The Holocaust Centre

The contribution that the Centre has made to the teaching of the Holocaust to schoolchildren is beyond question. Its unique character, in Great Britain anyway, is based upon the interaction between pupil and survivor, and that in turn is the result of the unique relationships between one family and an enormous network of survivors. Indeed, both these elements have melded together into a family association.

Even for adults, the feeling that they have touched hands with someone who can say, "I was there and this is what I experienced" is an essential part of understanding the impact that the Holocaust had on those who went through it. It is not enough to have learnt about the past; it only becomes possible fully to appreciate its impact through such links. The danger inherent in learning about the past is the loss of perspective, the difficulty in placing events into a proper perspective and context. Thus there are many people who can teach very effectively the events between 1933 and 1945, which have made up the whole story of the destruction of European Jewry, teach them to children of various ages and to adults alike. But it is the direct evidence, the personal testimonies which underline the bald narration of facts, which makes the difference between historical appreciation and "dry-as-dust antiquarianism". Schools and universities, however good they may be, museums and collections, however complete they may be, cannot perform this task of personal linkage. And that to my mind has been the supreme achievement of The Holocaust Centre.

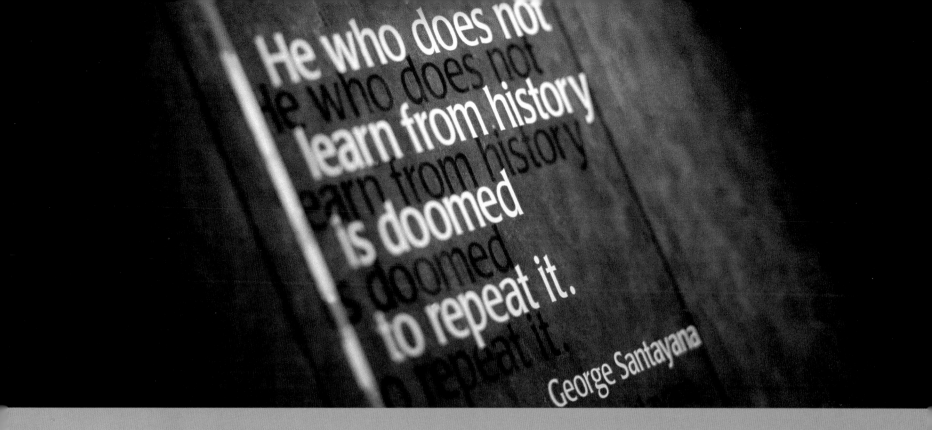

> He who does not learn from history is doomed to repeat it.
>
> George Santayana

Gunter Wimmer
Visitor

"I had the chance to see and experience The Holocaust Centre when I visited my friends – and I was overwhelmed!... You see, I have done a lot myself of finding out about the Holocaust in my home town, Karlsruhe, and am still active arranging talks, study-tours and lots of other things. I have been to lots of Holocaust Museums including Yad Vashem and to many places like Auschwitz, Theresienstadt and so on… So before coming to your place I was a bit sceptical about what I would see in the middle of Nottinghamshire. I was very much impressed and I would like to express my deepest respect for what you have done and are doing.

One experience was nearly unbelievable: When we arrived, we were urged into the hall where a talk of two survivors was just going on. After listening to just a few words of the gentleman speaking to school-kids,... an alarm-bell went off in my head. Wasn't he speaking of Lithuania, of Kaunas and its ghetto and all his experiences there? After the talk and discussion, I had to talk to the gentleman in order to ask him if he just by chance in Kaunas had heard of a certain Helene Holzman (a teacher and artist who had been married to a Jew killed by the Nazis). I had arranged an exhibition of her works of art. I went up to the gentleman and asked him the question. He looked at me as if struck by lightning and answered. "She was my teacher."

applying history

When the German people went to the polls in early 1933, they were voting in what they considered to be national and personal best interests. They were not knowingly voting to become the perpetrators of genocide. Micro-choices led to macro-consequences. The history of the Holocaust provides salutary observations about society, democracy, political policy and personal choices.

We decided to construct a narrative to outline the process that led to the Holocaust. We wanted to ensure that visitors are alerted to the fact that it did not happen in a vacuum, that it did not occur overnight, and that it was never inevitable. In so doing, the museum questions the alternatives, presenting the possibility of a set of choices which might have led to vastly different outcomes.

The memorial museum encourages visitors to think about the role that each of us plays in conditioning the society we create. Whatever lessons there might be from the Holocaust seem scarcely applied if repeated acts of genocide are any indication to go by. But behind every act of genocide lie prejudices conditioning people's choices and attitudes. It is these underlying attitudes and choices which the museum attempts to tease out.

Sir Ian Kershaw
Department of History, Sheffield University

... I have spoken here almost entirely about the Holocaust, which is the case of genocide I know best. I need no convincing about its many unique facets. And I think it is good that so much is done now, compared with only a few years ago, not least through the important work being carried out by The Holocaust Centre, in educating especially young people about the Holocaust in schools and universities, as well as through impressive permanent exhibitions such as those in the Imperial War Museum and the Holocaust Memorial Museum in Washington D.C. All this forms an important component of "remembering for the future".

But I could wish, without diminishing in any way the historic importance and singularity of the Holocaust, to widen the focus to other genocides much more than is normally done. To recall an earlier comment I made: the Holocaust will not repeat itself. But the potential for future genocides is, unfortunately, still very great...

In "remembering for the future", we need not just to look to the past, but also to do our utmost to understand the deeply inhumane and utterly alien mentalities that are likely to produce genocidal atrocities in times to come, and to understand better the types of conditions which are going to breed those 'fires of hatred' which can have such devastating consequences. These mentalities are as strange to us as the mentality of Himmler. But not only do we need to understand them; we need to do something about them. I am a historian, not a politician. So I can only comment on the present and potential for the future as a layman, on the basis of newspaper or television reports and analysis. But it seems to me that the rich and powerful capitalist countries of the Western world have for the most part been content to bury their heads in the sand until serious trouble which threatens the international order (and the prosperity of the West) flares up. Aid to developing countries has been for the most part little more than a plaster on a gaping wound.

Meanwhile, international capitalism operates in many regions of the world in ways which can only too easily be perceived by the indigenous peoples as rapacious economic imperialism. And, at the same time, the sale of arms or military support of recognisably dangerous regimes and highly dubious paramilitary organisations (which have a particular propensity to genocidal actions) often predictably leads to human calamity. More and faster international cooperation, diplomatic as well as military, where trouble is seen to be brewing, is vital. The United Nations Organisation is certainly not lacking in will or effort. But national interests usually prevail, and it is hard to describe it as a body capable of brisk, executive action. National interests will also presumably continue as far as the eye can see to limit a stronger European capacity for swift humanitarian – or united military – action. Above all, far more needs to be done by the wealthy and powerful 'West' on all fronts, not just purely economic, to overcome the largely

North-South divide, in which the intense economic and social deprivation of impoverished populations under often corrupt and despotic governments provides the best breeding ground for the building of genocidal – and global terroristic – mentalities. It is a huge task. Will the rich and privileged liberal democracies of the Western world be up to it? "Remembering for the future" might also involve reminding them that they must, in our own interest, be up to it, and of what might happen if they are not up to it. But it is hard to be unduly optimistic. Replication of the worst genocidal horrors of the 20th century might be avoided. But future generations will be fortunate indeed if they can look back in a hundred years or so and speak of the 21st century as having overcome the genocidal mentalities which had so blackened the benighted 20th century.

Extract from the Remembering for the Future Lecture, 2002

Yehuda Bauer

Academic Advisor to Yad Vashem, the International Task Force for Education and the Aegis Trust

The Holocaust (*Shoah*) was the most extreme form of genocide to date – the Nazi project, developed in stages, was to identify, register, mark, dispossess, humiliate, concentrate, transport and kill every single person the perpetrators identified as a Jew; everywhere in the world. The ideology was based on a genocidal mutation of Christian antisemitic (Christian antisemitism was never genocidal) fantasies, such as blood libels, the supposed Jewish desire to control the world (a distorted mirror image of the Nazi desire to do so), and racism – i.e. the belief that one so-called 'race' (there are no races, we all come from the same stock) has the right, even the duty, to rule over the other, and that 'race' is determined by 'blood'. These are irrational notions, but a whole great, civilized nation was persuaded and bribed into not only believing them, but acting upon them by murdering Jews wherever they could.

In addition, the *Shoah* had characteristics that one can see in other genocides, the most important of which is the suffering of the victims: there is no gradation of suffering; murder, torture, atrocities are the same wherever they are enacted, and there is no 'better' or 'worse' genocide or mass murder. Because of this, and because the *Shoah* took place in the centre of Western civilization, it has become – rightly so – the paradigmatic case of genocide generally.

Genocide, whether one does or does not accept the definition of the 1948 Convention on Genocide, has been with humanity since the beginning of time, though the name is modern. It has continued to be the bane of humanity after World War II. Biafra, Cambodia, Southern Sudan, Bosnia, Rwanda and now Darfur are further proof of the human capacity to engage in mass murder and genocidal acts. The *Shoah*, the best researched genocide, must serve as an exemplary warning, motivating us to apply history to at least attempt to put brakes on this development. The Holocaust Centre and Aegis Trust are, I know, dedicated exactly to this.

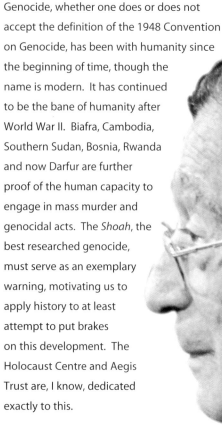

Karl A. Schleunes

Professor of History, University of North Carolina, USA

The Holocaust and the multiple genocides that have followed in its wake represent the darkest parts of the human past. This past demands that we extract from it lessons that we can apply in shaping our understandings and responses to the continuing evils in the world of our day. Unless we understand, we will be in no position to act. For the past decade, The Holocaust Centre has been at the forefront of precisely these endeavours, both in extracting the lessons and in applying them to places in the world where people continue to be subjected to torture and terror.

The Holocaust Centre's primary concern is to educate, and to have that education generate knowledge that will be shaped into understanding. The efforts of The Holocaust Centre in this regard range from the promotion of high-powered scholarly lectures and conferences to sustained programmes for children sponsored by its Primary Learning Centre. Its sponsorship of *The Aegis Review on Genocide*, the early issues of which focused on "Genocidal Mentalities" and "Genocide Prevention", point clearly to

the Centre's interest in dealing with the most fundamental questions raised by the human capacity to produce a Holocaust and subsequent genocides.

By extending its involvement to genocides in Asia, Africa and Eastern Europe, The Holocaust Centre has emerged as a leading institution not only of scholarly renown, but also one rooted in compassion and conscience.

history

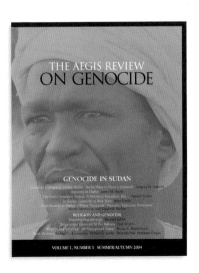

Alf Wilkinson
Professional Development Manager, Historical Association

History is about remembering. But it is about much more than that – it is about making sense of the past. If we don't learn from the past, then we are bound to repeat it, as someone much wiser than myself once said. At a time when the study of history in schools is limited – nearly 66 per cent of pupils give up history at the age of 14 – and when the role of history in a modern society is so widely debated, it is especially important to remember, and to understand.

In some senses history has become an industry – the "heritage industry" – neatly packaged and presented. Or a feature film – where the facts are never allowed to get in the way of a good story. Or a television programme designed to win the ratings war. Or a newspaper article with which to berate the government over something or other. In such circumstances where do people get an objective view of the past, the chance to put things into perspective?

The Holocaust Centre has an important part to play in all this. It offers the testimony of survivors, it offers a calm and measured place to think and be. It is independent. It doesn't preach. It lets you make up your own mind.

history

"A student once asked me, 'Miss, what was the worst thing that happened to you?' I told her, it was the day when I was sent to the back of the class because I was a Jew. Not because of that, but because when I left the class I expected my good friend Susi to be waiting for me. And Susi was not there. That was the day I lost hope, because I knew if she could not give me a hug and say everything would be fine, then anything could happen. It is the small things that count when big things are happening."

Lisa Vincent, Kindertransport Survivor

testimony

"What is not acknowledged cannot be healed." Waldemar Ginsburg

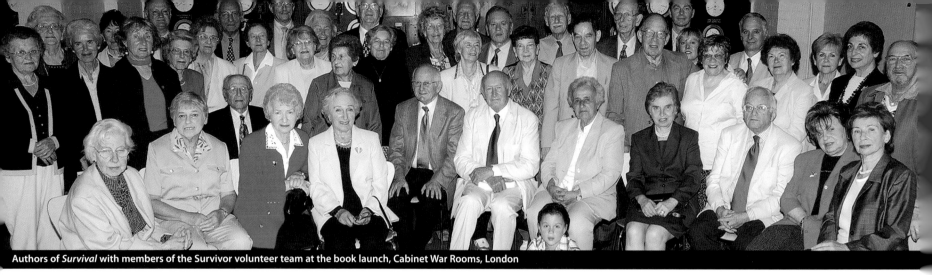

Authors of *Survival* with members of the Survivor volunteer team at the book launch, Cabinet War Rooms, London

the place of
testimony

33

testimony

We realised early in the development of the Centre that survivor testimony was critical to representing the story with integrity.

Survivors know.

They know what it felt like to be there. They know how detailed the plan was, how systematic its intent. They know how the plan tore their own world apart, crushed their dreams and ruined their childhood. They know how their mother and father reacted, what happened to their neighbours and friends. They know what their classmates and business associates said, who collaborated, who did not. They know what it means to starve, to fear, to hope, to survive.

They know what it felt like to be there.

They know well the consequences.

That is why memory, testimony and witness have been at the heart of the Centre's activities every day, without fail.

Marina Smith
MBE, Founder

The Holocaust Centre is much more than a museum.

It is a community.

When we sat down to discuss the creation of The Holocaust Centre, we decided that it should be a place to reflect the memory of the survivors. It seemed that for the memorial to have any meaning, it must first and foremost be meaningful to those whose families, friends and communities it represented. The Centre expresses something deeply painful, but we wanted it to be somewhere where survivors felt welcome, understood and at home.

It was a risk. What if Holocaust survivors did not want a memorial or a place of reflection? What if Holocaust survivors felt it was not our place to make such a place and felt we were imposing something inappropriate on them?

The gracious and enthusiastic way in which survivors from across the country embraced the Centre has been one of the most rewarding and enriching parts of our lives. Over the last ten years, I have personally developed close and lasting relationships with many survivors of the Holocaust who have visited the Centre or volunteer on a regular basis. Through sharing sorrows, deep understanding has emerged and gathered itself around the vision to remember and teach.

Survivors who associate with the Centre are much more than a collection of people involved in daily programmes or commemoration. We have become a community of friends with lasting personal relationships. We share birthdays, weddings and other celebrations; we swap photos of grandchildren, write to one another and meet at the Centre, sometimes regularly, sometimes not. Although we have not formalised into an association, through the Centre many survivors have met one another, made new friendships, rediscovered old ones, too.

As founders, the Smith family has been hugely enriched through this extension to our family life. My grandchildren have received such love, and have at a young age begun to sit on the survivors' knees, literally, and learn things beyond their normal experience.

The next ten years are going to be more difficult. With most of our survivor friends in their late seventies to mid-eighties, there will be fewer celebrations and more funerals. This is going to punctuate our lives with sorrow and immense pride. When we look back on the work that our dear friends have done, their legacy will endure.

They not only survived, but they then had the courage to tell their story to another generation.

Without these courageous, upstanding, determined individuals, the Centre would not be what it is today.

Nor would I.

voices

Survivors speak at the Centre every day of the week.

Every schoolchild who has visited has had the opportunity to listen to the story of someone who personally experienced the effects of National Socialism. Some speak of their time in Nazi Germany prior to the war; others describe conditions throughout the years of occupation. Every story is different. The survivors construct their narratives in different ways, have different styles of delivery and different ways of reflecting on the issues that come out of their experience.

We chose to make survivor narrative integral to the programmes to root the learning experience of visitors in real lives. The museum provides historical context. The survivor provides personal insights. The specific detail of the eyewitness, the lingering pain and the human struggle of individuals cannot be conveyed through displays in the same way.

35

testimony

Members of the Hendon Survivors' Centre visit The Holocausat Centre shortly after its opening

Testimony is fraught with the fallibility of memory. After 60 years, at times details can be eroded, facts blurred. But considering the displacement time has enforced, distant memories are remarkably accurate. Detail is tattooed into memory.

The survivors' voices at the Centre bring depth. The response of the students is to empathise with one individual, one family, one community, one set of questions, one set of answers. Personal experience is the cornerstone of learning.

Steven Frank
Holocaust Survivor

I first went to The Holocaust Centre , Beth Shalom, in 1996 with the Holocaust Survivor Centre from Hendon. As it happened it was Marina Smith's birthday. From the start, I felt that I would like to be involved in this unique venture

My first "talk" was an "away" one to a school in Newport, South Wales, and I have been going there ever since. My first talk at The Holocaust Centre was on 2 March 1998 and I have given over 100 since then. I got wonderful support from the organisation and they made all the transparencies for the overhead projector for me. Later on, Glen from the IT department made a CD disc which I have used ever since – and has been "updated" three times since then. This is the sort of support you dream about!

I have found the response from mainly 13-year-old students quite remarkable. A transformation from a totally self-centred teenager to a thinking, caring and grateful one, who suddenly feels so lucky to be living in a reasonable and tolerant society. As well

as the talk the students have at the Centre, the exhibition, through its narrow passageways, gives a feeling of overcrowding which was so prevalent in the camps.

Outside, the dedicated white roses, which in summer exude a lovely perfume, perfectly complement our desire to remember those whose lives were cut so short, and as I stroll through the gardens, I can remember them when they were vibrant and alive. These lovely gardens give a sense of tranquillity and remembrance, and then suddenly you are confronted by a monument, a statue around the corner and it takes me away from dreams to reality.

For me personally, the most moving thing is the "Terezin Sycamore", which, with its history, represents for me my children and the triumph of the human spirit over adversity, and that, despite all the devastation, life continues as we who were spared have children, and our children have children, just like the tree.

Renee Salt
Holocaust Survivor

I am proud to have been asked to contribute to the commemorative publication on the occasion of The Holocaust Centre's tenth anniversary. I first became involved when I visited the Centre about eight years ago, and immediately felt the warmth and hospitality emerging. Realising what important work was being done there, I volunteered to speak to the schoolchildren who visit The Holocaust Centre almost every day.

I now feel very much at home there and believe that I am doing an important service to the children, who need to know what happened during the Holocaust. We must prevent such atrocities from ever happening again. I find the children are very attentive and interested, and I know from the feedback that I receive from so many of them how thought-provoking they find it. I would like to quote from one of the many very special letters I have received:

"The Holocaust Centre is a wonderful place in the sense that you can really start to understand the horrible events of the Holocaust. The garden with all the roses and water was so peaceful, a place to contemplate the events. Reading some of the plaques by each rose brought a slight tear to my eye –

men, women, children, just ordinary people. The stone pile was especially touching where you can lay an eternal stone to remember a child who tragically died. I felt very privileged to lay a stone there, even if that is all I could do to help relatives of someone who was in the Holocaust, even if I helped a Holocaust survivor like yourself."

My husband Charles and I very much hope that The Holocaust Centre will continue its wonderful work for years to come.

38

testimony

Steven Mendelsson
Holocaust Survivor

testimony

I am one of the ever-diminishing number of "survivors" who frequently are invited by The Holocaust Centre to share our personal experiences with up to 100 pupils at a time, at the outstanding premises in rural Nottinghamshire.

Thanks to the British Government of the day, I was welcomed as a Kindertransportee, together with my younger brother, Wally, aged eight, in April 1939. At the time I was 12 years old. Britain was the only country that made huge efforts to rescue 10,000 Jewish children from the prospect of ruthless extermination.

I consider it an honour and a duty to relate my escape from Nazi Germany, emphasising the initial culture shock during the first few months in England. Alone without our parents, hearing a foreign language, having to eat different foods and being unused to different customs all added to the trauma and confusion. Very similar experiences are, of course, encountered by today's asylum seekers. In an ever-growing multiracial society as ours is today, it is essential that tolerance and understanding is practised by all, natives and newcomers alike.

Young people are most receptive to these ideals and the relating of Nazi atrocities is intended to show the horrors, humiliation and the futility of such policies. After all, today's pupils will be running the country and its society in the not too distant future.

The Holocaust Centre is making a truly remarkable effort in that direction and I am proud to still be able to make a positive contribution in that field.

Furthermore, I consider it my absolute duty to impart such information that I have of the tremendous degradation and terror suffered by six million innocent Jewish victims who are no more able to tell the world of their experiences.

Barbara Stimler
Holocaust Survivor

As a Holocaust survivor, upon my arrival to the United Kingdom, I did not anticipate that anyone would ever consider it important to record the testimonies of the remnants of European Jewry that had survived the Holocaust.

Although the Survivors' Centre was in its infancy, films of the *Shoah* prompted the educational authorities to introduce studies of the Holocaust into the National Curriculum. Subsequently, this created a demand for Holocaust survivors like myself to share our experiences with younger generations.

The London Jewish Cultural Centre undertook the task successfully of training prospective survivor speakers to lecture and liaise with schools and other institutions of learning.

My first knowledge or encounter with The Holocaust Centre, Beth Shalom came when I was invited to deliver a lecture of my Holocaust experiences, which I accepted with trepidation. The support and encouragement of the Smith family will be with me for the rest of my days.

To meet with people whose aim in life is to sacrifice themselves for their fellow man, especially the remnants of European Jewry, is remarkable. To erect at their own expense a magnificent memorial which has achieved worldwide fame due to its information and educational departments, deserves the highest order of merit. I am certain that the fruits of their labours will instil visitors of all ages with the enormity of the tragedy that this museum represents.

We cannot alter the past, but we can shape the future for all mankind.

Bob Norton
Refugee Survivor

To have had the vision to create The Holocaust Centre, Beth Shalom was remarkable. For its founders, the Smith family, to have achieved its many objectives in only ten years is even more remarkably to their credit. In spite of their achievements, they have a vibrant vision for the Holocaust Centre's future.

For many of us who make a small contribution to the Centre's work, it has become a form of spiritual home. We share that link to our past, we remember our lost families who did not survive. Importantly, it is a place which gives us each a voice to teach tolerance and understanding to younger generations.

*"Just remember, whether you are a Christian, a
Muslim or a Jew... this could happen to you."*

Victoria Vincent, Holocaust Survivor, 17 September 1995

*Victoria Vincent was a Nottingham resident who was one of the first
survivor speakers at the Centre from its opening in September 1995. In
the year that Victoria spent at the Centre before her untimely death, she
spoke to thousands of schoolchildren and was foundational in
establishing the role of survivors within the Centre.*

testimony

"When I left the Centre, I thought about the survivor for a very long time. It affected me very greatly. I want you to know how privileged I feel to have been to hear the story. It is something that needs to be done and is done best by survivors."

Lyndsey, Mount School

Clarke with her mother, Anka Bergman

Eva Clarke, telling her family's story

Eva Clarke
Holocaust Survivor

Although you have said not to sing the praises of The Holocaust Centre, that is precisely what I would like to do on behalf of myself and my mother, Anka Bergman. What you, the Smith family, have created at The Holocaust Centre is something unique and of immense value to all who visit, whether student, researcher, teacher, survivor or member of the public.

The Centre has had an enormous impact on my life insofar as it has given me the opportunity to tell the story of my mother's wartime experiences and in a unique setting. In fact, the first time my mother ever heard me was at the Centre and was I nervous!

The Holocaust Centre has also made a much valued contribution to my talks in the form of a CD-Rom disc containing family photographs. This has travelled all around the British Isles and across the Atlantic, and has certainly helped to bring my story to life.

Gina Schwarzmann
Holocaust Survivor

When I first heard about the Holocaust Education Centre project back in 1994, I was very sceptical. There would be many difficult hurdles to climb if the project was going to get off the ground and I assumed that the young man leading it, Stephen Smith, would inevitably lose interest, not having Jewish backing or financial support. However, when I met Stephen, his passion and energy shone through and I began to believe that this institution stood a chance.

In September 1995, the impossible was achieved and The Holocaust Centre, Beth Shalom was opened. I remember the unbelievable warm welcome of Stephen's mother, Marina. Her famous hugs have not weakened since! Stephen's father, Eddie, and brother, James, were just as welcoming and

their sincerity continues to humble all who know them. That first visit to Beth Shalom was for me an unforgettable experience; it remains deeply engraved in my memory.

When it was first set up, the Centre provided a clear guide to the Holocaust. Now, with the rich research material it has managed to source, it provides access to study causes of antisemitism and the active part of clergy, politicians, university lecturers and criminal elements that helped spread an environment which directly led to the Holocaust.

The Holocaust Centre's role has expanded to act as a centre of excellence in study and research, as well as remembering the horrific crimes against mankind. Brutal leaders ordered legalised killings of the Jewish population, denying the victims life, and worse, denying the victims an identity in death, and denying the dead a marked burial place. The Centre remembers all the victims – the innocent children, the ghetto child smuggling, the young and the old who perished. It remembers the ghetto fighters, the partisans and those who gave a helping hand to the hopeless Jews.

For most of us, creating The Holocaust Centre would have been more than a life's achievement. Not so for the Smith family. As the Balkan war raged and the people of old Yugoslavia faced genocide, they tried to influence governments to take action against these horrific crimes.

And if all this was not enough, the Centre played an important role in bringing the injustices committed to the Jews to the notice of politicians in this country who, in turn, played an important role in bringing about the annual National Holocaust

Memorial Day on 27 January, the day Auschwitz was liberated in 1945.

My personal contribution to the Centre is modest. I was interviewed about my ghetto experiences for the museum. The Centre was also involved in making the film *The Power of Goodness*, which shows the decency of a Christian family who hid me for two years and nine months, saving me from certain death. It is also promoting the sale of my book, *The Disappearance of Goldie Rapaport*, my childhood story under the Nazi occupation. I speak at the Centre whenever I am invited.

On 17 September 2005, The Holocaust Centre, Beth Shalom will celebrate its 10th anniversary. Without question, it has become a world authority on the Holocaust. Its immense contribution for all is evident. It is slowly changing people's attitudes and relaying the important message that all need to be treated with respect, dignity and religious tolerance. It is calmly creating a better world. I have no doubt that this beacon of knowledge called Beth Shalom will continue to be a source of inspiration for generations to come.

testimony

"The Association of Jewish Refugees regards
The Holocaust Centre, Beth Shalom as a natural
partner for collaboration and has been delighted to
work together in various educational projects. Our
cooperation with the Centre is of major importance to
us and to our members."

Andrew Kaufman, Chairman, Association of Jewish Refugees

Lady Amélie Jakobovits
Holocaust Survivor

"As a survivor of the Holocaust which took place some 65 years ago, no memorial or museum in memory of that most horrendous period in human history offers me more 'comfort' than when I am standing amidst 'Beth Shalom'. I know of no other place which brings the reality of those miserable years to life with more sensitivity. If it was located closer to where I live, I am sure I would be there very often – on the one hand to learn more and more, and on the other, to search for and receive emotional sustenance. No one can thank the Smith family enough for giving humanity this precious gift, The Holocaust Centre.

47

testimony

"My experiences have not destroyed my belief in humanity's goodness. What they have done is make me feel peripheral, always on the outside. After all these years, I still feel as if I'm in transit. I have watched the world unhinge itself and sometimes when I wake up from my nightmares, I wonder, was I really that little boy who saw all that?"

Josef Perl, Holocaust Survivor

Douglas Greenberg
President and Chief Executive Officer, Survivors of the Shoah Visual History Foundation

First-person accounts of survivors and other eyewitness to the horrors of Nazi terror have long been among the centrepieces of Holocaust education. Schools in Britain and in other countries around the world regularly invite survivors to speak with classes and augment the more traditional elements of the curriculum.

The presence of so many survivors so willing to share these deeply traumatic memories with young people has immeasurably enriched and deepened the teaching of the *Shoah*. Soon, however, those with eyewitness memories of the Holocaust will be gone. No one will be left, in other words, who suffered the privations of Buchenwald or actually saw Mengele select victims for the gas chambers and crematoria of Auschwitz. Lacking any other record, the memory of the Holocaust will be carried in the memories of those who remember the survivors and their stories: a memory of those who remembered.

Fortunately, the future need not rely exclusively upon the second-hand accounts of the past. There are now extant some 75,000 video testimonies of survivors of the *Shoah*, about two-thirds of them collected by Survivors of the Shoah Visual History Foundation. These video testimonies can never replace the presence of living human beings, but they can reproduce faithfully their faces and voices. For the first time in history, video recording has offered us the opportunity to see and hear those whose voices are now gone, whose voices are now silent.

These acts of human witness have an undoubted value for scholars and researchers, and an even greater value to teachers and educators who wish to communicate the immediacy of personal narrative to their students. Those who died under Nazi rule were not nameless numbers; they were real human beings. The same is true of the survivors. Although the individual stories of the victims can never be fully known or told, the survivors have bequeathed a precious legacy to those they leave behind in the form of video and oral history. We owe them and the future a commitment to preserve their testimonies for all time.

testimony

testimony

generations

Memory is shared by those who choose to share it, as well as by those who have no choice. The children of survivors have a legacy which is inescapable, at times confusing, painful, debilitating and oddly empowering.

Children of survivors are involved in the life of the Centre, whether through programmes, activities shared with parents, seminars, films and publications.

As time progresses, the responsibility for memory passes a generation. Some children of survivors will become their own bearers of witness. The Holocaust Centre is committed to becoming a place to channel their energies in years to come.

51

testimony

Nick with his sister Judith lighting a memorial candle at Bergen-Belsen, where his grandparents died in 1945

Nick Oppenheimer

Son of Paul Oppenheimer

Sometime 1985

We all joke about potato soup around the family table. Dad makes another comic reference to concentration camp food.

I laugh, Belsen has always been in the background of my family life.

I never want to see a concentration or death camp, I'm never ready to see Belsen; I anticipate it will be too overwhelming an experience. Places in Europe and Israel of Holocaust history, remembrance and education create a strength of unwelcome emotions, so I never linger but hurry through them – and just don't think too

hard about it. I'll put off carrying out a duty and obligation to pay respect, to unknown grandparents, to the thousands who did not survive... I'll visit Belsen when I'm ready.

May 2005

I am invited by Aegis to accompany a group of survivors including Dad (Paul), Aunt Eve and Uncle Rudi to commemorate the liberation of Bergen-Belsen concentration camp. So this is where they were kept, where they slept, where they died. I cry; Belsen is now the foreground.

It is overwhelming, as I had anticipated. Unwelcome waves of anger, frustration, grief,

disgust. I am a humbled witness to the dignity, courage and resolve of survivors as they recall their memories. Freedom and protection from atrocities is largely taken for granted by me, my friends, my colleagues, my generation... I linger, I think hard, I offer respect.

July 2005

Around the family table my young children are talking about unfairness. "It wasn't fair what happened to Biki (that's Dad) in the war, was it, Dad?" I smile, Belsen will always be a part of the background to my family life.

Katherine Klinger
Founder of Second Generation Trust

In the past decade, our understanding of the enormity and legacy of the Holocaust has finally begun to be grasped, not only by those directly involved, but the outside world as well. This is particularly noticeable in the context of the 'second generation', the children of survivors and refugees of Nazi persecution.

The notion that those born to parents who suffered and survived might themselves bear some of the scars and traumas of their parental experiences, is an idea that has taken a long time to be recognized. But finally, I believe that there is greater understanding and sensitivity to the idea of generational transmission of trauma, if and when the parental experience has been so brutal and devastating.

With hindsight, I think we can legitimately ask, "How could it have been otherwise?"

How can one generation possibly absorb and integrate what happened without collective, personal and generational consequences? If a nuclear bomb is dropped in one's home territory, the fall-out reverberates across a very wide space, and for many years the soil is contaminated. So is it also with genocide.

There is no doubt that the work of The Holocaust Centre, Beth Shalom has contributed greatly to Holocaust education in this country and supported the work of the second and subsequent generations with respect and care. This is greatly appreciated. None of this work is easy. As the *Guardian*'s leader article commented on 8 May 2005: "It remains the war that shaped our lives, including those who were born long after it ended. We are all, to some degree, victims of Nazism and its legacy."

Anita Peleg
Daughter of Naomi Blake

Since I was very young, I listened carefull to the stories that my mother told me about her Holocaust experience and I resolved that I would one day write that story. However, there were very few people who seemed able to tell their stor publicly and the task seemed almost unattainable. Since the opening of The Holocaust Centre, I have heard many survivors talk and watched others find the confidence to publish their stories. I am sure that without the support and encouragement of The Holocaust Centre, would have been much more difficult for them to do so. Listening to these people, their strength, determination and optimis has given me the confidence to start writing and achieve my goal.

Every time I visit The Holocaust Centre I ar amazed and humbled by the work being done by the Smith family and all those involved. It demonstrates to me that people still want to know about these events, that everybody's story is unique and everybody's experience is significant. Most of all, it reminds me of what is really important today, how important it is to pass on experiences for others to learn from, and this gives me renewed resolve to complete my mother's story.

Gaby Glassman
Daughter of Holocaust Survivors; Psychologist, Psychotherapist and Facilitator of Second Generation Groups

For me, the remarkable thing about The Holocaust Centre, Beth Shalom is that it exists. Ten years after its foundation, the indomitable spirit of each individual member of the Smith family continues to pass on its fundamental message of tolerance. Perversely, had their humanity prevailed more widely 70 years ago, there would have been no need for the Centre.

As a beacon of enlightenment in a still-prejudiced and belligerent world, its light shines brightly in the places that matter. For the survivors, it provides a testament to their suffering. For the second and subsequent generations, it exhibits unbiased facts that enable their parents' and grandparents' backgrounds and experiences to be understood, often for the first time. Its documentation is impeccable for the historian and the curious alike. For the wider world, it disseminates information and influences opinion-formers – because we do not want to have to relive our mistakes.

Beth Shalom was established as a living memorial to the lessons of the Holocaust and its victims. While it continues to honour its founding aims, subtly, it extended its remit to cover later genocides. In doing so, it broadened its audience, increased its impact and made its message more relevant to a new generation which can now understand "Never again".

Most personally, the roses I planted in the garden in memory of all four of my grandparents who perished are their only tangible memorials. I recorded my gratitude in the same way for my father's rescuer and protector. Thank you.

questions

Testimony is the first half of a conversation.

We wanted the Centre to facilitate that dialogue and create the space and time for learning together. After hearing testimony, visitors ask questions, which are discussed in open forum.

Questions which are asked include the practical questions of survival, such as, "How did you keep up your hope that you would survive?", "How did you survive the freezing temperatures?" Then there are moral questions of survival, "Did you ever steal anyone else's rations?", "Why did you not fight back?" Such queries probe the detail of memory and the moral complexes the survivor faced, the human dilemmas of such extreme circumstances.

Interestingly, the majority of questions focus on consequences. "Can you forgive your perpetrators?" "Have you ever been back to your home?" "Can you believe in God after your experiences?" "Are you proud to be a Jew?" "How do you feel when you see genocide occurring in the world today?" Over 70 per cent of schoolchildren's questions are about moral, spiritual and psychological consequences.

55

testimony

Trude Levi
Holocaust Survivor

In 1994, shortly before my first book, A *Cat Called Adolf,* was published, I spoke at an International Teachers' Conference at the then Spiro Institute, now the London Jewish Cultural Centre, about my experiences as a slave labourer in an outcamp of Buchenwald and survivor of Auschwitz and a death march.

This was when I met Stephen Smith. He told me about the plans they – he, his mother Marina and brother James – had to build their future Holocaust Museum and Holocaust Education Institute. He asked me if I would consider working with them when the Centre opened up. I gladly agreed.

Before long, I had a call to go and speak to groups of pupils who were coming to the Centre to visit the museum and hear a survivor telling her story. Even before the Centre opened, I was occasionally invited to a teachers' seminar. Many of the teachers who heard me speak on those occasions later invited me to go and talk in their particular schools.

I believe I was the first eyewitness speaker at the Centre when it opened in 1995. As I had spoken to groups previously and answered questions, I encouraged pupils to write or e-mail to me with further questions. I answered each individual question fully in writing.

Stephen then encouraged me to prepare these questions for publication and this resulted in my second book, *Did You Ever Meet Hitler, Miss*? This was done with the help of the Centre's editor, Dr Wendy Whitworth. The final publishing was then a co-venture between the publisher of my first book and The Holocaust Centre. Another achievement due to the efforts of the Centre's devotion to Holocaust education.

I have always felt privileged to be able to play a small part in the life of The Holocaust Centre and have gained the friendship of this wonderful family.

"

Did suicide come as an option? I personally think I would have considered it many times.

Do you think you could ever forgive the people who did this to you?

Do you still feel hatred when you come to Germany?

If you met Hitler face-to-face today, what would you say to him?

What was it about the Jews that made the Germans dislike them?

Do you feel that since the war people have learnt to treat other people as equals?

What do you think of Germans now?

Did you ever want to go back and live in Germany again?

What effect has your experience had on your religious beliefs?

Did you try and hide the fact that you were a Jew?

How did you feel when you found out what had happened to your family?

Why do you think some people are in denial about the Holocaust?

What do you think of Hitler?

Did you ever deny being a Jew?

Did you ever think of killing yourself in Auschwitz?

Who do you blame the most, Hitler and the SS, or the bystanders?

Do you think the world has learnt from the Holocaust?

What do you say to those who still follow Nazi ideology?

Did you ever go back to Auschwitz and see it again?

Did you hide your Jewishness in Sheffield growing up?

How should we react to bullying or racism?

Do you forgive the Germans?

What was your reception in this country?

"

"Some of the questions that are asked are tough... the answers tougher still. Survivors all have their own unique way of answering. We decided early to leave it entirely to them how they answer. I am always astounded to see how considerate they are to their audience. Sometimes the answer should be, 'There really is no hope. We live in a world where it seems some people are born for the single purpose of being fodder for the next person's hatred. Beware! Defend yourself, put up the barricades, live for yourself, learn to hate back, give as good as you get, because no one out there is going to protect you.' Instead, they say, 'I am hopeful that together we can learn from the past mistakes and create a better to world to live in.' How humbling is that?"

Stephen Smith, Founder

Avram Schaufeld
Holocaust Survivor

By far the most demanding question students and teachers ask me is whether I hate the Germans and if I have forgiven them.

I tell them that the war has been over for 60 years and that now there are two more generations of Germans who were not involved or responsible for what happened during the Nazi era. While I cannot forget what happened, nor is it my task to dispense forgiveness. I feel no hatred for those not involved.

Gina Gerson
Holocaust Survivor

Some years ago, I heard a talk Stephen Smith gave and after a visit to The Holocaust Centre, I knew I very much wanted to be associated with the Centre and contribute to its invaluable work in whatever small way I could.

I hoped my story of a 13-year-old being sent across Europe alone to escape the Nazis would be of interest – what it must have meant to my parents to let me go, my frightening ordeal at the frontier, the race against time to get my parents out of Germany and how the race to save them was lost by three days. I found a rapt audience of children of approximately the age I then was, able to identify with me and my experiences.

I was reluctant to talk about these painful events – yet there was also a sense of satisfaction to have held the attention of an audience of sometimes 100 children and to have visibly moved them. The questions

afterwards were amazing and surprising. One tearful girl apologised for having made me relive what was so upsetting for me. Some questions I am asked every time: "Are you sorry you were born a Jew?" "Do you still believe in God?"

The only time in my whole life that I have felt really safe as a Jew (even in England) was immediately after the war, when all the horrors of the extermination camps emerged. I felt then – everyone felt then – that such inhumanities could never happen again. Now, 60 years on, with the *Protocols of the Elders* again in circulation, I fear once again for my children, my grandchildren, for the world.

Rudi Oppenheimer
Holocaust Survivor

I have been privileged to give my testimony more than 150 times at The Holocaust Centre. A barrage of questions are always asked at the end of my talk, of which the most frequent are:

Have you now become an observant Jew?
What is your attitude towards the Germans today?
Have you been back to the camps?
How/why did you survive?
Were you ever beaten or hit by the Germans during your captivity?
Did you try to escape? Did others try to escape?
Did you see anyone being shot or killed?
What was the worst experience you encountered?
Are your brother and sister still alive?
Do you still have contacts with schoolfriends from the pre-camp days, or friends you made in the camps?
Did you visit the people who helped you in Amsterdam?
Where do you consider your home now?

This inspiring, appreciative response from the audience motivates me to tell my testimony again and again.

Simon Winston
Holocaust Survivor

As a supply teacher working in the area, I sometimes receive the sympathy vote with pupils saying to me, "Sir, I saw your 'statue' at The Holocaust Centre. I didn't know you were in Auschwitz." This gives me the opportunity to explain to them that, no, I wasn't in Auschwitz. The sculpture actually depicts two little boys who escaped the horrors of life in a Nazi ghetto for two years and then spent two years in hiding.

When I talk at The Holocaust Centre, I refer to my family's experience to delineate the wider context of the Nazi killing machine, which varied according to time, place and availability, but always with the same final objective. And, no, not just the Jews, I explain. Communists, Gypsies and mentally handicapped people were also selected for extermination. After them it could have been – it could have been you!

At The Holocaust Centre these same, sometimes naive, students are made aware that, sadly, the problem has not gone away. The challenge for them is what are they going to do about it – and awareness is a very good first step.

62

testimony

words

Documenting testimony occupies many forms of media.

Audio-visual documentation has become the fashionable means of creating historical document and is used extensively at the Centre. We use this medium because of the way in which testimony shapes itself on camera, and the multiple uses it has in multi-media settings.

More traditional methods of documenting personal narratives, such as memoir publications, personal archival collections, diaries and letters form an important part of the collection. The mosaic of sources which make up any single individual's life story mesh together to form a more complete picture.

Words that emerge from discussion are also testimony. Survivors telling their story chronologically emphasise different aspects of their lives than when responding to questions.

Presentations, poetry, publications, film, journeys 'home', letters, paintings, sculpture, discussion, debate... all of these 'words' – spoken, printed, published, presented – make up testimony at the Centre.

63

testimony

Michael Lee, who contributed his 'words' in many different ways, at home in his studio

Exodus

For all mothers in anguish
Pushing out their babies
In a small basket

To let the river cradle them
And kind hands find
And nurture them

Providing safety
In a hostile world:
Our constant gratitude.

As in this last century
The crowded trains
Taking us away from home

Became our baby baskets
Rattling to foreign parts
Our exodus from death.

Lotte Kramer, Kindertransport Survivor
Reprinted with kind permission of the author
from *Black over Red*, The Rockingham Press, 2005

Paul Oppenheimer
MBE, Holocaust Survivor

Every Holocaust survivor testimony comprises words. They may be spoken words or they may be written words. Each version offers certain advantages.

Oral testimonies can present a powerful and emotional image, which the audience may never forget. Such oral testimonies may also be recorded and reproduced. I first met Stephen Smith in 1994 and I started speaking in schools for The Holocaust Centre even before the Centre's inauguration in 1995. I have continued to present my personal account of the Holocaust in schools and at The Holocaust Centre, and to local adult groups, on more than 600 occasions.

Written testimonies in book form can provide valuable historical documents. The first Holocaust survivor testimony published by The Holocaust Centre was *Beyond Imagination* by Victoria Ancona-Vincent in 1995. I was privileged to submit my story, *From Belsen to Buckingham Palace*, in the following year. I had no writing experience except engineering reports and minutes of technical meetings. My knowledge of English was confined to the office, factory and sports arena and I knew no long words. Nevertheless, with the assistance of Stephen Smith, I completed the text in less than six months and the first edition of my book was published in 1996. The publication of my book created some surprising benefits. For example, the worldwide distribution of the book initiated contact with pre-war school friends from Holland and fellow camp inmates from Westerbork and Bergen-Belsen.

The book was republished in 2000 with a new cover illustration and there have been several reprints. It has been an outstanding success and more than 10,000 copies have been sold, the vast majority to teenagers in schools. I must acknowledge the assistance of my brother, Rudi Oppenheimer, who also sells my book after his presentations in schools and at The Holocaust Centre. The substantial sales of my book to students reflects their interest in the subject – they are spending their own pocket money! Many students use my book for Holocaust and history projects and I have received many kind comments from students, teachers and historians: "This unsentimental and very readable book presents a fascinating life-history of a Jewish family before, during and after the Holocaust. The book reminds us how much history consists of stories."

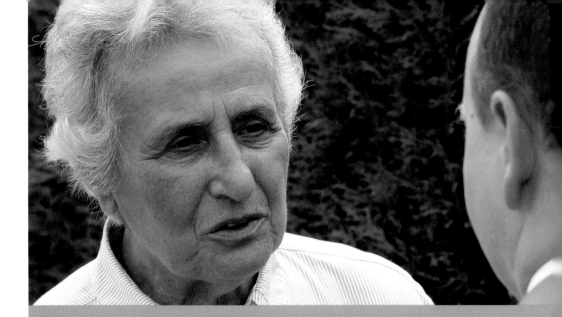

Anita Lasker-Wallfisch
Holocaust Survivor

testimony

I was asked to write a brief comment about the role of The Holocaust Centre "without singing its praises". It is hard to think of a more unreasonable request.

The Holocaust Centre is without any doubt one of the most important centres of education in the art of "How to be a Human Being".

For nearly half a century, Holocaust survivors had to suffer the additional trauma of keeping their experiences to themselves because no one seemed to be interested or prepared to listen.

At The Holocaust Centre countless people of all ages and nationalities are given the opportunity to meet survivors face to face, hear their individual stories, talk to them and ask questions.

I know from my own experience of speaking to young people that dialogue is the only way of relating this cataclysmic event to "here and now" and possibly shape attitudes towards others who may be "different" according to some preconceived concept of what is "normal" and acceptable.

By creating The Holocaust Centre, Beth Shalom, the Smith family have achieved not only a House of Peace but a House of Hope.

Shlomo Venezia
Holocaust Survivor

Six years have passed since I was at The Holocaust Centre to give my testimony. This happened because my good friends Michael and Morven Heller told me about the place, saying that you are serious people, working hard for the *Shoah* so that the memory will not be lost. I know that many children and adults come to visit you and listen to the lectures of other survivors, too.

It was quite difficult for me to give the testimony in English, but at the end of more than one hour, I was tired and happy because my story is very important as I am one of the six survivors of the *Sonderkommando* in the world, and what I tell about is my own experience in the crematorium in Birkenau.

Since 1991, when I began to tell my story in schools and public places, I have been 36 times to Auschwitz-Birkenau with all kinds of people to explain to them what happened there – and hopefully will never happen again. The students listen with great interest and I do it like a mission, with great pleasure. Even if it is like a drop in the ocean, I do it always.

Sholom Aleichem
Peace be unto you

*Candles flutter in the night
days of laughter, gone
thinking of those out of sight
only their names live on.*

*Stars shine in a blackened sky
like a velvet screen
we who watched our loved ones die
walk life in a dream.*

*Lighting candles in their name
helps to create gladness
that their life was not in vain
peace comes after sadness.*

Anne Kind née Anneliese Rosenberg
Refugee from Nazi Germany

"It is easy to look at figures and pictures and feel distant from them... I would particularly like to thank Susan Pollack, who was our speaker... I found her courage and fortitude completely inspiring. It helped put my own little worries into perspective."

Kerry, age 16, Lady Manners School, Bakewell

"When you're reading it in a book or watching a film, you don't really feel all the pain and misery they were put through, but hearing someone speaking who survived such a terrible ordeal really made me think."

Pupil, age 13, Abbotsholme School, Rochester

"Dear Val and Ibi,
Just hearing the way you spoke and the brave way in which you did it really touched me. From the beginning we felt sympathy for you, but the way you smiled and made all the girls smile made us happy that you had survived. We hope you have happier times in the future and keep on enjoying your life in the way you always should have."

Pupil, age 14, Bury Grammar School for Girls

"The Holocaust Centre has a special atmosphere of peace and reconciliation, both so important to the learning in our hurting world. Despite the sometimes graphic images of violence and death that we witnessed in the museum and through our meeting with Mrs Stimler, it is life you are celebrating, and its triumph over death and suffering. It is so important to remember the past events of the Holocaust; for some pupils it was the first time they had been confronted with anything like the full impact of their significance."

Stephen Milne, Head of English, St Peter and St Paul Catholic High, Lincoln

"The whole experience, your talk, Wasted Lives, the Memorial Gardens, the challenging/ questioning exhibition and, last but not least, Freda Wineman's story of her life raised many thoughts. Thoughts that will help challenge our own role in making a difference to our society."

Mrs Kali Case-Leng, Harrogate College.

"Deep emotions stirred as the suffering and sacrifice Paul Oppenheimer spoke about became a reality. The pupils showed an empathetic understanding in their faces that no textbook could convey... What's so special about this oral living history project is that it allows pupils to relate to other human beings who have been pushed to one side and yet are still fighting for their voices to be heard... The 'personalisation' of history inspires a degree of awareness as pupils are encouraged to learn empathetically by imagining what it would be like in a given situation."

Alison Morris, Head of History, Manor Farm Community School, Walsall, published in *Guardian Education*, 10 June 1997

"The talk by the survivor, Trude Levi, was a captivating and incredibly moving learning experience. The links from the Holocaust to Rwanda were very challenging, but also useful as my understanding and knowledge have increased considerably."

Trainee Primary Teacher, Leicester University

testimony

testimony

Bob Rosner
Kindertransport Survivor

Regularly speaking as a *Kindertransport* survivor has helped me to come to terms with my background, recognising and confirming my faith and identity in historical context. My participation in The Holocaust Centre educational enterprise has proved personally most rewarding.

The constantly developing approach that combines archive material created by recordings of surviving participants during their lifetime, together with the sensitive deployment of additional published factual information, will ensure that the impact of 'testimony' access to history can always be available in the future.

Audiences are especially appreciative of accounts given to them in person by individuals to whom they can relate and who can answer questions. Intent on presenting my own experience in a telling manner that is readily grasped by students, I have always felt comfortably supported by the impressive information technology and resource centres within the ambience of The Holocaust Centre.

Reality history easily captures attention and memory can activate future intent.

Accessing history through individuals who recount their experiences cannot be bettered.

John Chillag
Holocaust Survivor

Most survivors kept their Holocaust experiences 'bottled up'. For me the cork was removed following my first visit to The Holocaust Centre, Beth Shalom some ten years ago. From then on, I was able to share the past first with my own family, then also with students at the Centre, schools, universities and others throughout the UK and also on the Continent. In these ten years I have talked to over 20,000 people, to try and make them learn from the Holocaust, so that history does not repeat itself.

My book was written so that the life and fate of my forebears is not forgotten; and for future generations to learn the need to fight apathy, intolerance and hatred, so as to avoid Holocausts in the future.

back ^{going}

The testimony survivors describe did not take place in Britain. The events took place in Hungary, Lithuania, Germany, France and many other countries across Europe. Their experiences describe Drancy, Westerbork, Warsaw, Kaunas, Auschwitz, Belsen. Sometimes, the only way to explain these places is to go there again, to rediscover the past in the place where it occurred.

We decided that part of our role would be to take survivors back to the original places where their stories unfolded. Sometimes these visits have been to explain their testimony to mature students and teachers. On other occasions, they have been for commemorative purposes, for personal family reasons or to document testimony on film.

Going back is a living experience in which survivor and surroundings take on their own unique dialogue with the past in an intensely personal remembering.

Kitty Hart-Moxon returns to Salzwedel, the place of her liberation

as Gutter returns to Poland for the first time

Michael with a group of students during a Holocaust camp trip, 1997

testimony

Michael Lee
Holocaust Survivor

I have tried to analyse how I dealt with it… probably it's by forgetting… erasing a lot of things from my mind. When I went to Auschwitz some years ago, another member of the group asked me, 'How come you are so normal?' Now I never considered myself to be either normal or abnormal. So maybe the answer is that I've erased a lot of things from my memory.

My family who all died in the *Shoah* have no grave. Whenever I go to The Holocaust Centre, I somehow feel that their souls are residing there. It is for me an important place of calm – *Shalom* – dignity and spirituality. I hope that it continues to be that in times to come.

Freda Wineman
Holocaust Survivor

Why did I go back? In one sense, I am not sure myself. It felt like the right thing to do. I might regret it if I didn't go. When would I have the chance again?

In another way, I was very clear. This was to be a return to one of the places of my oppression in order for me to declare, without uttering a word, that I had survived Bergen-Belsen and Auschwitz, and other centres of humiliation and extermination. Despite the Nazi machine, despite the attempt to crush all human spirit, I was still here, having rebuilt my life, brought up a family and lived to see grandchildren born and develop into adulthood. The continuity of our people is the loudest and most articulate response to the attempt to wipe us out. Just by being there, in Bergen-Belsen, I would be confirming life instead of mourning death, something we have all done so much of these past 60 years.

These were indeed my feelings when I stood in what is now the open space that was the site of our oppression. Yet it was impossible to escape the flashbacks to cruel beatings and the stench of death, images made all the more vivid by my presence on the very spot where it all happened. On the plans of the camp I identified the location of my hut and the place where I was beaten within an inch of my life by a Nazi criminal, a memory I had previously repressed.

No "closure", but a painful, yet meaningful and life-affirming experience.

Mala Tribich and Freda Wineman at Bergen-Belsen, April 2005

Mala Tribich
Holocaust Survivor

My own feelings about being back in Belsen on this 60th anniversary of the liberation were very strange. At first I could not get my mind round to the horrors I experienced; it all seemed very surreal.

However, looking at the concentration camp site as it is now, a vast cemetery of mass graves and large and small memorials, it became overlaid with the picture which is ingrained in my mind – that of sitting by the window of the children's barrack and seeing the unending stream of people dragging dead bodies, the people looking barely alive themselves, and throwing these corpses on to the heap of other corpses in the hut opposite.

I am thinking of all those people who suffered such an unnatural and horrific death and feel an overwhelming sense of loss. The least we can do is to make sure that they are never forgotten.

Although this trip was very painful and emotionally draining for me, I am glad I made it. It gave me the opportunity to mourn all those who died and are buried there, in a more personal way – may they rest in peace.

It meant a lot to me to have the presence and support of Stephen Smith and his team from The Holocaust Centre and I would like to thank them, not only for being there, but also for organising it so well, with such sensitivity – and obtaining the funding, which came as a very pleasant surprise.

testimony

Survivor Toby Biber finds the headstone of her sister, Sarah, during The Holocaust Centre's visit to Bergen-Belsen. Sarah died shortly after liberation in 1945.

In addition to survivors going back to their home and places of incarceration, regular visits with mature students and trainee teachers have taken place. These visits are far more than field trips; they are an opportunity to confront oneself with the Holocaust and its challenges in the places where it occurred. The experience for those privileged to attend such visits is intense and demanding physically, emotionally and psychologically. They are visits which leave an indelible impression, with questions that linger for many years thereafter.

"I take groups of young people to Poland because it is so important to teach them what actually happened during the Holocaust. The visit changes them fundamentally.

The first time I went with an organised group was with The Holocaust Centre. I now go annually with Nigel Flanagan and his team at the Sefton Holocaust Project in Liverpool, which also has a long and close association with the Centre."

Arek Hersh

"It was, for me, a profound experience and one which I am unsure how you might improve for future visits."
Phil Smith, Advice and Inspection Service, Education Dept., Leicestershire Council

"Along with the grimmer images of the trip, I have some very warm and positive ones – like debriefing over poppyseed cake, being serenaded by the plump Russian singer and discovering the unexpected, even when we didn't want to any more, thanks to your indefatigable spirit. It was a real pleasure getting to know you and being one of the recipients of your exhaustive knowledge of the Holocaust."
Reva Klein, Journalist

"You have enabled us to have a deeper understanding of the rich Jewish culture in Poland of the past centuries – which, of course, makes its loss even more poignant. All who took part have shared in an indelible experience which would not have been possible without you."
Ruth Sotnick, former Chairman, British WIZO

"How could you possibly expect me to criticise five days that I will remember for the rest of my life as an important experience that has made a lot of things clear to me? An incredible trip. I could write pages (I have) or I could write nothing and be satisfied with an undisturbed memory."
Nathan, Student

"The first time I went to Birkenau, it was an intensely personal experience. I was lost, physically, emotionally, spiritually. Soon enough, I was taking groups to Auschwitz twice a year. One day I stood at the end of the Rampe where the best part of a million people had walked to their deaths and realised I had became accustomed to the place. I had become a tour guide. I vowed never to take groups there again. I never have."
Stephen Smith

testimony

memory

"I learned the value of life and how precious it really is." Sophie, age 14

architecture

Memorials mark places where things happened.

But nothing happened here.

Unlike memorials at Auschwitz, Treblinka, Majdanek, Sobibor, Belsen, Dachau, Westerbork or Sachsenhausen, The Holocaust Centre is not situated on a site of historical significance. No one left from there or returned to there. It is dislocated geographically, unusually English, improbably rural.

We were well aware of this when creating the Centre. We knew that its displacement was likely to be a drawback. We also knew it might well be a strength. We wanted to underscore the universal nature of the Holocaust, to make the point that all can share in the duty to remember, whoever they are, wherever they are. Its remoteness forces visitors to make their journey purposeful. No one arrives at this memorial because they are passing.

You have to make the journey.

Memory is embedded in the Centre's name, Beth Shalom – the House of Peace. It emphasises its purpose to dignify memory and the otherwise forgotten. Its architecture, gardens, tranquillity and beauty do not allow the need for memory and reflection to be lost on its visitors.

memory

memory

Stephen Adutt
Architect, Professor Emeritus, University of Brighton

Westwood Farmhouse was built at the close of the 19th century on a ridge running north-south among rolling Nottinghamshire countryside. The sturdy three-storey building of local brickwork did not need to be architecturally 'designed'. An established local vernacular tradition ensured sensible orientation, strong pitched roofs to throw off rain, high chimneys to dispel smoke, generous and practical internal spaces.

A sense of historical continuity remained when, in 1979, the farmhouse was converted to make a family home for the Revd Edward Smith, his wife Marina and their two sons, Stephen and James. The family's faith spurred them to establish a Christian Retreat programme. Then, following a trip to Israel to see the Holy Land, a new vision emerged and with it a new building. They built a

Memorial Hall and Exhibition Gallery for survivors and students of the European Holocaust, a new function reflected by the uncertain style of the building, part church, part village hall, part cricket pavilion.

Today a vista along the ridge and against the skyline reveals in sequence: pine trees, the memorial hall, the farmhouse, a cottage and, in the adjacent farmyard, a barn, two asbestos cement-clad sheds, then more pine trees. The whole setting, this combination of buildings, trees, land and sky, in this most rural of English landscapes, is a place of utter peace and tranquillity.

Roman Halter
Holocaust Survivor, Architect and Artist

One year after Beth Shalom opened to the public, I went to see it and found it sited amongst fields. Made up of small, interlinked buildings with a few trees around them, Beth Shalom Holocaust Centre looked domestic, inconspicuous and rather attractive. This was a view from the outside and my first glimpse of it. Inside, leading to a lower level, were carefully chosen photographs, objects and descriptive posters which gave a clear and concise history of the Holocaust.

What struck me immediately and forcibly was the fact that the tragedy that befell European Jewry under the Nazis, the gruesome murder of so many Jewish people, was displayed in that relatively small space in such a way that children could study the material and understand it, without the fear of them being traumatised by it. Quite a commendable achievement, I thought.

The ground floor housed a library, cafeteria and an auditorium which could seat up to 80 people. There were other spaces on the first floor which were equally and economically allotted to what is a very important Holocaust Centre.

In the past, in my capacity as an architect and artist, I have assisted with certain works at Yad Vashem. I also created, together with my son Ardyn Halter, the Yad-Layeled museum at Beit Lohamei Haghetaot, Israel, which was then developed and its construction supervised by the Israeli architect Ram Karmi. I therefore studied The

Holocaust Centre with a critical and professional eye. But I could not fault a thing! Neither could the people whom I met there. The Hebrew word for "very well done" is "*Kol Hakavod*" and we said "*Kol Hakavod*". It is a truly praiseworthy achievement.

It was just at the time when the government was considering having the Holocaust taught in schools. I wondered whether this, the only Holocaust Centre in this whole country of ours, would be able to cope with busloads of children, in addition to adults, visiting on a daily basis. Should it not also have a very large auditorium capable of seating up to 200 pupils, to be used for lectures and discussions? Leaving the place, one is full of questions which merit discussing and answering in a space where one is free to do this.

The Holocaust Centre has over the years become an internationally important place. It serves not only this country but people from all over Europe. They come to visit, to see, to learn; and they leave impressed. It now vitally needs expanding.

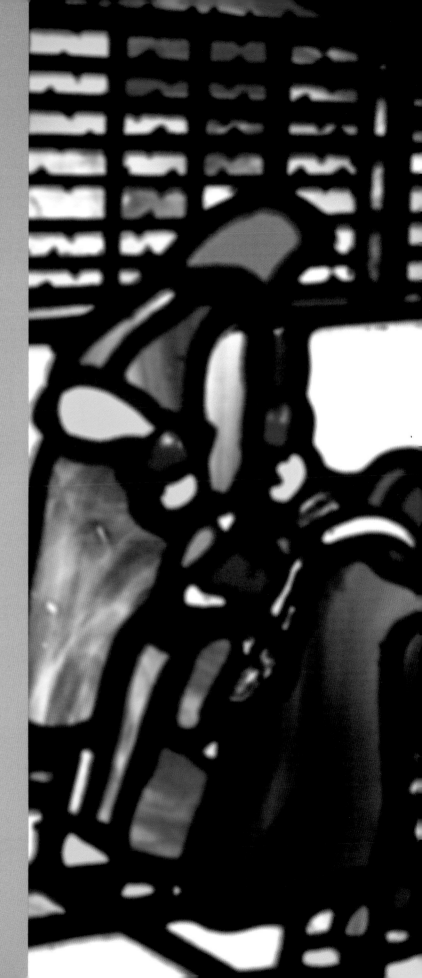

gardens

The history of the Holocaust is intense.

At times it is overwhelming.

We planned the gardens at the Centre as a counterpoint to the historical museum. They provide space for reflection, places for individuals to remember their families, an opportunity for visitors to sit in the midst of a living, growing world and to absorb the demanding challenge that the Centre presents.

The memorial rose garden has become a place of pilgrimage in its own right. Survivors and their families have planted roses to remember family murdered during the

Holocaust. For many, it is the only place where the names of their parents and siblings are permanently inscribed. For some, their return journey to the Centre is simply to come and sit in the garden, perhaps on a date of some significance, and to have time alone.

memory

"The gardens provide both
testimony and healing –
important because it is a
traumatic experience to immerse
oneself in this issue."

Aostre Johnson, Assistant Professor of Education,
St Michael's College, USA

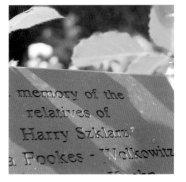

memory of the
relatives of
Harry Szklarz
a Fookes - Wolkowitz

Judith Hassan

Director of Services for Holocaust Survivors and Refugees, Jewish Care

Through Jewish Care's therapeutic services at The Holocaust Survivors' Centre and Shalvata, we are helping survivors to live next to the trauma which never really leaves them. As they grow older, however, it is important to work alongside other organisations that will help to carry the legacy that the survivors will leave. We become the witnesses of their suffering and have to ensure that it will not be forgotten.

The Holocaust Centre plays a key role in ensuring that the memory of the horror does not fade over time. Through the museum, the past is recorded for posterity. Through the schools' programme, in which the survivors participate, the past, present and future are brought to life, and help to give meaning to their survival. This has helped to bring peace of mind to many survivors.

However, it is the rose garden that stands out as unique. With no gravestones to commemorate those who were murdered in the *Shoah*, the roses that are planted allow those relatives to be remembered. Watering the roses and nurturing them gives a sense of care to those with whom they can no longer share their lives. The roses symbolise regeneration out of the destruction, life rather than death, hope rather than despair. In the future, when the survivors can no longer visit The Holocaust Centre, they feel that the care will continue.

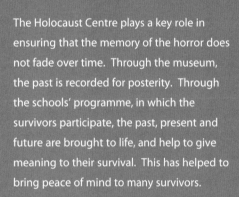

Alf and David Vincent

Family of Victoria Ancona-Vincent

In the summer of 1995, at our home, Stephen Smith told me and my dear late wife Victoria that they intended to include a memorial garden in their plans for the building of The Holocaust Centre, Beth Shalom. As a survivor of Auschwitz and two death marches, she was deeply moved. She said, "A memorial garden with roses and name plaques, with place names and camps, granite and stone memorials, a children's memorial with round stones to be placed on the site. They will teach in their silence about the Holocaust, to the young and not so young." The first stone laid at the Children's Memorial was on a wet Sunday afternoon in April 1997. We are pleased to have a photo record of this moving ceremony.

Several years have now passed and added to that first stone are thousands, forming a silent mountain. It is silent but it speaks to us now and in the future when the witnesses are no longer, and the Holocaust truly is history.

Victoria passed away on 5 August 1996. A small corner of this special garden was set aside where we could remember her. Each year my son and I visit the Centre at Yom Ha Shoah, the annual lectures and other events where possible. The memorials in the garden continue to increase. Dear Victoria was right. Each and every visit is like a first visit. There is always a new photo record to be taken – to remind us of the garden. This is what the memorial gardens mean to us.

Reflections

"Looking at the tributes and adding a pebble to the pile gave a far greater impression of the immense number than seeing figures in a textbook."

Trainee Primary Teacher, Leicester University

"When stepping into the gardens, the horror of the Holocaust actually hit me. Seeing all the flowers and memorials made me think. I loved being there even though it was so sad."

Pupil, age 13, Nottingham High School for Girls

"In the Memorial Gardens I felt so very sad. I picked up a stone. Why? To remember all the children who died in the Holocaust."

Pupil, age 14, Exeter Royal School for the Deaf

"I always find it a haven of peace and find consolation in the beautiful gardens; it was a real joy to catch the roses at their best, filling the air with their sweet perfume."

Hana Eardley

"I loved the chance to spend some peaceful time in the garden – the way your golden stone is like Jerusalem – the way you humanise the people whom the Nazis tried to rob, not just of their lives but of their dignity, by placing names and faces and following threads."

Leonora Samuel

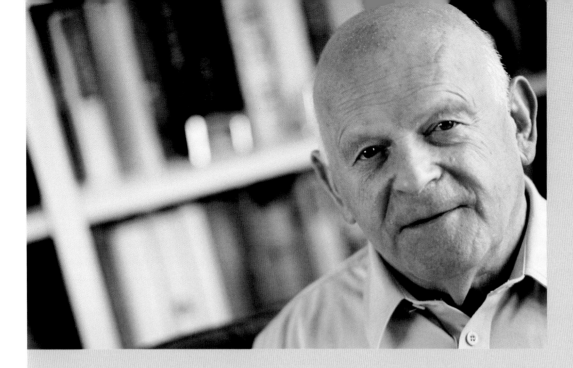

Ben Helfgott
Holocaust Survivor

memory

At The Holocaust Centre, Beth Shalom the exhibition is in stark contrast to the memorial and rose gardens. After looking at the harrowing exhibits, the cruelty inflicted on so many innocent people and the destruction of whole communities, one feels completely drained and lost for words.

It is to the credit of the Centre that they thought to develop and nurture the memorial and rose gardens. They have proved a valuable adjunct to the Holocaust exhibition and an indispensable place for visitors, without which the purpose of their visit would be incomplete. The quiet and the serenity that prevails in the beautifully landscaped gardens are conducive to contemplation, self-searching and reflection. In addition, it has become a place where families of whom there is no trace are remembered.

It is an acknowledged fact that when visiting the Holocaust exhibition, reactions differ from person to person.

They are essentially subjective and depend largely on the state of mind of the viewer. On one of my visits, I went through the museum and continued to the memorial and rose gardens. There in a peaceful and contemplative mood, I found myself reflecting on what I had just seen. Although it was all familiar to me, I could not help thinking – apart from the moral and human savagery – about the wealth of talent that was destroyed which could have contributed so much to the welfare and prosperity of society at large.

It was particularly poignant to me when I considered it in the light of my arrival in England nearly 60 years ago, together with 732 youngsters who had miraculously survived the concentration camps. I thought about our recuperation, rehabilitation, life in hostels, the Primrose Jewish Youth Club and about the wonderful people who helped us to integrate in society. With that help, we soon became independent, began to settle down and established

our own families. We formed the '45 Aid Society with the intention of helping our members, as well as others less fortunate than ourselves, and to promote Holocaust education and remembrance.

I spent some time in the gardens reflecting over those years, thinking of our collective achievements, our successes, our complete integration into normal life and our commitment to helping others. It was with gratitude that I concluded that Britain has been good to us; it gave us an opportunity to develop our potential in spite of having to overcome so many hurdles. We, in turn, can be proud of the fact that we have made a positive contribution to the Jewish community and to society at large.

Perhaps the most significant achievement of The Holocaust Centre, and the family who founded it, is to remind us not only of the depths to which mankind can descend, but also of the heights to which we can aspire.

94

memory

95

memory

96

memory

"The beauty, peace and tranquillity is like a tonic when visiting Beth Shalom. The empathy and understanding one receives is greatly appreciated."

Trudy Murray, Kindertransport Survivor

sculpture

"Abandoned" tells more than one story. It depicts the individual abandoned by the world, by the absence of moral values and by humanity. It also depicts the human spirit unbroken despite its abandonment.

It depicts the story of its artist, Naomi Blake.

It is also the story of the ten cousins who arrived in Auschwitz with her in 1944 and who did not make it. Red roses in their memory encircle the garden.

Naomi Blake, with daughter Anita Peleg and granddaughter, Lucy Blake

99

memory

"Hidden" depicts two children, Simon and Joseph Winston (Weinstein), hiding in the Radzivillov ghetto.

Stanley Bullard cut the sculpture from local Mansfield sandstone in memory of those many children who hid to save their lives, and for those who did not emerge from hiding alive.

Today Simon is one of the survivors who speaks to visitors at the Centre, telling his story of hiding and escape.

memory

Artist Gustav Kreitz and Marcus Storch (right) installing the Raoul Wallenberg piece

101

memory

"The Briefcase" is an unsuspecting piece placed just outside the exit to the Holocaust museum.

It depicts the life of Raoul Wallenberg, and with him, the stories of rescuers during the Holocaust.

On the side of the bronze briefcase, sculpted by Gustav Kreitz and designed by Ulla Kreitz, are the initials RW, in memory of Raoul Wallenberg, the Swedish diplomat who filled his briefcase daily and went to the railway station in Budapest to hand out Swedish identity papers. He secured the safety of some 100,000 Hungarian Jews.

Marcus Storch
Chairman of the Nobel Committee

After World War II, when the Allies questioned Oscar Schindler, two questions they asked him have stuck in my mind. The first was, "Why did you join the Nazi Party?" Schindler answered, "I am German; I am loyal to my country. That's what was expected of me." The second was, "Then why did you save Jews?" Schindler thought for a long while, then answered, "I don't know."

These answers excellently represent something that in my view is even worse than evil: indifference. Just as Schindler acted out both his evil and good sides, so we all have complicated, often instinctual, mixed motivations for our responses to events. We are after all animals and largely abide by the genetic and social rules of the animal kingdom. Our one advantage over other animals is that we can observe, learn and judge ourselves. We can learn from our personal experiences and from our historical mistakes. The only problem is that our memories fade faster than our instinct.

More than half a century has passed since the Holocaust, and despite survivors still alive today, that era is beginning to slide into the realm of ancient history. Some years ago in Sweden the Holocaust was considered such a worn-out topic that nobody wanted to watch television programmes or read about it. But then a big neo-Nazi – and openly anti-Jewish – demonstration took place in Stockholm. Suddenly everyone realised that the memory of the Holocaust was not etched in our collective consciousness. It was gone.

This is why the memory of good deeds in times of evil has to be reinforced, as a model of how human beings can be good, even when the world around them is turning lethally evil. Raoul Wallenberg was not predestined to be a hero. He was not even known for sticking to his tasks. Today we know why my father and his Jewish friends chose this young, diplomatically untrained man for the mission to try and save Hungarian Jews. One of my father's collaborators had had Wallenberg as a junior business partner and was impressed with his intellect. This is all we know, but perhaps it was obvious to them that Wallenberg was a free thinker with integrity and a potential for courage.

Thus, a monument to Wallenberg's memory serves as a reminder of the capacity within each one of us. We do not need to be armed or have an army behind us to fight evil. Sometimes, all we need is a briefcase and a load of courage. That is Wallenberg's significance. He is not only a Swedish symbol, a symbol of courageous acts in Hungary, but also a symbol of the potential for good within each one of us. This is the message of The Holocaust Centre.

"Anne Frank" has become a symbol of youth lost during the Holocaust. The vivid descriptions in her diary prior to her deportation to Auschwitz and Belsen have captured the imagination of generations of teenagers.

Sculptor Doreen Kern's depiction of Anne Frank anchors that story within the gardens of the Centre and it particularly resonates with many of the younger visitors who have read and relate to the significance of her story.

Anne Frank: by Doreen Kern

102

memory

commemoration

We felt that the Centre should also act as a place for regular commemoration and reflection.

Each year there is an annual Yom Ha Shoah commemoration at which survivors light candles and remember their own families. It is a day of deep emotion and reflection, which is shared by survivors, their families and members of the Centre together.

Holocaust Memorial Day is a day of reflection and learning for younger visitors who attend

events with their school and share with the survivors, civic dignitaries and local community members their thoughts on the meaning of Holocaust Memorial Day for them.

On significant anniversaries the Centre also holds special commemorative events. This might commemorate a significant anniversary marking, say, the liquidation of the Lodz ghetto, the liberation of Bergen-Belsen, the events of *Kristallnacht* or the creation of the Nuremberg laws. These are

often accompanied by exhibitions, book launches, films or other presentations, as well as a time to reflect on their significance for those directly affected by them.

103

memory

Holocaust survivors and their families attending the 60th anniversary commemoration of the liberation of Bergen-Belsen

Rabbi Moshe Perez
Minister and Chaplain

The beginning of The Holocaust Centre, Beth Shalom has brought education to hundreds of schools, to the young and old, not only to Nottingham but also to the whole of the United Kingdom.

Some had a different idea that it would not last – because it is isolated, it is in the middle of nowhere, and a non-Jewish family runs it.

The Smith family's determination has proved that you don't have to be Jewish to teach Jewish history and be compassionate about it. Because they got a sense of purpose from this tragedy that happened to the Jewish people – six million lives destroyed just because they were Jewish, among them one and a half million children. We are so lucky that they were so determined, and we

congratulate them for making the souls of those six million people live on in our hearts and minds. And we hope and pray that it should not happen again to anyone, no matter what their religion or beliefs.

To everyone I say, a big thank you. As I said a few years ago, you are true Righteous Gentiles and our community is grateful to all of you for bringing The Holocaust Centre to Sherwood Forest. Each year we come to pray as a community and remember the victims of the Holocaust at Yom Ha Shoah. Beth Shalom has become the *beth shalom* of our whole community.

memory

Susi Bechhöfer
Kindertransport Survivor

"It is a great privilege to be asked to light
this candle here today. I want to dedicate it
to this very, very special place of Beth
Shalom.

For me this place has an angel in every
corner. It had those angels when I first came
and still has them now, those angels of love.
For the candle that I light, I hope the flame
will symbolise and give clarity to the
wisdom, to the future of Beth Shalom. May
the flame shine brightly. May it be the
pathway for all those who come here, and
may the flicker of that flame be the love and
peace and reconciliation that we need in our
hearts. And when that flame dies and fades,
as it will, may we never forget to remember."

Henri Obstfeld

Holocaust Survivor, Association of Child Survivors, Great Britain

memory

After I had agreed to light a candle, I reflected on what to say. On a number of occasions during my early years in optometric practice, I had met British soldiers who recognised my Dutch accent. That gave me the opportunity to explain that without their help, I might not be alive today... Hence, I dedicated my candle to the Allied soldiers, in particular, the Canadians. They liberated me and my foster family, and the other inhabitants of the Veluwe region, on Sunday 29 April 1945. But how did we come to be liberated twice in one day?

In September, we had escaped from Arnhem during the battle for the bridge across the Rhine, to the hamlet of Harskamp. Every Sunday afternoon we walked from Harskamp along the main road to the hamlet of Wekerom, to visit friends. This particular Sunday, without knowing it, we had walked through the battle lines, from German-occupied territory into the liberated part... There was a troop carrier full of Canadian soldiers in the drive of the house where our friends were staying. This called for celebrations! Came five o'clock and my foster parents said that it was time to go back because dinner would be served at six. On the advice of the locals we walked along farm tracks, crossing into occupied territory again. Just after dinner, all hell was let loose: the Canadians attacked. That didn't last long because the German soldiers fled, and so we were 'free' for the second time that day.

Had it really been necessary to return for that meagre meal?

I lit my candle in memory of them, because either way, I would not have been alive without them.

memorial day
Holocaust

Holocaust Memorial Day was instituted in January 2001.

Since its inception, we have played an active and significant role in ensuring that it is adopted as widely as possible.

The Centre has run its own commemorative events, as well as providing support to the Home Office and other organisations in the delivery of a meaningful national commemoration.

The Holocaust Centre has developed and published materials for use in Holocaust Memorial Day commemorations across the country, such as posters, reflections and poetry.

In local communities, the Centre has involved itself in supporting commemoration by training event organisers in how to hold commemorations which are dignified, meaningful and relevant to their respective audiences.

107

memory

Stephen Smith at HMD in 2003. Edinburgh City Council ran a successful national ceremony. A year later, Martin Hutchison worked with Aegis to direct the Rwandan Genocide tenth anniversary ceremony in the National Stadium at Kigali.

Neil Frater

Lead Home Office Official, Holocaust Memorial Day, 1999-2004

The Holocaust Centre, Beth Shalom, played a key role in the establishment and development of Holocaust Memorial Day. And with Stephen Smith's recent appointment as first Chairman of the new Holocaust Memorial Day Trust, it will, I am sure, make a significant contribution to the future sustainability of the Day.

As lead Home Office official, I was also very grateful for the resources, support and efforts of the rest of The Holocaust Centre team; in particular, Wendy Whitworth who developed the guidance for local activities and built a network of supportive councils and other organisations across the country, and David Brown who designed the well-used and regarded website.

The Holocaust Centre team also worked well with other Holocaust experts – including David Cesarani, Ben Helfgott, Paula Kitching and Karen Pollock – to ensure that the contemporary relevance of the Holocaust was understood. I was also delighted when Marina Smith was awarded the MBE for her support of Holocaust survivors. The five years I spent working with them and many others to establish Holocaust Memorial Day were the most personally rewarding in my 41 years' service in the Home Office.

Fahmia Huda
Lead Home Official, Holocaust Memorial Day, 2005

I really came to HMD in a position of ignorance. I was brought up in a small town in the north, in a small mining town, not really knowing very much about the Holocaust. I had very little knowledge about what it was, and about Jews in general, and I think I was really only first challenged when I made my visit to The Holocaust Centre early last year. I went around the exhibition and I started to understand some of the reasons why HMD should be a message for all of society; it's not just a Jewish experience. And then I also had the privilege of going to Auschwitz at the invitation of the Holocaust Educational Trust, slightly later in the year, which really made me confront who I am and what I believe in. It was my road to Damascus, I think, because I learnt that I had been making all sorts of assumptions about what the Holocaust was, what it meant for Jewish people, and I have to say that most of my assumptions were wrong. It really did challenge me, and for the first time, I was able to empathize with the Jewish community in a way that I had not experienced before, to feel their profound sense of grief and loss, to understand it and to actually share that as a human being...

109

memory

"Fahmia's address was very relevant in making the links between the Holocaust and present-day issues around the topic of community cohesion. When there are examples of good practice given, it is reassuring to people that it can be done!"

Balbir Sohal
Regional Adviser for Citizenship, West and East Midlands

It has been my pleasure to work closely with The Holocaust Centre, and in particular with Dr James Smith, Dr Stephen Smith and Dr Wendy Whitworth, who were all involved in the delivery of Holocaust Memorial Day (HMD) when I took over responsibility at the Home Office in late 2003.

The Holocaust Centre, Beth Shalom had been intimately involved in the discussions and consultations prior to the inaugural event in 2001 and continued this collaboration with the Home Office to shape the structure and content of the Day in successive years. In 2004, with their understanding and in-depth knowledge of the Rwandan genocide forming the bedrock of the commemoration, and in 2005 through their work with survivors, the team at the Centre have been indispensable in producing poignant and contemporary commemorations.

The Holocaust Centre has also been responsible for the year-on-year growth in local activity around HMD through the auspices of Dr Whitworth, who produced the local activities' packs for HMD over the last three years. This is an integral element of the support infrastructure for the national event, as is the website, for which the Centre was also responsible until 2004.

Last year, I had the privilege of attending the seminar for local practitioners to interpret the "Survivors and Liberation" theme and explore how HMD can be a tool for community cohesion and awareness-raising of issues on racism and intolerance. This has been invaluable in helping people with the practical application of the concept, which has changed annually to reflect different facets of the Holocaust.

Now that the responsibility for HMD has passed to a newly-created charitable trust (of which Stephen Smith is the Chair), I feel confident that the expertise and creativity that The Holocaust Centre has brought to HMD will continue and invigorate and nurture this important event in the national calendar.

"The Council has been holding a Civic Event on Holocaust Memorial Day since 2002 and we are very grateful for the excellent advice and support The Holocaust Centre, Beth Shalom has given us in arranging these events. The seminars run by the Centre have been particularly helpful, acting as conduits for developing ideas and exchanging good practice."

Bob Wearing, Head of Members' Services,
London Borough of Hounslow

110

memory

Wendy Whitworth, Holocaust Memorial Day Local Activities Coordinator

111

memory

"It was particularly relevant to be at The Holocaust Centre just before 27th January 2005 to prepare for the 60th anniversary of the liberation of Auschwitz, to listen to survivors, be inspired by the Smith brothers, to have access to material, both written and on video, and above all to exchange views and experiences with others involved in preparing for Holocaust Memorial Day. It was a privilege to take part in the seminar and it gave me renewed enthusiasm and courage to continue organising the event for the London Borough of Merton."

Helen Bramsted

General Vaslily Petrenko, Red Army liberator of Auschwitz

Karen Pollock

Chief Executive, Holocaust Educational Trust

We continue to be delighted to work alongside The Holocaust Centre, Beth Shalom to ensure Holocaust Memorial Day is commemorated throughout the country in schools, local communities, colleges and universities.

It is so important that Holocaust Memorial Day is marked, not only by a national event, by our politicians and our community leaders, but also at a grassroots level. By working together we can ensure that all sections of society are learning about the Holocaust and its relevance today.

Cooperation between our organisations enables us to reach many more people, which results in increased awareness and activity to commemorate and educate about the Holocaust.

Lord Greville Janner, who as Chairman of the Holocaust Educational Trust recognised early the value of The Holocaust Centre and awarded Stephen Smith the Holocaust Educational Trust Award, along with Lord Bramall and Hugo Gryn (posthumously). From left: Lord Bramall, Greville Janner, Stephen Smith, Jackie Gryn

Major Dick Williams, liberator of Bergen-Belsen with Belsen survivor Anita Lasker-Wallfisch

Sean Silver

Community Leadership Manager, Northampton Borough Council

In Northampton, Holocaust Memorial Day is seen not only as a programme of activities focusing on 27th January, but ranging around it, engaging a wide variety of local communities.

The Holocaust Centre has proved to be an inspiration and significant support in developing our local programme. The materials produced have been visually stimulating and also thoughtfully produced, such as documentaries lasting under 15 minutes, which can easily be incorporated into public events. Stephen Smith has also supported us directly, being our Keynote Speaker in 2003 at our annual Holocaust Memorial Day lecture hosted by our local synagogue.

We have always engaged young people in our memorial programme and visits to the Centre have been tailored to our needs, from exploring literature in the library to workshops developing memorial events.

We have now become established in the local calendar. Each year's programme of events has been well received, and we now have an established Steering Group representing local faith communities, as well as our Race Equality Council, Lesbian, Gay and Bisexual Alliance and Ability Northants.

David Goldberg
Rabbi Emeritus, St John's Wood Synagogue

Perhaps it was convenient, a facile excuse, to label the Holocaust as a unique occurrence. Unique means one of its kind. Describing the Holocaust as 'unique' lets us off the hook, it suggests that it was an extraordinary aberration, in no way typical or symptomatic of human behaviour. Certainly the Holocaust was unique in its use of science and technology to industrialise mass murder, so much more efficient than firing squads or haphazard massacre. But the motives behind the Holocaust – a generalised hatred of a particular people who are held responsible for all the world's ills and then steadily dehumanised, reduced to objects, as a prelude to disposing of them as one would of vermin – such motives have been all too common throughout history in our response to the alien, the outsider, the scapegoat.

But that does not absolve us from our responsibility to do whatever we can to fight against prejudice and discrimination, whether against an individual or whole communities. On the wall of this lecture theatre at Beth Shalom from where today's service is being transmitted are words taken from the rabbinic literature known as the Talmud. They read: 'He who saves a single life, saves the world entire.' They are inspiring words, encouraging us to positive action, which is why the altogether more sombre second half of the quotation is not included. That goes: 'And he who destroys a single life, destroys the world entire.'

To save or to destroy: that has always been the choice facing human beings. Holocaust Memorial Day is a necessary reminder of the duty we owe to our own and all peoples to learn from a terrible past and not repeat it.

BBC Radio Four's Sunday Worship programme being recorded at The Holocaust Centre to mark Holocaust Memorial Day 2005. Guest speaker was Rabbi David Goldberg.

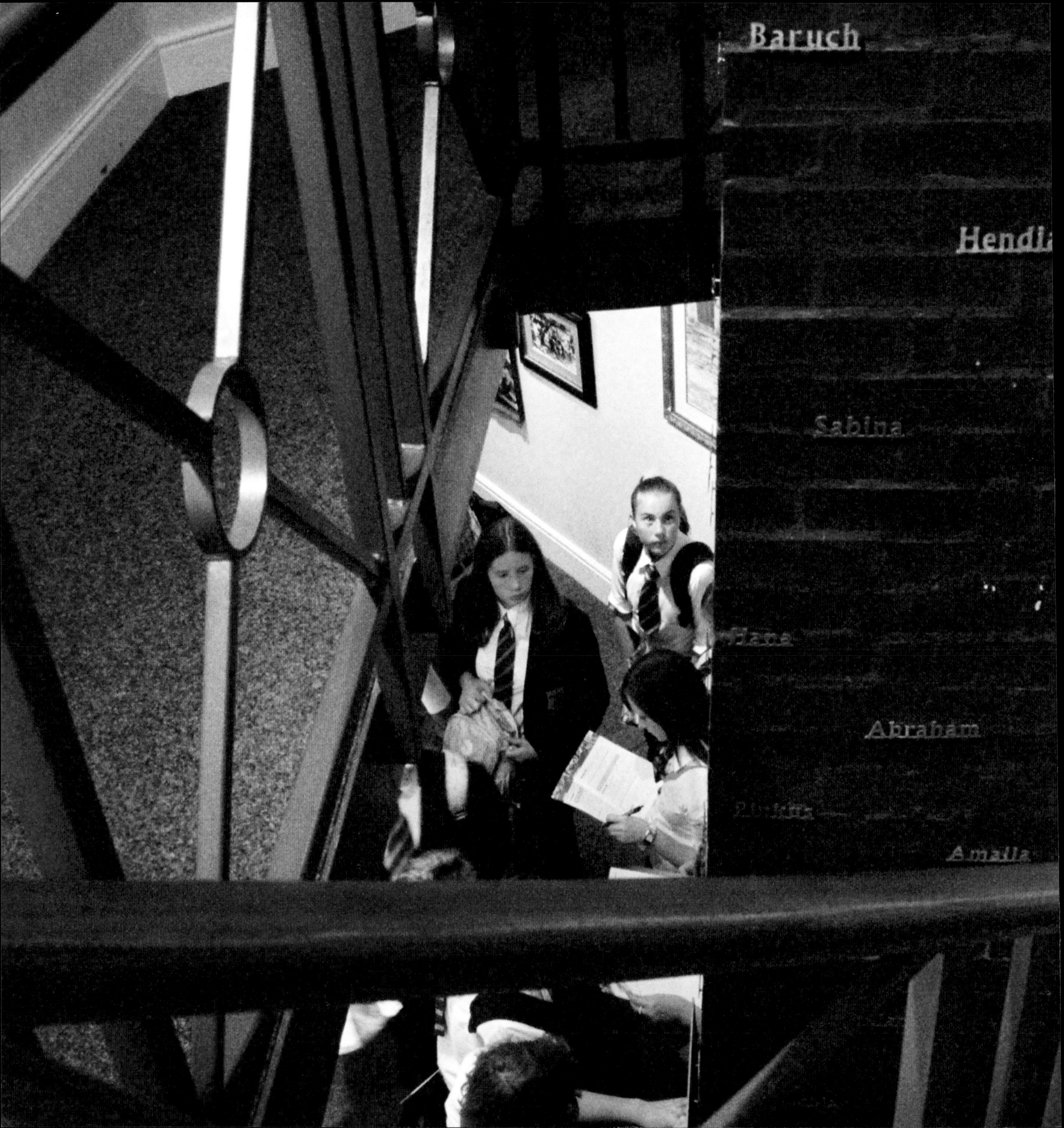
Baruch
Sabina
Abraham
Amalia

education

"We cannot understand genocide unless our hearts have been broken. This is a valid piece of learning."
Mark Chater

education
the place of

We first opened The Holocaust Centre as a memorial and education centre. We did not publish opening hours for the general public or describe the Centre as a museum. Its principal function was as a place of learning for young people to attend as part of their formal education.

The emphasis we place on education hinges on the assumption that learning how to approach the Holocaust, to formulate questions and begin the struggle with its difficult dilemmas are best done while young.

The experience of the Centre working with young people every day has been a very positive one. The museum and its programme of talks provide the framework for activities. Within this setting, students find their own questions, dilemmas and dialogue. Each day is entirely different from the next, because students make their visit personal in their own unique way.

Education is central to the Centre's life and activity. Some 500 schoolchildren a week have visited the Centre to attend day seminars since its opening. Our only regret is that we are not yet able to accommodate more.

education

Departure

Separation, devastation
The devastation of separation
Hunger, cold, discrimination
Segregation and exploitation.

Strutting, proud, confrontation
Resentment, enmity and humiliation
Realisation, termination
Extermination.

Pupil, age 13, Abbey Grange Church of England School

secondary

Since the early 1990s, the Holocaust has been a part of the National Curriculum for schools in England. It has typically been taught in Year 9 when pupils are 13-14 years old. Usually this is as part of their studies in history. The Holocaust is also taught in secondary schools in religious education, literature and citizenship, among other curriculum areas.

The demand for the Centre to support pupils engaged in these various curriculum areas has been noticeable. The majority of the school visits to the Centre are by Year 9 pupils, although very few come under the auspices of a single discipline. Teaching staff typically cover a wide range of disciplines and explore the Holocaust as a cross-curricular activity. An increasing number of schools view their visit to the Centre as an extra-curricular activity for the benefit of their students as young adults. A number of schools insist that every pupil visits the Centre as a part of their learning experience at the school.

The key issue for us is how to deliver a meaningful educational programme in a single day that will benefit the pupils over an extended period. To facilitate this, the visit is usually developed into a programme with the school, so that activities which take place in school prior to and following the visit complement the day, thus extending its effectiveness over a longer period of time.

Balbir Sohal
Regional Adviser for Citizenship CPD, DfES

"The Holocaust must be understood and *remembered*. By preserving that memory we assume our responsibility to *actively transmit* this knowledge in every generation to the children."[1]

Itzhak Tatelbaum's words remind us as educators that we have the responsibility to develop this important area of work in schools with students. Teachers do need support to "actively transmit" this difficult and complex subject and here in the West Midlands we have been very fortunate that The Holocaust Centre, Beth Shalom has allowed students and teachers the opportunity to study, access training, participate and reflect on the lessons of the Holocaust.

The Centre offers a positive active learning environment and its educational work has had a ripple effect, from providing INSET opportunities to teachers in order to raise the profile of teaching about the Holocaust to hosting regular conferences for sixth-form students focusing on personal testimonies of Holocaust survivors, the latter of which has made a deep and profound impact on many of the young people and adults who took part. Looking back over the personal and professional relationship with the Centre, the most memorable event was the planting of a rose in remembrance of Regina Franks, a survivor. Regina will be remembered and her memory will live on for Coventry children.

Recent work with the Centre has included the use of many of the excellent resources, many of which have stimulated work on other crimes against humanity, in particular genocide. At this present time this is particularly pertinent and issues of racism, prejudice and the abuse of power do need to be explored with young people and adults. A centre such as Beth Shalom allows these issues to be explored as part of the study of human society, in so doing allowing us to examine ourselves.

1. Itzhak B. Tatelbaum, *Through Our Eyes – Children Witness the Holocaust*, Yad Vashem, 2004

"I was arguing with my Dad the other day and I stopped and thought about my experiences at The Holocaust Centre and thought, 'Why argue?' I should be enjoying my time with the people who are dear to me."

Pupil, age 13, Caistor Grammar School

Susan Pollack
Holocaust Survivor

When I first addressed a group of students at The Holocaust Centre, almost at the opening of the Centre, I had no clear definition of the purpose nor of the interaction that only gradually unfolded, and made me realize the importance of Holocaust education.

Secondary education includes as part of the Second World War an overview of the Holocaust. Factual information is essential before a personal survivor's own experience is told, or the knowledge gained will be limited and perhaps unsatisfactory for the survivor. Issues on related subjects, i.e. democracy, the power of propaganda and everyday conduct of living, morality and so on, became topics that were discussed later.

My own role in speaking was that my experience was valued as a living witness, and thereby the students listened and absorbed history that was still current and part of their lives. How do students now experience the painful effects of persecution or bullying? By placing my own tragic past in their lives, I hoped they would also become witnesses to what may result in an unequal society.

The responses to my talk have created stimulating enquiries. I have felt that some of the students will further their studies of the Holocaust with greater interest and enthusiasm.

Deirdre Burke
Student Support Coordinator, Religious Studies, University of Wolverhampton

The Holocaust Centre, Beth Shalom has made a significant contribution to secondary education by responding to research concerns and developing a pedagogical approach to teaching about atrocity. During their visit pupils experience the historical museum, gain some understanding of the communal dimension of the Holocaust in the memorial gardens, and encounter the Holocaust personally in their encounter with a survivor.

These experiences are pedagogically supportive in linking facts, feelings and actions. The historical museum anchors the Holocaust in pupils' historical consciousness, with exhibits taking pupils on a journey through a range of Holocaust experiences which are linked to contemporary survivors. The talk by a survivor brings the past events into their present day, often making a link to contemporary concerns. This living contact with the Holocaust clearly makes the Holocaust a part of their lives in a way that other historical study cannot, as survivors can "tell it like it was".

The structured mix of inputs helps pupils turn the experience into learning:

completing the student workbook provides a sound historical foundation, the emotional impact of the Holocaust is developed through the personal encounter with a survivor, and the space to reflect and discuss issues with friends is evident in the memorial gardens. The dedications in the memorial gardens, "For those who have no one to remember them" had such an impact on Sinead that she said, "I don't think I will ever forget my visit." A pupil made an analogy between the nurture of plants in the memorial gardens and the way The Holocaust Centre, through the museum and the survivor talk, keeps the memory of the Holocaust alive.

A rough estimate of the number of pupils who have visited the Centre puts the figure close to 200,000. This figure, whilst substantial, is but a small percentage of pupils who have been influenced by the Centre, either directly through a visit, or by hearing about it from friends, or using the vast range of book and electronic learning materials.

"I don't think I can put into words how upset, angry and confused I am, but when I ask myself if I'd stand up against the leading power of my country, I'd probably not do it. This proves that unless we are prepared to stand up for what we believe is right, then history will repeat itself."

Rebecca, age 14, Mayflower School

122

education

education

"It makes you wonder what you would do in that situation. How would you feel and what side of your personality would come through? You ask yourself, 'Am I strong enough?'"

Matthew, age 13, Caistor Grammar School

Shulamit Imber

Pedagogical Director of the International School for Holocaust Studies, Yad Vashem, Israel

During my several visits to The Holocaust Centre, Beth Shalom, I have always been impressed with the commitment of their staff to foster an educational experience and dialogue with teachers and students. As leaders in Holocaust education, we place an emphasis on how to instil moral values through learning about individuals who had names, voices and faces. An in-depth inquiry about the identities of the victims should also not be limited to their pre-war lives and Holocaust experiences. We also need to examine the post-war journeys of the survivors – their return to life. After all, how did they rebuild their lives in the dark shadow of the Holocaust? By carefully reading their diaries, letters and memoirs, we gain a glimpse into their life stories.

Needless to say, we must be vigilant in ensuring that Holocaust education will be based on historical accuracy, but we also need to guide our students to question how the destruction of European Jewry occurred in a modern, western world and consider universal questions about how racial hatred and indifference endanger society as a whole.

The observations, thoughts, poems, hopes and dreams of the victims and survivors are very important pedagogical tools for teachers, and The Holocaust Centre has developed excellent educational programmes and materials in this direction. Their didactic methods and educational materials will hopefully provide additional teachers in Great Britain and around the world with invaluable skills that will better prepare them to teach the Holocaust to young minds in the 21st century.

Phil Smith

Adviser/Inspector, Leicestershire County Council Education Department

The Holocaust Centre has an extraordinary and special place in the field of anti-racist education and it has been our privilege to work in partnership with them over the past ten years. As an LEA with a strong commitment to race equality and the opposition of racism, many Leicestershire schools have benefited from their education programme and, in particular, the opportunity for Leicestershire students to hear survivor testimony.

The education work of the Centre is never, and was not designed to be, comfortable. Confronting young people with the horrors of the Holocaust is not easy, but the approach taken at the Centre, which focuses on the tragic real-life experiences of real people, rather than overwhelming learners with images of mass murder and destruction, is very effective. This helps students to learn to empathise, to understand the possible process of moving "from prejudice to genocide" and develops a strong commitment in many students to ensure that this never happens again.

A further and key development in the programme at the Centre is to help young people engage with the idea that Hitler's war against the Jews has mirrors in modern history and connects to Rwanda, the Balkans and Sudan, amongst others. The understanding of this continuum, however uncomfortable and challenging for young people, ensures they do not see the Holocaust as an isolated historical event, but as a continuing feature of some societies' mistreatment of their citizens, which needs to be challenged at a personal, local, national and global level.

"If I ever hear a racist comment, I will tell them what little remarks lead to."

Nisha, age 14

education

"

I feel that I am lucky to be alive. That sounds like a cliché but I now know when I say 'I have had a bad day' that I don't really know what that means.
Daisy, age 13, Eaton Bank School

I left at the end of the day with the feeling that we should all make our own effort, however small, to prevent anything like the Holocaust happening again.
Alexandra, age 13, Nottingham High School for Girls

It made me think how lucky I am. To know when I wake up I will be with my Mum and my sister. To know I am going to be safe and that I am not going to be judged for what I believe in.
Sarah, age 13, Caistor Grammar School

I will no longer take my life for granted.
Tom, age 13, Oakbank Sports College

This visit made me realise that my actions can contribute to a big thing, so I have to think carefully about what I do before I do it.
Emily, age 13, Oakbank Sports College

I now realise how lucky we are today and how much we should respect people and how important life is.
Kirby, age 17, Hucknall Life Skills student

"

Kevin James

Head of Humanities and Head of Religious Studies,
The Ecclesbourne School, Duffield, Derbyshire

I recall The Ecclesbourne School being one of the first secondary schools to visit The Holocaust Centre, Beth Shalom shortly after it opened. We brought along all our Year 9 pupils and originally just Humanities Faculty staff to experience this new centre's atmosphere, educational value and the work it was trying to promote in those early days. I can't remember any of our pupils not being struck by either the excellent exhibition, friendliness of the staff and above all the valuable witness testimony when we entered the main hall to hear a survivor speak.

Once again, the importance of the Centre came home even more to me quite recently when I met a former pupil who, after the usual formalities of "Hi Mr James, how are you doing?" said, "Do you still visit Beth Shalom? That was the one trip I can really remember and above all, how much it affected me and my classmates and I shall never forget the experience." This former pupil is now 24 and it was immediately clear how the Centre had had a profound influence on this young person's life. She went on to say how she had told all her family about the visit and how it will stay with her for the rest of her life. Just think, if that is only one former pupil from one school, what the magnitude of the Centre's work is when you multiply it by all the pupils that have visited the Centre over the years, not just The Ecclesbourne School!

Now some ten years on, hundreds of our pupils have visited. They have written their experiences up at school, but sometimes for local papers and magazines they are involved with, for the school newsletter and the like, and the impact of the Centre is the same now as it was when we first entered through the gates. As importantly in my view, virtually all our staff from all the different faculties have now visited and it is never a school visit where I struggle to get staff to accompany the pupils!

The rose we planted on a visit by staff, parents and friends of the school, one evening some eight or so years ago now, is something I shall cherish, as are the many survivor testimonies I have heard. No one can underestimate the value that The Holocaust Centre is in our society today.

education

Don Rowe
Director of Curriculum Resources, Citizenship Foundation

For some years the Citizenship Foundation has been pleased to develop formal and informal links with The Holocaust Centre in recognition of the high quality work done by the Centre on the important area of genocide education. The Foundation has sought in a number of ways to address issues of racism and xenophobia. Carrie Supple, who now manages CF's Youth Act! project has published a well respected book for students on the Holocaust, *From Prejudice to Genocide*. The Holocaust Centre's interactive multimedia learning tool about genocide drew on Tony Thorpe's recommendations. Tony Thorpe is the Citizenship Foundation's principal associate writer and editor of the *Young Citizen's Passport*, CF's flagship publication for young people.

When the Department for Education and Skills recognised that the education for diversity strand of the National Curriculum framework would present teachers with significant challenges, it commissioned the Citizenship Foundation to survey existing resources in all media and develop recommendations as to the most effective ways to address racism and xenophobia. That review, led by Don Rowe, CF's director of curriculum resources, suggested that

although much attention has been focussed on structural racism within schools, there is remarkably little robust research into 'what works' most effectively in terms of shifting attitudes away from prejudice and towards toleration and acceptance.

The Holocaust Centre's CD-ROM on genocide provides a powerful way for teachers to address one aspect of this issue, namely, first-hand witness accounts of atrocities, which, whilst harrowing, do powerfully harness both the affective domain as well as the cognitive.

The Citizenship Foundation believes that no amount of preaching or moralising will produce 'good citizens'. Rather, they need a range of practical and rich class-based learning experiences which are real and relevant, which move students sufficiently to want to make sense of issues and develop personal responses to the challenge of how every individual can play a part in making the world a better place.

responses
student

129

education

It makes you think
Could I or would I have done such evil things?
You hope you would not
But you watch the videos and look at the displays and you realise!
The Nazis were not just a small group of evil people
but a large group of normal people who were made to believe
that their problems were caused by others.

Pupil, age 13, Caistor Grammar School

'In a day, all the blank unbelievable statistics became people: men, women and children like myself. It was a real insight."

Lindsay, age 15

"The talk by the survivors was extraordinary, I was totally lost for words. The fact that they sat on that stage in front of a group of teenagers, just looking like normal, average people, but sharing their horrific past with us, was the best part of the day... It has to be said that this was the best school trip we have ever had."

Laura

"Racism still exists in our society because some people cannot accept the fact that there are different kinds of people. They think that new people coming into the country are taking away their jobs. When this is going on, the 'good people' just sit and watch."

Pupil, age 13, Bluecoat School, Coventry

"In my opinion, it is very important to share this idea with pupils and people all over the world. Not only about remembrance, but also as an illuminating of stereotypes, it is very interesting."

Denise, Pupil, Woherlschule, Berlin

"I think that The Holocaust Centre is a wonderful tribute to the six million Jews who died. If it makes just one person like me think about it, it has fulfilled its purpose."

Rebecca, age 14

"I hope to make a very conscious decision to make sure that I myself never become even a small part of discrimination against others."

Stevie, age 15

"You learn more from a survivor than from a book."

Robert, age 13

"The experience not only touched me, but it also touched all my family when I told them Rudi Oppenheimer's horrific story."

Matthew, age 14

"I do not know how to explain how much your Centre has affected me. Hearing the unique tale of an incredibly brave woman who survived Auschwitz, looking into her eyes, trying to find the words to express to her my feelings – that was without a doubt the most important experience of my young life."

Tahnie, Pupil, Cannock Chase High School

"It's kind of hard to
See your mum and dad get shot
But I guess I'm next."

Pupil, Carlton Le Willows

"It took a long time for me to realise how important the Holocaust was to civilization today, but... I promise you that I will never forget the impact it had on the world and how many individuals were the victims of this dreadful experience."

Yasmin, Pupil, Bablake School

sixth form

The Centre has an annual programme of conferences for high school seniors who are considering issues of the Holocaust in more advanced contexts. Topics include "What was the Holocaust?", "The Problem of Evil" and "Theological Responses to the Holocaust". These fall under several disciplines:

History: Students engage in recent historiographical debates. Conferences focus on recent publications, new sources of knowledge or historical controversies. Within the Advanced Level history curriculum, students opt to study the development of racial policies in the Third Reich. The conferences attempt to complement and expand on these courses of study.

Theology: A number of students opt to study Judaism within Advanced Level Religious Studies. One of the topics under consideration is how the Jewish community has struggled with the theological implications of the Holocaust for Jewish faith, belief and practice. Conferences on this topic also raise the issues faced by Christian theologians.

Moral Philosophy: As a more recent subject within the Advanced Level curriculum, Moral Philosophy conferences provide students with an opportunity to explore the philosophical implications of the Holocaust. The nature of good and evil, issues of personal and social responsibility, the complexity of failing societies and ethical considerations all form part of conference discussion sessions.

131

education

Isabel Wollaston

**Senior Lecturer in the Department
of Theology and Religion,
University of Birmingham**

Since The Holocaust Centre introduced its sixth-form conferences in 1998, I have been involved in running annual day conferences on Jewish religious responses to the Holocaust, and the Holocaust and the problem of evil. Educationally, the structure seems to work, combining a visit to the museum with the opportunity to watch a video, hear a lecture, listen to survivors, and discuss the issues both formally (in the main hall) and informally (during the breaks).

Whilst standing in as my Department's Admissions tutor, I noticed that a small but significant number of applicants used the personal statements on their UCAS forms to reflect on the impact these conferences, or a visit to the site of a ghetto or camp in Europe, had in prompting them to want to study the Holocaust as part of their degree.

We asked teachers to specify what questions or issues they would like addressed, in the hope of tailoring the sixth-form conferences to their specific needs. What is noticeable over the years is that whilst interests have remained broadly constant, a number specifically requested more information on Orthodox and Progressive responses, reflecting the changing requirements of their exam boards. Whilst providing information on Orthodox responses is relatively straightforward, doing so in relation to Progressive responses is less so, given that the term is rarely used in the literature. Hence, teachers' questions over what should or should not be covered under this rubric. Other teachers asked that the more formal or theoretical religious/philosophical issues be related to contemporary issues, such as the current educational preoccupation with civil society, contemporary examples of genocide or attitudes to Islam. The sixth-form conferences at the Centre, therefore, illustrate how the demands of 'the education market' evolve whilst retaining constant elements.

education

"What happened to being individual and following one's own morals? How did the world let this happen? How does the world allow genocide to happen still? Do we not learn?"

Katie, Pupil, Toot Hill Comprehensive

"I feel very aware of the fact that we are one of the last generations who will be able to hear first-hand about the experiences of Holocaust survivors... It's really depressing to think that even with the wealth of information available to us today, genocide on similar scales has still taken place post World War II."

Lucy, Pupil, Toot Hill Comprehensive

"It's the first time I have ever listened to a direct account of the Holocaust. It really does emphasise the importance of being your own person and having freedom of speech, and how just one person can make such a difference."

Danielle, Pupil, The Becket School

Waldemar and Ibi Ginsburg
Holocaust Survivors

It was quite by accident that my wife and I discovered the existence of the newly established Beth Shalom Holocaust Memorial Centre. To our delight it was situated in North Nottinghamshire, not far from our place of residence in West Yorkshire. For both of us, survivors of the Holocaust, this discovery was of vital importance. We were alarmed at the lack of knowledge among the general population and especially among the young generation about the history of the Second World War and the events leading up to it. There were some efforts made to remedy the situation but without much success. The real change in attitudes came about in 1995 with the creation of The Holocaust Centre. It came into existence thanks to vision, initiative and huge effort. Within a short time, it became a leader in the field of Holocaust history and education. Schoolchildren, students and adults from all walks of life started arriving in their thousands to learn about the Holocaust.

In 1996 we were introduced to the Centre and its work. We established a rapport and were invited to join the survivor speakers. To tell our own stories takes nearly one and a half hours, but they are quite different and that helps to keep the attention of the listeners. An important adjunct to our talks are the questions. They allow us to assess the reaction and comprehension of the audience and to adjust our talk. Question time is usually a lively and interesting affair. The questions range far and wide but the most popular are: a) Can you forgive the evildoers? b) Did the experience of evil affect your religious beliefs? c) Do you hate the Germans? We particularly enjoy discussing these difficult topics with more advanced students during sixth-form conferences.

We consider it a privilege to be allowed to join the speakers of The Holocaust Centre and to be able to contribute to the educational effort of the Centre.

education

"This is an uplifting and essential experience, which has been appreciated by us all."

Ruth Lodge, Teacher of Religious Studies and Psychology, Brighouse High School

tertiary sector

University students from a variety of disciplines use the Centre, either in groups with their tutors or as individual research students. From the outset, facilities were provided to suit the needs of undergraduates. The library collection was selected to ensure that students from the range of disciplines studying the Holocaust would have access to core texts to meet most needs.

Students come from departments including history, theology, English, philosophy, law, criminology, psychology, cultural studies, politics, fine art, museum studies, education, humanitarian aid studies, war studies, peace studies, among others.

The structure of the visit for university students is twofold. Initially, students are provided with historical background, including the opportunity to hear a Holocaust survivor. The second part of their visit is discipline-specific, in which discussion focuses around the issues pertaining to their particular course of study.

The association with some universities, such as Wolverhampton University, Leeds University School of Education, The University College of Ripon & York, St John, goes back to the early days. Increasingly, the Centre is now formalising its affiliation with higher education institutions, including Nottingham University School of Education, Middlesex University and Bishop Grosseteste College in Lincoln.

135

education

Mark Chater
Reader in Education, Bishop Grosseteste College, Lincoln

In my experience of bringing higher education students to The Holocaust Centre for ten years, there have been many moments of grief, pain, discomfort and embarrassment. Rightly so, in view of the story it has to tell and the challenges it offers to its visitors. Holocaust and genocide education should not end in tears, but tears should form a part of it. We cannot understand genocide unless our hearts have been broken. This is a valid piece of learning.

Students from several undergraduate and postgraduate programmes at Bishop Grosseteste College, Lincoln, have to make a visit to The Holocaust Centre as part of a module. They go as theologians or education specialists, or teachers in training. They are welcomed in the hall – an arresting place; "Who saves a single life…" They walk through the permanent exhibition – and begin to understand not only *how* it happened, but how it *could* happen, and what failures of the human spirit, and of education systems, and of politics, and of the whole European modernist project, brought us to that point. They research in the library

and make connections with other failures of history and of our time. They listen to survivor testimonies – with a fresh young empathy that turns, sometimes, to wondering and incomprehension, and sometimes even to embarrassed silence – what does one say to a survivor? What can one give, how can one make it better? Often there are tears. Often I am uncomfortable, and I have done it many times. I hope I never lose the discomfort.

May we always take the lead of The Holocaust Centre and educate our scientists, historians, lawyers, teachers, police, military personnel and all citizens to recognise and name the nascent tyrannies of our own time before they engulf us; may our discomfort stay with us; may we use education to "tame the savageness of man and make gentle the life of this world,"[1] and to work for *tikkun olam*, the repair of the world – which is also the repair of ourselves.

1. Robert F. Kennedy borrowed this phrase many times from its original in Greek philosophy (M. Kennedy, *Make Gentle the Life of this World: The Vision of Robert F. Kennedy.* NY: Broadway Books, 1998, p.43).

education

Hugo Slim
Chief Scholar at the Centre for Humanitarian Dialogue in Geneva

One of the most important moments in our Oxford Brookes Masters Programme in Humanitarian and Development Practices was the annual visit to The Holocaust Centre. Each visit started before dawn. About 40 students ranging from 25-55 years of age, and from a wide variety of different nationalities, would board a bus wondering why on earth they were going to spend six hours travelling to a small Nottinghamshire village and back. Most of them already had considerable experience working for agencies like Oxfam, *Médecins Sans Frontières*, the United Nations or Red Cross. By the end of the day, many had received one of the most important educational experiences of their lives.

They had learnt in detail about the Holocaust and the process of genocide – something about which aid workers are still surprisingly ignorant. They had listened to an extraordinary survivor. They had wandered quietly through the memorial gardens and then discussed the role of humanitarian agencies in preventing and responding to genocide. Above all, they were moved: moved to think about how extreme violence comes about; moved to reflect on their particular responsibilities, and moved to feel for the millions of victims of such violence. The extraordinary hospitality of the Smith family and their team gave these seasoned aid workers a uniquely private, pensive and surprisingly positive space in which to remember victims they had met in their work, alongside those named in the garden whom they had never known. Many were moved to tears. And every year, unfailingly, a group of committed humanitarian workers emerged with clearer understanding, new resolve and a better mix of heart and head with which to approach their work in today's wars.

Martin Stern, Holocaust Survivor, speaking to trainee teachers

"The experience has been an emotional one, especially listening to Dr Stern's experiences. It is easy to become complacent and apathetic about the Holocaust but by using modern-day examples, such as Darfur, it gives us the ultimate question: 'Have we really learnt from the Holocaust?'"

Amanda Bradford, PGCE Student

138

education

"Sempo Sugihara, the Japanese diplomat, could not treat the Jews as 'nameless, disposable nothings'. Issuing transit visas cost him his consular position but saved 1,600 lives. How many others could have done likewise?"

Student, Middlesex University

Joanna R. Adler
Postgraduate Programme Leader, MSc Forensic Psychology, Middlesex University

The postgraduate students who come from Middlesex University to The Holocaust Centre are mainly from two academic backgrounds: Applied Psychology, mostly forensic; or Criminology. They are diverse in terms of age, experience, nationality, race and profession. In one visit, we had a range including German lawyers, English prison psychologists, inspectors and civil servants, an African probation officer and a Chinese new graduate. Before Beth Shalom, their understanding of genocide also varies widely. From third generation survivors to people who ask "What's a Holocaust?" or "Where's Rwanda?" when they see the outline of the field trip.

The field trip to The Holocaust Centre is part of several MSc programmes that share a module called "Criminological Psychology". When we designed this module, we were clear that we did not want to focus on the aetiology of offending behaviour, juvenile crime and victims of crime in an affluent democracy, to the exclusion of considering some of the most heinous, difficult to comprehend crimes. As psychologists, we wanted to ensure that our students were given the opportunity to consider the impact of hate, persecution and prejudice, as well as the power of mediation in justice, alongside the more predictable elements of the module.

As students, without exception, they love the visit. They find it emotionally draining, physically exhausting but intellectually stimulating, and they find a way to respond as individuals. It is not surprising that every year, our module evaluation forms sing the praises of the Centre, its staff and the work that is done there.

Letter from first-year university students at Nottingham University, History Dept

"Thank you so very much for your time and efforts given to us on our visit to The Holocaust Centre to aid us with our history project. The use of your library and the lectures have provided us with valuable and necessary material with which to approach the question of myth and legend within the modernist/post-modernist debate, using *Schindler's List* as a case study...

The Centre is a truly worthy testament of the *Shoah* and all the lives lost in it, and we were very moved by the memorial rose garden and the sculptures. It performs a function that is essential if people are to be educated as to the events of the Holocaust – that is perpetuating the memory of millions and telling their story. In the face of antisemitic deniers, such a Centre becomes crucial if man's cruelty to man is to be understood and an awareness created that genocide is always possible as long as humans exist, as the events in Eastern Europe and Africa sadly testify."

Bernard Barker
Leicester University

"I write on behalf of the primary and secondary history postgraduate students and myself to express our thanks for a precious, invaluable two days. Your rich gift of time, trouble, scholarship and ideas is deeply appreciated and has stimulated all of us in our different ways to face the meaning of the Holocaust and to re-examine aspects of our response. Special thanks, too, for the survivors, whose courage and commitment to telling the story aids the next generation with a personal connection...

I have come away this time with the idea of The Holocaust Centre representing the very opposite of what government demands from schools – an approach that touches the soul, not just test-answering cells of memory..."

Barry Dufour

Teaching Fellow in History at the School of Education, University of Leicester and Visiting Lecturer in Education at De Montfort University, Leicester and Loughborough University

In the summer of 1995, following a short feature on the local East Midlands TV news about the opening of Beth Shalom Holocaust Memorial Centre, I made contact with the Smith family the very next day to declare my interest and support. At that time, I was running a Postgraduate Certificate in Education course at Loughborough University for students preparing to be History teachers in secondary schools. Like other teacher educators, I saw myself in a pivotal position to influence new teachers in the quality, authenticity and relevance of the kind of history curriculum they presented to secondary school pupils in order to enable them to become better-informed citizens.

Every year since then, I have made a day-long visit with each group of PGCE students, the high point being our opportunity to meet and listen to a survivor. I always prepare the students back at the university by running a day-seminar on current research on the history of the Holocaust, usually presented by a visiting scholar such as Professor Aubrey Newman of the Stanley Burton Centre for Holocaust Studies at the University of Leicester, and I combine this with a session that I run on how to teach children about the Holocaust and its implications.

The immediate and longer-term impact on these new teachers has been tremendous. They are deeply moved, not only by the historical content of The Holocaust Centre

and with meeting a survivor, but also by the ambitious conception of the facilities, including the memorial garden. They also comment, with some awe, on the commitment and breadth of knowledge of the Centre's team. In the longer term, many of them, now established teachers, bring their own pupils to the Centre.

Since 1995, there have been major changes at all levels. Nationally, we now have a National Curriculum in History that requires the study of the Holocaust for 11-14-year-olds. Since 2001, the UK has had a National Holocaust Memorial Day on 27th January, the anniversary of the liberation of Auschwitz-Birkenau. Both of these developments were influenced by the Centre. Since 2002, we have had the new subject of Citizenship in the National Curriculum that opens up endless possibilities for the exploration of the wider issues that the Holocaust presents us with. Linked with this, the Centre has also expanded with the inception of Aegis, which concentrates on the broader areas of genocide and fundamental human rights. In 2001, I transferred to the School of Education at the University of Leicester where I was delighted to discover that Dr Mel Vlaeminke and now Dr Ruth Lee, the new PGCE History Tutor, also shared the same priority in placing a visit to The Holocaust Centre as one of the essential features of the PGCE year. The good work thus continues.

Pauline Elkes
Senior Lecturer in History, Staffordshire University

The Holocaust Centre, Beth Shalom performs a crucial and increasingly important role in Holocaust and genocide education. As a historian, I spend time with undergraduates considering and debating the theoretical approaches, historical interpretations and controversies that surround this sensitive and difficult area of history. Taking students to the Centre offers a unique experience – to immerse themselves in the Exhibition Centre and Remembrance Garden, to talk and listen to survivors, to have discussions with other students, often from other areas of life – all in a completely different learning environment. The visit is always enriched by the extremely professional and friendly welcome, ensuring that the visit is both positive and informative.

Christine King
Vice Chancellor, Staffordshire University

The study of the Holocaust in Further and Higher Education has a number of faces. It may be the concern of the specialist undergraduate or postgraduate student or of the researcher. It may also be the focus of interest for non-specialists, for whom the area of study raises personal or intellectual issues. At any level, the challenge is to balance the precision of critical enquiry with the recognition that this is history that still lives to haunt and to heal.

At The Holocaust Centre, the complex and subtle needs of such students and their studies are met in a unique and powerful way. The Graduate Summer School is a perfect example of the mix of rigour with empathy which permeates all that happens at the Centre.

Here, as in other consultations, people of a wide mix of backgrounds, of many faiths and of none, come together around a series of academic inputs to explore a range of detailed studies. What is valuable and precious about the Beth Shalom experience is that the words of those who have strong personal commitments and life stories to tell sit alongside and articulate with the intellectual debate.

This same diversity of input, from speakers and participants, characterises the public lectures and seminars, as well as the contact individual students or groups of students have with the Centre.

The Holocaust Centre, Beth Shalom inspires all of us not only to remember, but to take seriously the responsibility to embed our remembering in the questioning of our students.

education

outcomes

Students visit The Holocaust Centre on one day in their lives.

As educators, the question we really would like to answer is the impact the Centre has on pupils' lives in the years that follow.

education

Recent research into the long-term effects of the Centre shows a marked influence on pupils' understanding of the Holocaust, and their willingness to engage with issues which raise similar questions.

It is because of these positive long-term outcomes that the Centre intends to increase its through-put of younger visitors.

"There is no purpose for my letter other than to say that my visit to The Holocaust Centre has quite literally changed my outlook on life and for that I thank you."

Kate Cordingley, Visitor

Marcia Sachs Littell

**Professor of Holocaust and Genocide Studies, The Richard Stockton College of New Jersey;
Executive Director of the Annual Scholars' Conference on the Holocaust and the Churches**

The first "Remembering For The Future" (RFTF) conference took place in Oxford and London in July 1988. Prior to the opening of the RFTF conference, I was asked to join Elisabeth Maxwell and Yehuda Bauer to testify before the Education Committee of the House of Commons. The MPs on the Education Committee wanted to know what was being taught in the United States. The government officials asked how Franklin Littell developed the first interfaith, international, interdisciplinary Holocaust education programme in 1975 at Temple University, how we trained the teachers, disseminated information and pioneered the Annual Scholars' Conference on the Holocaust and the Churches in 1970. Their challenge was how and where to begin in the UK in 1988. Until that time, a deafening silence regarding *Shoah* education had prevailed in the schools and universities of the United Kingdom.

The "Remembering for the Future" conference provided the climate for change by creating high visibility and public awareness. It also initiated the first ever Survivors' gathering in the United Kingdom. But the vehicle for the actual introduction of the subject matter in the schools, universities, communities, churches and synagogues in the UK was still in the distance; it did not appear until 1995 when The Holocaust Centre, Beth Shalom was established.

A bold and dramatic beginning such as Beth Shalom established might best be viewed as an interactive process. The "Remembering for the Future" conference can be seen as preparing the philosophic and ideological first phase of Holocaust awareness and education in the United Kingdom. The second more radical phase of this interactive process came a few years later. The interfaith educational initiatives ushered in by the selfless dedication of the Smith Family in 1995 created the dramatic beginnings in the UK. The Beth Shalom Centre served as the model for all other Holocaust education projects which were to follow.

A third and stabilizing phase of this interactive process can be identified in the growth and expansion of Beth Shalom. The Centre educated and influenced the community as well as government officials. The magnificent gem in Laxton served not only to teach as well as to honour and memorialize the victims of the Holocaust, it presumably also served as the inspiration for the Imperial War Museum in London. In the ten years of its existence, Beth Shalom has clearly caught up with – and surpassed – many of the teaching centres established in the US decades earlier.

The Holocaust Centre, Beth Shalom has reached out to Eastern Europe, training teachers in countries where two totalitarian regimes – Nazism and Communism – had built the wall of silence about the Holocaust and the destruction of the Jewish people. As a Holocaust educator, I am grateful for Beth Shalom's leadership and teaching in countries where Holocaust education did not previously exist. Most important is the understanding the Smith family brings to the work. The Holocaust is a tragedy that happened to the Jewish people, but it is also a spiritual tragedy for Christendom. The leadership of the Centre teaches how Christianity should function – concerned with the dignity and integrity of the human person – regardless of race, religion or ethnic origin. May their work continue to grow and flourish around the world!

"It has been a very eye-opening and moving experience, highlighting the plight of many millions around the world, and teaching us that lessons from the past have not been learnt."

Pritpal Garcha, PGCE Student

Paula Kitching
Education Consultant

The Holocaust Centre, Beth Shalom opened its doors ten years ago, a significant time in the historiography of the Holocaust. In the years just prior, the Holocaust became a statutory subject in History for English schools. *Schindler's List* was viewed by millions worldwide and there was the 50th anniversary of the end of the Second World War.

Many of the survivors then began to talk for the first time and, as some people listened, others began to ask questions: "What was the Holocaust?"; "Why do we not know more about this?"; "Who are the victims?"; "How can we stop this from happening again?" "How do we teach others about it?" A small number of organizations raised their heads to try and respond to the questions.

We all knew some of the answers, or part of the answers, or we at least tried to find answers, but most importantly we were prepared to tackle the questions and tell people that as we were trying, they must try and listen.

I first went to The Holocaust Centre, Beth Shalom as one of the people from another

organisation as we all worked together to try and provide the knowledge needed. I have continued to work with the team there throughout the last ten years. We have shared ideas, taken part in discussions, listened to testimony, worked with teachers. Most importantly, we have all worked together to ensure that education about the Holocaust, the racism that created it, the prejudice that supported it and continued after it, reaches as many people as possible, across the UK and abroad.

A lot has been achieved in ten years. Holocaust Memorial Day was a significant step especially for education, but the work continues. Unfortunately, a greater awareness of the Holocaust has not yet stopped racist atrocities, either here or abroad. However, Holocaust education does provide a platform to begin to explain why we must be vigilant, why we must continue to learn, why those terrible events of the past have a relevance to now and the future, why we have to keep educating for the next ten years and on.

"I have visited Theresienstadt and Auschwitz, but exhibitions about the Holocaust are for me still moving, especially as a German. It is a special exhibition and carefully collected. Beth Shalom should be an example."

Mathias, University of Warwick

146

education

primary

Following repeated requests of teachers and parents, we decided to introduce a learning centre for primary school pupils. "The Journey" tells the stories of children during the Nazi period for 9-12-year-olds. It takes the form of a second permanent exhibition and learning centre on the site.

Each child survivor of the Nazis has his or her unique story to tell. They take younger visitors on a journey back into their homes, to their classrooms, to their streets, on trains, in hiding and in barracks, before their ultimate survival.

Carefully telling these difficult experiences, the exhibition avoids the worst excesses of the Holocaust, ensuring that children are not traumatised by their visit.

"The Journey" is the journey of the children who lived through the Nazi period and survived. It is the journey of the children who visit and learn. It is a journey through the choices that face us all in life. It is a journey of discovery about ourselves.

"I was really delighted to hea *about this project... I did have r* *doubts at first as I do not wish :* *burden children with our difficu* *history too young.. but the wa* *this is being put together... it i* *beautifully executed... it will so* *seeds for many years to come."*

Lisa Vincent, Kindertransport Survivor

"I think that other children should come here as well because you learn a lot. I learned more about the Holocaust and not just the history of religion, but about other people as well."

Adam, Glasgow

education

"I think they should really speak to youth about it because they're the next generation and should not forget about this. It's a very important time in history."

Primary School Pupil

Dorothy Fleming
Kindertransport Survivor

It is important for pre-teen children to begin to learn about the Holocaust because this is an aspect of recent history that needs to be part of everyone's understanding, so that nothing like it should ever happen again. All children need to understand what happens with discrimination, scapegoating and the development of prejudice, and what can happen to ordinary people in extraordinary situations. They need to learn not only about the terrible depths to which human beings can sink but also about the heroism and idealism people can demonstrate.

Because The Holocaust Centre, Beth Shalom, provides many opportunities for primary-age children to learn about the Holocaust in age-appropriate ways, it is the ideal setting for such learning to take place. Seeing the exhibition and the memorial garden; meeting a survivor with a personal story to tell; taking part in "The Journey" to bring to life the experiences of *Kindertransport* and hidden children – all these help young children to gain a foundation of knowledge and understanding on which their secondary school curriculum and their later life can build.

At the primary school stage, particularly at around ages 9-11, children learn to formulate their own identity and relationship to others; how their "here and now" fits in with "there and then", and they are beginning to grasp how the world works and their own place within it. They are interested in similarities and differences in people and are developing ideas of morality – of good and bad, fair and unfair, kind and cruel, and so on. They are also honing their skills of observation, recording and presentation, both individually and in groups, and they thrive on opportunities for expressing feelings and imagination creatively. They need active learning as well as many and varied experiences, together with time and space, to reflect on and react to such learning experiences. All of these opportunities can be found and made sensitive use of at The Holocaust Centre; an ideal educational setting – but not a school.

Susanne Pearson
MBE, Kindertransport Survivor

The Primary Learning Centre will be opening in response to many requests and considerable time spent in consultation, planning and fund-raising.

I have felt privileged to be part of this process, drawing on my own experience as a Kindertransportee at the age of 11 and having had a career in primary education. My involvement in Holocaust education was prompted by the Anne Frank Exhibition, which came to Sheffield in 1987. I feel very much in tune with its stated aim "that the rejection and prevention of discrimination must start at an early age". Since then I have spoken of my experiences to many groups, including both secondary and primary schools. When speaking at The Holocaust Centre, I have been most conscious of how much the ethos there contributes to the understanding of these difficult issues.

It is known that primary-aged children learn best through interactive and visual experience, and the planning of the Centre is based on this. It is also known that this is a most impressionable age, and I very much hope that the Centre will make a valuable contribution to how young people view the world around them.

Bela Rosenthal
Holocaust Survivor

I was a very young child who was the sole survivor of my family who lived in Berlin. I was incarcerated in Theresienstadt for two years, fourteen months of which was spent as an orphan.

For years, older survivors and well-meaning people assumed that because I was so young I could not remember, and therefore could not have suffered. This attitude was extremely hurtful and alienating. I was denied the right to my experiences. I was of no account.

It is because of this I realised that it is important to work with younger children. Adults often underestimate the sensitivities of children who are often fully aware of the world around them. Many suffer in their homes through domestic violence, divorce and the pain of lost relatives. They either experience or see the effects of bullying, prejudice and racism at school and in their everyday lives.

They are perfectly able to understand the issues raised by the Holocaust. Given the opportunity granted by the exhibition at The Holocaust Centre, Beth Shalom, children can see and hear about the effects on children of the horrors and hardships of the Holocaust. Survivors like me are very excited at the challenge of the new exhibition and being able to talk in an informal way to children. It will be a perfect setting to explore the issues raised by the Holocaust and to raise their awareness of the dangers of prejudice and racism.

150

education

Vera Schaufeld

Kindertransport Survivor

I came to England on the *Kindertransport* when I was nine. This definitely influenced the career choices I later made as a teacher. After teaching a range of subjects in primary schools, I started to work with children learning English as a second language. Later, I worked with English language teachers in the multi-ethnic London Borough of Brent.

During the last ten years, The Holocaust Centre has given me the opportunity to speak to many children and their teachers about my experience of coming to England as a child.

I am very pleased to see the imaginative way that the Centre has developed a large area for use with primary school pupils. It will introduce them to the lives of Jewish children who were born in Europe during the Holocaust years. Their visit will help them to empathise with the experiences of individual children and their families. Through this, the visitors of today will be able to see the results of intolerance and racism. They will be encouraged to think about the treatment of people in their own communities who may be different from themselves. The visit can lead to individual reflection as well as further classroom work and discussion. It will help to prepare pupils for a deeper understanding of the terrible events of the Holocaust when they come to study them as part of the secondary school curriculum. Importantly, it may also make them more sensitive to the ongoing suffering of people in minority groups.

151

education

Eve (behind) with Sonia Berenbaum, whose parents looked after her immediately after survival in Bergen-Belsen

Eve Oppenheimer

Holocaust Survivor

In this tenth anniversary of the setting-up of The Holocaust Centre, Beth Shalom, it is very good news to hear that a Primary Education exhibition is being created. It is very important that youngsters of the age of nine begin to understand what happened to so many children during the Holocaust – and what can happen if we are not keeping our ears and eyes open in the world in which we live.

The idea of arranging the exhibition in three different stages gives our young visitors an idea of what happened to different children who arrived in this country for a life that was completely different to what they had been used to. Each of these groups had different problems to deal with. The *Kindertransport* children came mostly from loving homes, where they were well looked after and cared for by their families. The shock of leaving them behind

must have been very traumatic. The hidden children were suddenly put with people who, in most cases, they did not even know and where the slightest sound could arouse the suspicion of people who did not know they were there. And lastly, the Camp Survivor children, especially the younger ones from the age of four, hardly knew what was happening. Being in the last group, I found it extremely difficult to adjust to a new way of life. It wasn't just the question of learning to live and trust people you didn't know, which was very hard, but a whole new way of life, starting with learning a new language; to go to school, to be able to go to the shops and park was a whole new experience.

I'm sure this new Centre will give the children a lot to think and talk about.

Lingfield House was the hostel where very young child survivors were housed and brought up after the Holocaust.

152

education

"It is more real when you are here, because when you are in class you are just learning about it and it does not really seem that it happened... After the visit I think I could talk about this kind of thing with my parents and my friends."

Sonia, age 11

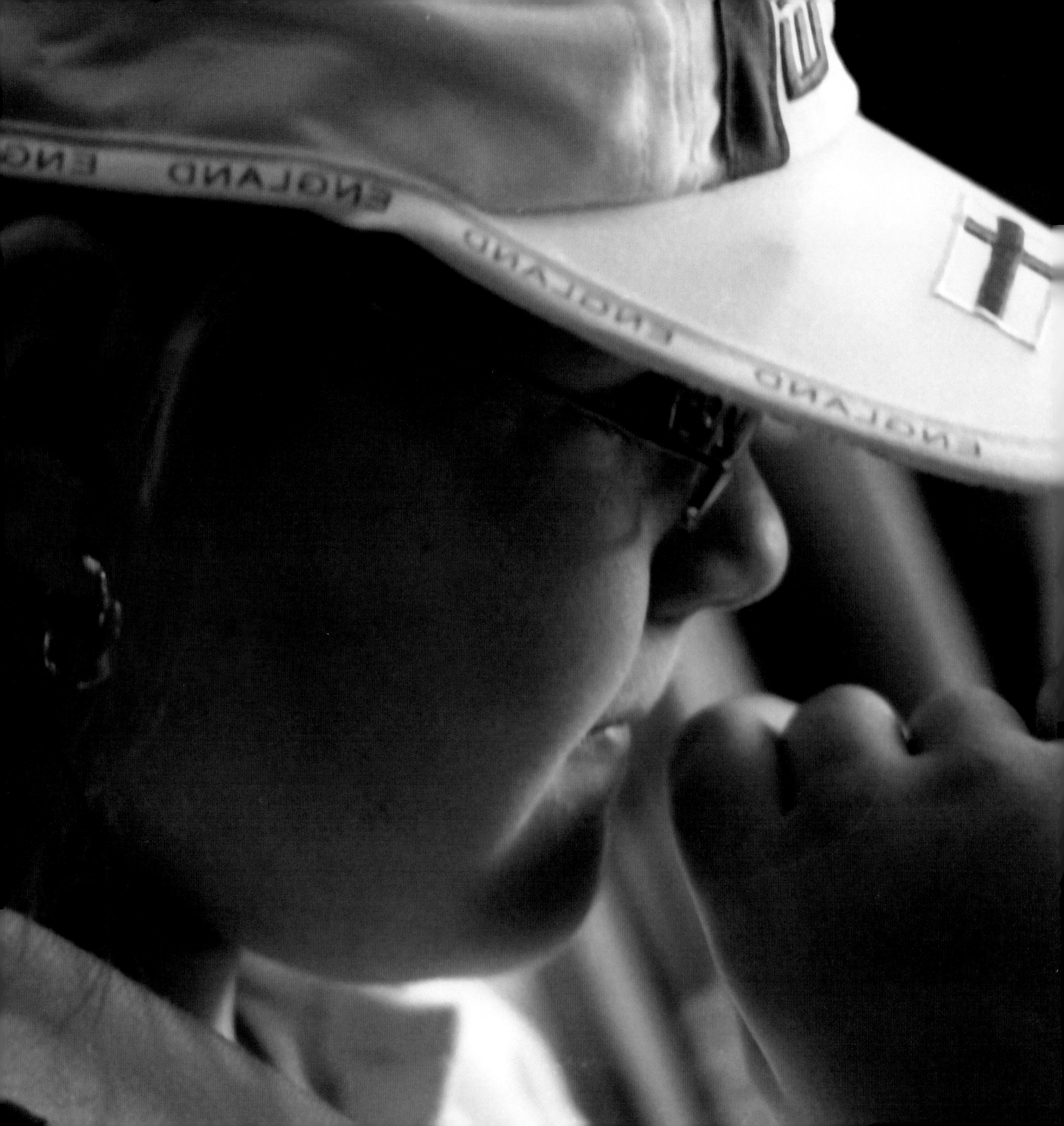
ENG
ENGLAND
ENGLAND
ENGLAND
ENGLAND
ENGLAND

Batsheva Dagan
Survivor, Child Psychologist, Teacher Trainer and Author, Israel

SHOAH – should this, can this be a topic for children? Yes, it should be – and The Holocaust Centre, Beth Shalom believes so, too, and provides the best setting and conditions to present it. The subject arouses existential anxiety which is linked to the fear of death. The encounter with the *Shoah* raises the basic conflict between man's tendency to repress the topic and the need and the obligation to remember. Today, the multimedia in the home dominate the lives of many children who are exposed to actual and fictional disasters and violence. Therefore, special attention needs to be paid to the *Shoah* in the education of primary and secondary schoolchildren.

Perception of the *Shoah* and the formation of attitudes towards it should be considered as a gradual developmental process, according to the child's own level of emotional and cognitive maturity. The role of identification in this process is crucial. Identification leads to the learning of patterns of behaviour. Identification with individuals can occur in two ways: either through admiration, fondness and respect, or through hate and fear which leads to identification with the aggressor. If our goal is teaching tolerance and love for our fellow man, this may be achieved through presentation of positive identification models. Therefore, selection of appropriate material is crucial. Children need hope. Life in hiding, parting and separation, all ending happily, are appropriate themes for our pupils.

The duty of the educator resulting from the child's exposure to the topic is to create a balance by emphasizing positive humane behaviour within the horrific events of the *Shoah*. Meeting survivors whose very survival is a happy experience, and teaching teachers how to deal with this complex subject are an important contribution to the education of the young generation.

Participating in The Holocaust Centre's innovative programmes has given me, personally, the opportunity to fulfil two of my aims as a survivor. I have been privileged to teach about the *Shoah* according to my educational and psychological tenets, and my presence and work in the Centre has given purpose to my survival and my testimony as a witness.

154

education

"I think the children's memorial is good because it shows that it wasn't just adults that were killed; there were lots of younger people as well."

Primary School Pupil

creative sparks

We felt that the Centre and its contents might be least accessible for some of the people who might well benefit from it most.

We created provision for special needs schools. We were delighted to welcome Ashley School from Widnes and the Royal School for the Deaf, Exeter, which have contributed creatively to the poignancy of remembrance events here. Many other special needs schools now also enrich the life of the Centre, including Shepherd School, Nottingham.

We created a programme to make the Centre available to children permanently excluded from school. The Creative Sparks programme enables young people with serious learning and behavioural difficulties to engage the history and the issues the Holocaust raises over a period of time, and to apply their learning creatively.

On one programme, the young people come to the Centre with the sole purpose of learning how to make a documentary film. Their topic is "What do people learn at The Holocaust Centre?" Across several weeks of work they make several visits, follow other school groups around, interview survivors, learn how to follow a brief, conduct interviews and construct a three-minute magazine piece on the lessons the Centre has to teach.

Creative Sparks has resulted in young people usually dislocated from society playing an active part in local politics, visiting Westminster to lobby their MPs on recent conflicts, and engaging peers still within the school system on citizenship issues.

"The experience that made me think a bit more is listening to a survivor, about his life and what happened to him... I have learnt to think of other people and what's going on in their lives, and not just think about myself or people around me...."

Debbie Payne, Newark E2E

Debs McCahon
Young Roots Coordinator, Heritage Lottery Fund

The Heritage Lottery Fund (HLF) awarded the The Holocaust Centre, Beth Shalom a grant of £20,000 to enable it to develop an exciting and interactive programme of events designed to excite and educate young people. The project, entitled "Creative Sparks", was new and innovative work for the Centre, who have traditionally hosted educational visits and more formal education programmes.

The children visited the Centre and had the opportunity to meet and talk to a survivor from the death camps and discuss their experiences. This proved to be a very powerful method of learning for the youngsters. The group devised and developed short films depicting their reflections on the project and what it would have been like to be a survivor.

Through this work, the children developed in confidence and strengthened their discussion skills, whilst also learning useful technical and IT skills. Aside from the Holocaust experiences, the children also learned about genocide and issues of equality, human rights and censorship.

The films are now being used as an introduction to the Centre for new school and community groups.

The team at the Centre also gained from the project, giving them an insight into how to effectively engage with young people. These learnings are now being used for future projects.

Comments on Individual Case Studies from Youth Workers:

"Young person, aged 17, with dyslexia and lack of social skills was able to fully engage in this programme. The learner really enjoyed making the CD-ROM and gained in self-confidence from this experience. The learner is very proud of her CD and shows it to all other agencies involved with her."

"Young person, 19 years old, has visited the Centre on a previous occasion. Being involved in the Creative Sparks project has helped reinforce his understanding of the Holocaust and the effects of genocide. It raised issues in himself from a personal perspective and helped him to overcome barriers around confidence and self-expression – it gave him the confidence to question others' values and morals."

"This was the first visit of a young person, 18 years old. The visit had a profound effect on her and it brought out her caring, compassionate nature which was brought out in the final product."

"An excellent day, highlighting the relevance of history to current issues. Particularly interesting were the resources available and the work already being carried out with young people."
Jan Hall, Notts County Council, Crime and Disorder Team

"When I was first asked to go to Beth Shalom, I did have reservations about how this would fit into my remit working with young offenders. Having sat through the seminar, I feel that there are many links and cross-threads that I could use with the young people, coming from a different angle."
Julie Slater, Youth Worker, Notts County Council, Crime and Disorder Team

"After watching about Rwanda... I felt upset that people could stand and just watch it happen, all the genocide being done…"
April Ward, Worksop E2E

"It is quite important because it is telling us what has gone on in the past and what is going on now in the world... "
Thomas Bramley, Mansfield E2E

"I think you should come and learn what actually happened because when you come here, they open your mind to what actually happened. Textbooks can only say so many things. Here they tell you everything."
Daniel Keetley, Newark E2E

158

education

outreach education

Before the Centre opened, we decided that outreach would be a part of the commitment we would make to ensure that as many young people as possible were reached, particularly those not able to access the museum programmes directly.

The outreach programme has now reached over 1,000 schools, listed on the facing page.

We created a mobile exhibition, which was duplicated four times to meet demand; we set up a survivor speaker bureau with survivors travelling to schools around the country; we created the Education Resource Department to create and distribute educational resources, posters and films for use in schools. We also created a website to give young people access to historical information, www.holocausthistory.net.

Schools associated with The Holocaust Centre during the last ten years...

Abbey Grange High School, Abbey Hill School, Abbey Road Primary School, Abbey School, Abbottsholme School, Abingdon School, Abington High School, Abraham Darby School, Acorn Initiative, Adam School, Adcote School for Girls, Ainsdale High School, Aireville School, Akiva School, Alcester Grammar School Aldenham School, Alderbrook School, Alderman Derbyshire School, Alderman Smith School, Aldersley High School, Aldridge School, Alexander Mcleod Primary School, Alfred Barrow School, Alice Ottley School, All Saints Allesley, All Saints Catholic High School, All Saints RC School, All Saints School, All Saints School,All Saints School, Allertonshire School, Alleyne's High School, Alleyn's School, Alun School, Amery Hill Secondary School, Ampleforth College, Ancaster High School, Andrew Marvel School, Anglo European School, Angmering School, Archbishop Sandcroft High School, Archers Court School, Armthorpe School, Arnold Hill School, Arthur Terry School, Ash LEA School, Ashby Grammar School, Ashley School, Ashton Under Lyne Sixth Form College, Ashville College, Aston Comprehensive School, Astor College for Arts, Audley Junior School, Aylands School, Aylesford School, Aylward First and Middle School, Bablake School, Baines School, Bannerman High School, Bar Beacon School, Barnard Castle School, Barnsley College, Barnwood Park High School for Girls, Barr Beacon Language College, Barton Peven College, Batley Boys School, Bay House School, Beacon Hill School, Beal High School, Beckett School, Bedale high School, Bedford School, Bedwas Comprehensive School, Belgrave High School, Belmont First School., Belper School, Belvidere School, Belvoir High School & Comm Ctr, Bennerley School, Bennerley School, Bentley West Primary School, Bentley Wood High School, Benton Park School, Berleigh comm. school, Bethany School, Beverley Grammar School, Beverley School, Bewdley High School, Bicester Community School, Biddulph High School, Big Wood School, Biggar High School, Bilborough Middle School, Bilbrook Middle School, Bilton High School, Bingley Grammar School, Birkdale School, Birley Secondary School, Bishop Auckland College, Bishop Grosseteste College, Bishop High School, Bishop Stopford School, Bishop Vessey's Grammar School, Bishops Castle School, Blake High School, Blake Valley Tech College, Blemrose Community School, Blenheim High School, Blue Coates School, Bluecoats School, Blurton High School, Blythe Bridge High SChool, Blyth-Jex School, Bohunt Secondary School, Boothville Middle School, Borough Bridge High School, Boston College, Boughton Leigh Junior School, Bourne Grammar School, Bowering Park Comp. School, Bracken Lane Primary School, Brackenfield Special School, Brackenhill School, Bradfield School, Bradford Grammar School, Bramcote Hills School, Bramcote Park Comprehensive School, Brampton Manner School, Branston Community College, Brantwood Independent School for Girls, Brentside High School, Brentwood Preparatory School, Bretton Wood Comprehensive School, Bridgewater Middle School, Bridley Moor High School, Bridlington School, Brighouse High School, Brimshaw Green School, Brinkley Grove Primary School, Brinsworth Primary School, Bristol Cathedral School, Bristol Grammar School, Brodeski Primary School, Brooke School, Brookfield Community School. Broomhill Junior School, Brownhills Community School, Brownhills High School, Brownhills School, Brownlees School, Broxborne School, Brune Park Community College, Brunts School, Burleigh Community College, Burleigh Community School, Burn Holme Comm College , Bury Boys Grammar School, Bury Grammar School, Buxlow School, Buxton Community School, Bydales School, Caister High School, Caistor Grammar School, Caistor Yarborough School, Calderdale College, Calderwood Lodge Primary School, Calthorpe Park School, Campion School, Campion School, Camprion RC School, Campsmount School, Cams School, Cannock Chase High School, Canon Slade School, Cardinal Newman Catholic High School, Carlton Digby School, Carlton Le Willows School, Carmel Technical College, Carshalton High School for Girls, Cartor Community School, Casterton Community School, Castle Hills Communty School, Castle Rock High School, Castle vale School, Castlehead High School, Castlehills School, Cator Park School for Girls, Central Technology College, Chamberlayne Park School, Chapel en le Frith, Charles Reed high School, Chase Terrace High School, Checkendon C of E Primary School, Chellaston School, Cherry Orchard Middle School, Cherry Tree School, Cherry Willingham Community School, Chester College, Chesterfield College, Chesterfield High School, Chethams School of music, Children's Hospital School, Chiltern Cantelo School, Chiltern Edge School, Chilwell Comprehensive School, Chingford Foundation School, Chitern lower School, Chosen Hill School, Christ the King School, Christ's College, Christ's School, Churchdown School, Churchfield School, Churston Ferrers Grammar School, City of Leicester School, City of London School for Girls, City of Portsmouth Girls School, City School, Claire Mount School, Clare Mount School, Claremount School, Clifton College, Clough Hall Technology School, Clover Reed's School, Coatbridge High School, Cockburn High School, Colchester High School For Girls, Colne Park High School, Colne Valley High School, Colonel Frank Seely School, Colton Hills Community School, Combe Down Primary School, Connaught School, Coombe Dean School, Cooper School, Coppice High School, Coquet High School, Cordeaux High School, Cotelands School, Cotswold Chine School, Coulsdon College, Coulsdon High School, Craig Mount High School, Cranborne Middle School, Crestwood School, Crispin School, Croesycilíog School, Croft Primary School, Crofton High School, Crofton School, Crookhorn Secondary School, Crossley Heath School, Crown Hills Community College, Crown woods School, Cuthbert Mayne School, Dagfa House School, Dalestorth Primary School, Dalkeith High School, Danecourt Grammar School , Danum School, Danum School Technology College, Darland School, Darton High School, Darwin Vale High School, Dawn House School, Dayncourt School, De Aston School, De Lisle Catholic School, Deincourt Community School, Dene Magna Community School, Denny High School, Derby High School, Derby Moor Community School, Derrymount School, Dewsbury College, Dinnington Comprehensive School, Dixie Grammar School, Dixons City Technical College, Don Valley School, Doncaster College, Dover Girls Grammar School, Dr Challoners Grammar School, Drayton School, Dronfield School, Duchess's Community High School, Dukeries School, Dumfries High School, Durants School, Durham High School for Girls, Dyke House School, Dyson Perrins School, Eaglescliffe School, Earl of Scarborough High School, Earlham High School, Easington Community School, Easingwold School, East Bridgewater Community, School, Eastbourne Technical College, Easthampstead Park School, Eastwood comprehensive school, Eaton Bank School, Eaton Comprehensive School, EBBW Vale comprehensive school, Ecclesbourne School, Eckington School, Edensor high School, Edgbarrow School, Edge End High School, Eliot Durham School, Elizabethan High Schoo, Elmsdale High School, Eltham Hill Technology College for Girls, Emmanuel School, Endeavour High School, Enderby Danemill Primary School, Endon High School, Enfield Grammer School, Ernehale JuniorSchool, Ernesford Grange School, Eton College, Etone Community School, Fairfax School, Fairfield High School, Fairham Community School, Fakenham High School, Falkirk High School, Fallibroome High School, Farfield Girls School, Farmor's School, Farnborough School, Farr Hill School, Farringdon Community College, Fearnhill School, Fearns Community High School, Fernhill Secondary School, Fernwood Comprehensive School, Fernwood Junior School, Fernwood School, Filey School, Filsham Valley School, Fir Vale School, Firth Park Community School, Fortismere School, Foulstone School, Foxhills School, Foxwood School, Framingham Earl C High School, Framwellgate School, Frank I Harrison School, Frank S Harrison School, Frederick Gent School, Frederick Harrison Infant School, ,Freesland School, Friary School, Friesland School, Frodsham High School, Fulbrook School , Fulford School, Fulhurst Community College, Furness College, Gable Hall School, Garendon School, Garibaldi School, Garstang High School, Gartree High School, Gateacre Comprehensive School, Gateways School, Gawthorpe High School, Gayhurst School, Geat Barr school, Gedling School, George Abbot School, George Spencer School, Giggleswick School, Gleed Girls School, Glyn Derw High School, Godley Primary School, Golden Hillock School, Goldings Middle School, Golspie high school, Gonville Primary School, Good Shepherd Primary School, Goodricke College, Gosforth High School, Graham School, Grange Middle School, Grangefield School, Grantham Church High School, Great Baddow High School, Great Bar School, Great Berry High School, Great Sankey High School, Great Wyrley High School, Great Yarmouth High School, Green Bank High School, Greendown School ,Greenshaw High School, Greenwood Dale School, Griff School, Grindon Hall Christian School, Grosvenor School, Grove School, Gryphin School, Gwindon Hall Christian School, Habergham High School, Halesowen College, Halewood Community Comprehensive School., Hall Cross School , Halstead Place School, Hammersmith & Twckenham School, Hampden Park School, Hampstead Hall School, Hamstead Junior School, Hanson School, Harl Laxton College, Harris C of E High School, Harrogate Granby High School, Harrow High School, Harry Carlton School, Hartford High School, Hasmonean High School, Hasmonean Primary School, Hastings High School, Hastingsbury School, Hatfield High School, Hathershaw Technology College, Haywood school, Hazel Grove High School, Headlands School, Heanor Gate School, Heart of England School, Heartseas High School, Heathcoat Primary Schoolm, Heathfield High School, Heathfield School GDST, Heckmundwhite Grammar School, Helenswood School, Heles School , Helsby High School, Henry Box School, Henry Cort Community School, Henry Mellish School, Henry Smith School, Henry VBeaufort Secondary School, Henry VII Senior School, Hereford Cathedral School, Hereford Tech School, Heritage Community school, Heritage School, Heronsgate School, Herts and Essex High School, High School for Girls, High Stones School, High Town Primary school, Highbury Grove School, Highfields School, Hightown Primary School, Highview School, Highworth Grammar School, Hilbre High School, Hill Head High School, Hindley Comm. High School, Hodgson High School, Holgate Comprehensive School, Holly Lodge High School, Hollygirt School, Holmfirth High School, Holte School, Holy School, Holy Trinity Catholic Primary School, Holy Trinity CE (A) Senior School), Honiton Community College, Honley High School & College, Hopwood Hall College, Horndean Community School, Horsforth School, Horsforth School, Houndsdown School, Howden Clough School for Girls, Hucknall Junior School. Hulme Grammar School , Hummersknott School & Language Coll, Huntcliff School, Huthbaid College , Huxlow School, Hydesville Tower School, Ilkeston School , Ilkley Grammar School, immanuel college, Immingham School, Intake High School, Isebrook School, Isleworth & Syon School, Ivanhoe College, Jack Hunt School, James Brindley High School, James Gillespie High School , Jewish Primary School, John Bentley School, John Cleveland College, John Fernley High School, John Hanson School, John Port School, John Smeaton Community High School, John Summers , John Taylor High School, Joseph Lecke School, Joseph Rowntree School, Joseph Susan School , Joseph Whitaker School, Jubilee House Christian School , Judge Meadow Comprehensive School, Kenilworth School, Kennel Lane School , Kennet School, Kesgrave High School, Kesteven and Sleaford High School, Kestgrave High School ,Keyham Lodge school, Kibworth High School , Kimberley School, Kimberworth Comprehensive School, Kimbolton School, Kineton High School, King David High School, King Ecgbert School, King Edward VI Camp Hill School For, King Edward VI Grammar School, King Edward VI Grammar School, King Edward VI Handsworth School,, King Edward VI High School, King Edward VI School, King Edward VI School, King Edward VI School, King Edward VI School for Girls, King Edward VII & Queen Mary School, King Edward VII Camphill School for, King Edward VII School, King Edward VII Upper School, King George V School, King James School, King Richard Secondary School, King Solomon High School, King William Street School , Kings High Schools for Girls, Kings Norton Girls High School, Kings School, Kings School, Kings School, Kings Secondary School,Kingsbury School, Kingsley Park Middle School, kingsnorton Boys School, Kingswood School, Kirkby College , Kirkby Kendal School, Kirkby Stephen Grammar School, Kirkham Grammar School, Knowsley Hey School, Lacon Childe School, Lady Manners School, Lakelands School, Lakes College, Lancaster Boys School, Lancaster Girls Grammar School, Landau Forte School, Langdon College, Langley Park School for Boys, Langley School, Lawnswood School, Lawrence Jackson School, Leeds Grammar School, Leeds High school, Lees Brook School, Leicester Grammer School, Leicester High School, Leicester High School for Girls, Leighton Park School, Leon School & Sports College ,Limehurst High school, Lincoln Christ's Hospital School, Lincoln Minster School, Lindsey School, Lindsey School & Communtiy Arts Col, Liskeard School, Little Heath School, Locksley Christian School, Lode Heath School, Lodge Park Technology College, Long Eaton Community School, Longbenton college, Longfield School, Longslade community college, Lordswood Girl's School, Lostock College, Loughborough Grammar School, Loughborough High School, Lourds Secondary school, lowestoft College, M.G.B School, Mackworth College, Magdalen College School, Magnus Church of England School, Maidenhill School, Malet Lambert School, Maltby Comprehensive School, Manchester High School for Girls, Mank's Dyke Technology College, Manning School, Manor C E School, Manor College, Manor High School , Manor Park School, Manor School, Maplewell Hall School, Market Bosworth High School, Market Weighton School, Marshlands High School, Martin High School, Masidenhill School, Matthew Holland School, Matthew Humberstone School, Matthew Moss High School, Matthew Murray High School, Mayfield School, Mayfield Secondary Schoolm Mayflower High School, Mcauley Catholic High School, Meadow Lane infant schoolm Meadowhead Schoolm Meadows Community School, Medeley Court School, Meden School, Medlock Primary School, Merchant Taylor's School, Mereway Upper School, Merlin Rees High School, Merrill College, Merton College, Methwold High School, Michael Sobell Sinai School, Middlefield School, Milais School, Milestone School, Mill Chase Secondary School, Mill Hill, County High School, Mill Hill School, Millfield C P School, Milton Keynes College, Milwards Primary School and Nursery, Minster School, Minsthorpe community Collegem Montagu School, Montsaye School, Moor House School, Moorlands School, Moorside High School ,Moreton Community School, Morley High School, Morley High School, Mortimer Comprehensive, Moseley School, Mosslands Schools, Moulton School, Mount Grace High School, Mount School, Mount St Mary's Catholic School, Mount St Mary's School, Mountbatten Secondary School, Murray Park School, Myers Grove School, Nantyglo Comprehensive School, National C of E Junior School, National C of E Junior School, NCC Prince William School, Nelson and Coln College, Netherfield Junior School, Netherthorpe School, Netley School, Neville Lovertt Secondary School, New College Nottingham, Newark E to E, Newark High School, Newcastle Community High School, Newcastle Community School, Newent Community School, Newfield School, Newland School for Girls, Newman College, Newnham Middle School, Newport Primary school, Newsome High School, Newton Primary School, Newton Regis Primary School, Newton School for Girls, Neyland junior school, Niddrie Mill Primary school, Noadswood Secondary School, Noel Baker School, North Cheshire Jewish Primary School, North Doncaster College, North Kesteven School, North Leamington School, North Lindsey College, North Notts College, Northampton School for Girls, Northcliffe School, Northfield Primary School,I Northfield School, Northgate School, Northumberland CollegeNotre Dame R C Girl's School, Notre Dame School, Notre Dame School, Nottingham Bluecoat School, Nottingham Emanuel School, Nottingham, High School For Boys, Nottingham High School for Girls, Nunthorpe School, Oakbank SchoolOaklands Catholic School, Oaklands Comprehensive School, Ockbrook School, Offwell School, Old Hall School, Orchard Primary and Nursery School, Orchard School, Ordsall Comp School, Ordsall Hall School, Ordsall Junior School, Orian Primary School, Orwell Park School, Ossett School, Oundle School, Ounsdale School, Our Lady and Pope John School, Our Lady's Convent High School, Our Lady's Convent School, Our Lady's High School, Oxclose Communtiy School, Oxted School, OYY Lubavitch Boys' School, Palatine High School, Pangbourne college, Park Community School, Park Primary School, Parkfield High School, Parklands Girls High School, Parrenthorn High SChool, Parrenthorn High School, Paul Hayes Community School, Paulet High School, Pencalenick School, Perins Community School, Pestatyn High School, Petersfield School, Pilgrim Hospital School, Pingle School, Plantsbrook School, Pocklington School, Polesworth High School, Pool Hayes Community School, Portchester Community School, Portland Primary and Nursery School, Portland School, Potway Community School, Prestatyn High SChool, Prestwich High School, Priesthorpe High School, Priestland School, Prince Harry Grammer School, Prince Henry's Grammar School, Prince William School, Putteridge High School, Quarrydale School, Queen Elisabeth High School, Queen Elisabeth High School, Queen Elisabeth School, Queen Elizabeth Grammar School, Queen Elizabeth Grammer School, Queen Elizabeth Mercian School, Queen Elizabeths School, Queen Ethelburga's School, Queen Mary's High School, --Queensbury School, Radcliffe School, Radford Primary School, Ralph Thoresby High School, Ramsey Grammar School, Raphael Independent school, Ravens Wood School, Ravenswood Primary School, Rawmarsh School, Read School, Reading School, Redhill School, Redland High School for Girls, Rednock School, Reed's School, Reepham High School, Regents Park School, Reigate Grammar Schoo, Reigate School, Repton School, Retford Upper School, Rhodesway School, Ridgeway school, Ridgewood School. Rippon and York St John College, Riverside Community College, Robert May's School, Robert Pattinson School, Rochester Math School, Romsey Secondary School, Rossett High School, Rossington High School, Roundhill community college, Rowan High School, Rowley Fields School, Royal Latin School, Royal School For The Deaf, Royal West of England School of the Deaf , Roydes Hall High School, Royshall High School, Rudolf Steiner School, Rufford School, Rugby High School, Rushcliffe Comp. School, Rushcliffe E to E, Rushden Community College, Rushden Community School, Ryde County High School, Rye Hill, School, Sacred Heart Catholic High School, Saint John Fisher, Salt Grammar School, Samuel Rhodes School, Sandbach High School, Severn Vale School, Shanwick Hall School, Shavington High School, Sheffield High SChool, Sheffield Sports College, Shenley Court School, Shepherd School, Shepshed High School, Sherburn High School, Sherwood Hall School, Shevington High School, Shire Oak School, Shirebrook School, Shireoak School, Sholing Girls School, Shotton Hall Comprehensive School, Shrewsbury School, Sir John Leman High School, Sir John Sherbrooke Junior School, Sir Joseph Williamsons Mathematical School, Sir Thomas Boughey High School, Sir William Robertson High School, Sir William Romneys School, Skegness Grammar School ,Skill force,Quarrydale School, Skipton Girls High School, Small Heath Lower School, Smithsdon High School, Smithswood School, Snaith School, Soar Valley College, Solihull School, Somervale School, South Charnwod High School, South Holdeness School, South Hunsley School, South Lands High School ,South Notts College, South Wigston High School, South Wirral High School, Southam College, Southend High School, Southlands High School, Southway Community College, Southwold Primary School, Southwolds School, Sparrowdale School, Spennymore School, Sponne School, Spratton Hall School, Springfield Junior School, Springfield School, Springwell Community School, Springwood High School, St Aidan's C of E School, St Albans High School for Girls, St Ambrose Barlow RC High School, St Anselin's college, St Augustine of Canterbury RC High School, St Augustines RC High School, St Charles RC School, St Christopher CE High School, St Christophers School, St Claire's Special School, St Crispin's School, St Edmund Arrowsmith School, St Edmund's Girls School, St Edmund's School, St Edward's School, St Felix School, St Francis College, St Francis School, St Francis Xavier's College, St Georges RC High School, St Georges RC Secondary School, St Gregory's Catholic High School, St Gregory's Catholic High School, St Hilda's CE High School, St James C of E School , St James's Catholic High School, St John College, St John Fisher High School, St John Fishers School, St John's Healthy School Project, St John's High School, St Joseph College, St Joseph's Catholic School, St Luke's School, St Margaret Ward High School, St Margaret's School, St Marks School, St Mark's School, St Marks West Essex Catholic School, St Martin's High School, St Martin's School. St Mary and St Martin Primary School, St Mary Cof E Primary School, St Mary's Catholic High School, St Mary's College, St Mary's High School, St Mary's Primary School, St Marys R C School, St Marys R.C High School, St Mary's R.C.School, St Mary's RC High School, St Marys School, St Mary's School, St Michael at Bowes School, St Michael RC School, St Michael's C OE Middle School, St Michael's c of E school, St Michael's Catholic High School, St Michael's CE Primary School, St Mungo's High School, St Ninians High, St Paul's Catholic School, St Paul's School, St Peter & St. Paul School, St Peter Port School, St Peters School, St Peter's School, St Peter's School, St Philip Howard School, St Richard Gwyn High School, St Robert of Newminster School, St Stephen Churchtown CP School, St Swithin's Girls School, St Teresa's School, St Thomas A Becket, St Thomas Moore RC School, St Thomas More Catholic Primary School, St Thomas of Aquins High School ,St Thomas - Becket School, St Walframs CE High School, St Wilfrid's RC High School, St. Margaret's School, St. Marys Catholic High School, Stainburn School, Stamford School, Standish Community High School, Standish High School, Stanford hall College, Stanhope Primary School , Stanwell Comprehensive School, Staunton Park School, Stephenson Way Primary School, Stockton Primary School, Stokesley Comprehensive, School, Stokesley School, Stoney Dean School, Streetly School, Stretford Grammer School, Stubbin Wood School, Stubton Hall School, Sudbury Upper School, Sunnyside Primary School, Suttton Ctr Comm College, Swanbourne House School, Swanley School, Swanwick Hall School, Swinton Comprehensive, Sydenham School, Tanfield School, Tarleton High School, Tarleton High School, Teesdale School, Teign School, Temple Moor High School, Temple Ewell C.E.P. School, Tendring Technology College, Test Valley Secondary School, The Alfred Barrow School, The Armthorpe School, The Aveland High School, The Becket School, The Bishop Stortford High School, The Campion School, The Chalfont Community College, The Challenge College, The Chase High School, The College of Ripon and York, The Community College, The Deepings School, The Divinity School, The Dronfield School, The Ecclesbourne School, The Edgware school, The Elizabethan High School, The Emmanuel School, The Ferrers School, The Foulstone School, The Gedling School, The Godolphin and Latymer School, The Green School, The Griff School, The Grove School, The Harry Carlton School, The Hartland School , The Hayesbrook School, The Hillcrest School Dudley, The Holgate School, The Holy Cross School , The Hulme Grammar School For Girls, The Jews Free School, The John Henry Newman School, The Joseph Rowntree School, The King David High School, The Kings High School, The Kings Schol , The Kings School, The Kings School, The King's School, The Kingstone School, The Kingswood School ,The Lakelands School, The Lindsey School, The Magnus C of E School, The Malet lambert School, The Marches School, The Market Wheaton School, THe Marlborough School, The McAuley School, The Meadows Community School, The Meadows School, The Michael Sobell Sinai School, The Minster School, The Mount School, The Old School, The Orchard Special School, The Peele School, The Petersfield School, The Pingle School, The Plume School, The Queens Foundation FOD, The Ridgeway School, The Royal School, The Royal School, The Royal School for the Deaf, The Royal Wolverhampton School, The Streetly School, The Swinton High School, The Thorpe Bay School, The Tong School, The Toynbee School, The Village Community School, The Weldon School, Therfield School, Thistley Hough High School, Thomas Adams School, Thomas Adams School, Thomas Alleyne's High School, Thomas Cowley High School, Thomas Estley School, Thomas Keeble School, Thomas Magnus C of E School, Thomas Tallis School, Thorden Secondary School, Thorn Community School, Thorn Hill high, Thorn Park School for the Deaf, Thornaby Community School, Thornden School, Thorne Grammar School, Thornhill High School, Thornton College, Thornton School, Thorpe Bay School, Thorpe St Andrew School, Thurso High school, Thurstable School, Tong School, Toothill School, Top Valley School, Tower College, Townley Grammar School for Girls, Toynbee Secondary School, Trent College, Trinity School, Trinity School, Tupton Hall School, Tuxford Comprehensve School, Tuxford Primary School, Upton Hall School, Vallerod Skolen (Danish School), Village Community School, Wales High School, Waltheof School, Walton High School, Warwick School, Wath Comprehensive School, Wavell School, Weald of Kent Grammar School, Wellesley School, West Bridgford School, West Graven High School, West Leeds High School, West Park School, Westborough School, Westhill College, Whitecross school, Whitesmore School, Whitgift School, Whittington Grange School, Wildern Secondary School, Wilford Meadows School, William Farr Comprehensive School, William Harrison School, William Henry Smith School, William Lovell CE School, Wilnecote High School, Windsor Boys School, Winton School, Woldgate School, Wolfreton School, Wolfson Hillel Primary School, Wolstanton High School, Wolverhampton Grammar School, Wombwell High School, Woodgreen School, Woodhouse Grove School, Woodlands Community School, Wortley High School, Wycombe Abbey School, Wymondham High School, Yarborough School, Yardleys School, Yardleys School, Yarm School

history
moving

It was clear to us from an early stage that the physical space of The Holocaust Centre was not going to be sufficient to provide resources for all those who wanted to access them. Visitors were travelling to the Centre from within a two-hour radius on the whole, which covers 37 per cent of the population. But for those outside the catchment area, a travelling exhibition was created to circulate around educational institutions.

"Another Time, Another Place" is a twenty-panel exhibit which condenses the permanent exhibition into a mobile format. The historical narrative is woven around the personal experience of survivor Kitty Hart-Moxon. As the history unfolds, the narrative returns to her story to provide continuity and a human dimension to the story.

The demand for the exhibition was such that it was reproduced in four copies and was used by schools and universities as far afield as the Isle of Wight, Glasgow, Cardiff and Belfast. Approximately 30,000 students a year used the exhibitions in school-based learning programmes, often with survivor speakers attending the school to participate in the programmes.

161

education

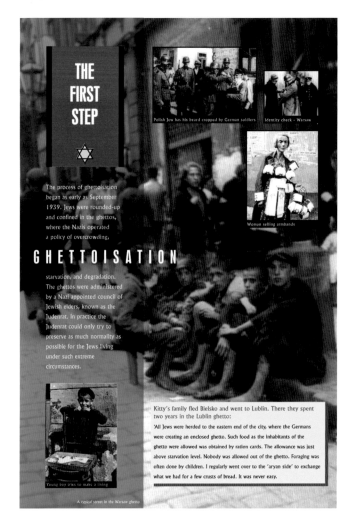

THE FIRST STEP

Polish Jew has his beard cropped by German soldiers — Identity check - Warsaw

Woman selling armbands

The process of ghettoisation began as early as September 1939. Jews were rounded-up and confined in the ghettos, where the Nazis operated a policy of overcrowding,

GHETTOISATION

starvation, and degradation. The ghettos were administered by a Nazi appointed council of Jewish elders, known as the Judenrat. In practice the Judenrat could only try to preserve as much normality as possible for the Jews living under such extreme circumstances.

Young boy tries to make a living

Kitty's family fled Bielsko and went to Lublin. There they spent two years in the Lublin ghetto:

'All Jews were herded to the eastern end of the city, where the Germans were creating an enclosed ghetto. Such food as the inhabitants of the ghetto were allowed was obtained by ration cards. The allowance was just above starvation level. Nobody was allowed out of the ghetto. Foraging was often done by children. I regularly went over to the 'aryan side' to exchange what we had for a few crusts of bread. It was never easy.

A typical street in the Warsaw ghetto

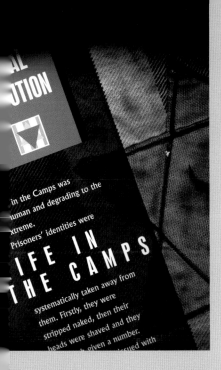

Life in the Camps was ... human and degrading to the extreme. Prisoners' identities were systematically taken away from them. Firstly, they were stripped naked, then their heads were shaved and they ... given a number. ... ssued with

Alan Brine HMI

Former Inspector for Religious Education in Hampshire

I first came across the work of The Holocaust Centre in the mid-1990s when, working with other colleagues in Hampshire, I visited their travelling exhibition. We were struck by its quality and by its potential as a resource in Hampshire schools. At that time, schools were seeking to make RE more relevant and challenging for secondary pupils and the theme of the Holocaust was proving a particularly effective way of achieving this.

Schools were desperate to find material on the events of the Holocaust which was honest, reliable, challenging and engaging. The travelling exhibition was ideal and The Holocaust Centre was kind enough to let us have a copy on long loan to move between Hampshire schools. I remember writing to all the heads of RE and history in the county offering them the opportunity to borrow the exhibition – wondering if the logistics of moving it around and providing display space would defeat us. We need not have worried.

The response was overwhelming and I recall Dawn Thompson, who at that time ran Hampshire's RE Resource Centre, spending many profitable, if at times stressful, hours organising the delivery and installation of the exhibition in schools across the county.

All the effort was worth it. The exhibition proved a great success and ensured that many teenagers had access to a resource which would stimulate their interest, support their learning, and serve as a moving and long-remembered experience.

100 nights

At the opening of the Cape Town Holocaust Centre, Justice Richard Goldstone remarked to us that there was yet to be a travelling exhibit on the Rwandan genocide, and that it would be valuable for us to think about creating such a resource.

The following year Aegis created the first international travelling exhibition on the genocide in Rwanda. Entitled *100 Nights*, the exhibit details the causes and consequences of the genocide in four five-metre folding panels.

The exhibit has toured the UK extensively as well as being displayed in venues in South Africa, France and Rwanda itself.

163

education

education

Universities
Organisations
Schools

Edinburgh

Newcastle
Upon Tyne

Kendal
York
Preston Hull
Leeds
Liverpool
Manchester Lincoln
Nottingham
Shrewsbury Norwich
Birmingham
Northampton Cambridge
Oxford
Cardiff LONDON
Bristol
Guildford
Salisbury Maidstone
Southampton
Portsmouth

Regions in which The Holocaust Centre has outreach
programmes.

*"I don't think it's something that
anybody will forget."*

Anna, Eastbourne Technology College

Joyce Miller

Head of Diversity and Cohesion Education, Bradford

Bringing The Holocaust Centre's travelling exhibition to Bradford gave us the opportunity to mark the first national Holocaust Memorial Day in a way which impacted on the life and work of many of our secondary schools.

The launch of the exhibition was held in one of our schools that serves a mainly Pakistani heritage community and they were the young people who acted as guides and hosts that evening. For many, it was a significant experience which challenged deeply-rooted ideas and stereotypes and caused them to begin to articulate questions that had never presented themselves in such stark reality before. Long after the guests had left, they remained – talking and sharing and puzzling over what they had learned. There was genuine engagement and empathy and a learning process began that evening which might well continue to exercise their minds and lives for a long time to come.

This brief description of one event represents one of the real privileges of teaching and working with young people where, particularly in religious education, there is the opportunity to explore issues about theology, morality, philosophy and human rights, which are of immense importance as young people are growing up and working out their own world-views. There are questions here that have no answers and that is another tension with which young people have to deal; despite the lack of simple solutions, these questions are crucially important for they are at the heart of being human, and therein lies hope.

Tricia Martin
Senior Lecturer, College of St Mark and St John and RE Adviser, Diocese of Exeter

My attendance at The Holocaust Centre, Beth Shalom's First Graduate Summer School in 1998 changed the direction of my life. I thought I knew what the Holocaust entailed; I discovered that I hadn't had a clue! Facts I could recite to some extent, but what became very clear to me was that they had little meaning unless the human stories behind them were encountered. At Beth Shalom I experienced these encounters. As a result, I arranged for the Holocaust Mobile Exhibition to tour eight schools in Devon and 35 teachers attended INSET training. Six years on, many schools in Devon have been visited by Holocaust survivors and the 'history' has become experience and the beginning of understanding rather than facts. On a personal level, I have been privileged to lead INSET at Beth Shalom, I am a Freelance Educator for the Holocaust Educational Trust and I am completing an MA in Jewish-Christian Relations. My initial visit to the Centre caused many 'ripples in the pond' and I know I am but one of many for whom it has had just such an effect.

Look at the Oceans

LOOK AT THE OCEANS!
Rolling with the blood of the innocent,
Staining Dover's cliffs red.

HARK AT THE STREAMS!
Bitter with the tears of millions mourning,
No more rushing, their joy is gone.

WALK THE STONES!
Skulls of human ivory,
Exposed by the wasted flesh.

FEEL THE TREES!
Shivering with fear,
Every leaf terrified of the slaughter.

STARE AT THE SKY!
Yellow badges of accusation,
Blotted out by the black spider.

LISTEN TO THE WIND!
Calling to the world leaders
"never again, no never again."

Kirsty Reger
Poem inspired by seeing "Another Time, Another Place", Soham Village College, Ely, Cambs

166

education

learning _for life_

In addition to formal education, the Centre has an active informal education programme, which encourages young people and adults involved in group-learning to access the Centre's resources.

For young people, the Centre provides services with opportunities to bring youth groups to pursue interests in the Holocaust, genocide, racism and prejudice, society and citizenship. The Centre is also used by Sunday schools and synagogue classes.

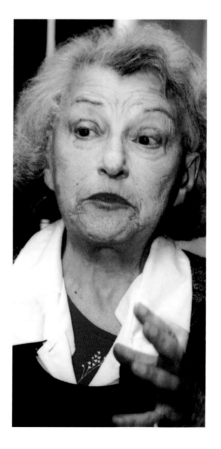

The Leicester Interfaith gardening group comes each year for an informal education seminar and spends several hours volunteering in the memorial gardens, organised by Sara Elkes, daughter of the former head of the Kaunas Ghetto _Judenrat_, Dr Elkhanan Elkes.

"*We are all human beings and have different ways of believing what to do, but we all have to respect one another. I've learned about different ways of understanding life and to tolerate other views.*"

Participant, Leicester International Interfaith
Gardening Work-camp

"Today we went to The Holocaust
Centre. I behaved well. That is
good because when I used to go out
I was usually told off. Today was
incredible. I had a wicked time. I
learnt a lot too! That survivor talk
made me rethink about all different
people."

Carrie Jones, Entry to Employment, Ollerton

visits

"If it was left to me, a visit for all within reach would be compulsory." Canon Ian E Gooding

visits
group

Since opening, the Centre has welcomed hundreds of organised coach parties for day visits. Groups have come from churches, synagogues, Rotary Clubs, University of the Third Age and Association of Jewish Refugees.

Volunteer groups that have used the Centre for informal training include Victim Support, East European tour guide training, interfaith groups, anti-racism and human rights groups.

Group visits are arranged as day visits and include talks, films and discussion, as well as seeing the museum and gardens. These visits are rarely enjoyable, but can be strangely stimulating. The rare opportunity to discuss difficult issues and to find a small way to remember the past in constructive dialogue is an important part of the experience for our visitors.

Groups may be as small as a dozen people or extend to as many as two coach-loads. However large or small the group, people come together to listen, to learn and to teach us too.

visits

Nitza and Robin Spiro
**Founders of the Spiro Institute and Directors of the Spiro Ark,
Holocaust Centre Group Leader**

We first heard about The Holocaust Centre, Beth Shalom from Geoffrey Wigoder, editor of the *Encyclopaedia Judaica,* a friend of the Spiro educational vision and a mentor of the Centre. He urged us to go and see this educational phenomenon at an early stage when it was hardly known.

We came, we saw and we were conquered.

Ten years on, we are all delighted to observe how the entire Smith family defied the sceptics who say that individuals have no power to make history. They have shown us how the concept of a family, united by a common, noble goal can be used for the good of thousands worldwide. This has been done through enormous commitment, selflessness, a deep feeling for humanity and an incredible ability to respond to universal issues of prejudice, discrimination and genocide.

We at The Spiro Ark are proud to claim immediate recognition of the Smith project and of our joint programmes with Beth Shalom, which we believe have had a significant impact on the public.

Ruth Jacobs
**Director, Israel Information Centre, Midlands and
Regional Coordinator, JNF UK, Holocaust Centre Group Leader**

Beth Shalom Holocaust Memorial Centre and the Smith family made an indelible impression on me when I first visited there in its infancy. Since then I have been privileged to bring many visitors, including Israeli ambassadors and diplomats, and I have encouraged senior Midlands Christian clergy, city councillors, educationalists and those involved with interfaith dialogue to experience the uniquely inspiring setting and message of Beth Shalom.

Through my involvement with JNF UK, the Midlands celebrated JNF's century in 2001 with a tribute dinner organised in Birmingham to acknowledge the extraordinary contribution made by Stephen Smith and his family to Holocaust awareness and education. As a result of the tremendous UK and international response, which raised over £55,000, the Stephen Smith Forest in the British Park was established near Jerusalem, with a separate plaque recording this installed in the beautiful garden at Beth Shalom. Sadly, as the need for the lessons learnt from the Holocaust has not diminished, may Beth Shalom continue to inspire and motivate people to work towards changing the world. Congratulations on the achievements of the last ten years and sincere good wishes for the future.

community local

The Holocaust was a global event which happened at a local level. We therefore run programmes for professionals working with local people. Our Communities Seminar Programme fulfils this need. These are attended by officers in local authorities who hold diversity, citizenship, race equality, public relations and events portfolios.

Holocaust Memorial Day seminars are held each year to give event organisers in local authorities, schools and community groups theme-related ideas for the delivery of their local programme.

Work with Race Equality Councils, equality officers and community cohesion coordinators for local communities results in seminars at the Centre in support of their work, or participation by the Centre's professional team in community-based seminars. These seminars aim to raise awareness about the Holocaust and apply the issues it raises to current and ongoing policies.

175

visits

Paddy Tipping
MP for Sherwood

The Holocaust Centre borders my constituency and has a significant role to play in the community which I serve as Member of Parliament for Sherwood. I was delighted to learn of its existence and the vision it has to teach about the Holocaust as a means to warn, to challenge and inspire.

For some time now, I have had a personal interest in the events which occurred in Armenia, the first of many genocidal events which scarred the twentieth century. To know that The Holocaust Centre, through its teaching, and Aegis, through its parliamentary work, are working hard to make genocide a thing of the past is something which gives me great pleasure to support personally and professionally. It is heart-warming to know that, on a daily basis, the local community of North Nottinghamshire is playing a small but significant role in these important global issues.

The Lord Mayor of Nottingham, Cllr Roy Greensmith, 1998

Bob Froggat, former Chair, Laxton Parish Council

176

visits

Cllr Stella Smedley, Notts County Council

guests special

All our visitors are special. Sometimes, though, official or high-profile visits bring particular activites to the life of the Centre. Such visitors demonstrate the relevance of the Centre to public life and keep it connected to contemporary issues, concerns and constituencies.

177

visits

"I think it's remarkable what you have created here. It really is a fascinating and wonderful place. I am sure a lot more people will want to visit the Centre in future."

HRH Duke of Kent

"What a delightful letter you sent us following our memorable visit to your remarkable Centre... I particularly liked your references to the choices yet to be made. Your reference to current affairs in the Balkans is indeed frightening. The line between sins of omission and commission is thin indeed, and one wonders what the judgement of history is going to be. We certainly found the Nottingham experience most stimulating."

The Rt Hon The Lord Jakobovits, 1999

visits

Sir Bob Geldof

Indifference grows from the commonplace. I hope this Centre can articulate the story of the Holocaust not just for young people, but for all of us.

I hope that the language of the Holocaust, the piety from the Holocaust, the images of the Holocaust never become worn-out with overuse, and that we become indifferent to them. The daily banalities of the news can't counter the horrors to which we should be alert, whether it's in Rwanda, in South America against the peoples of the Amazon, where genocide is perpetrated in the name of the god 'development', or in South Africa.

In Africa today, we can see what is happening, particularly in terms of the AIDS pandemic. Is this not a kind of genocide? In Zambia, 25 per cent of the society have AIDS. There you can see a society in collapse. In South Africa, the figure for those with AIDS is 20 per cent of the population. We know about it. We have the drugs to help these people, so why don't we? I'm telling you:

millions upon millions of children will be dying in ten years. Today, 10 per cent of all children in the affected countries are dying. Is that not genocide? They live in far-away countries about which we know next to nothing, and for whom we do little. It's the articulation of our indifference.

We can go on and on about killing. All of us know we human beings do it, and we know we are going to keep doing it, and that's why The Holocaust Centre, Beth Shalom and the new Aegis Institute are so important. Because unless we're confronted in the most direct and brutal way, using the clearest and most shameless language to describe genocide, genocidal events and mass killings, we shall not take notice and do something about stopping these horrors – and then all those lights of human genius in so many parts of our fragile world will just wink out.

From a speech at the Centre, September 2002

180

visits

professional

"Who they are is more important than what they teach…"   Frank McDermott

training

The Holocaust was perpetrated by professionals.

It also has profound implications for professionals today.

During the Nazi period, lawyers, doctors, teachers, clergy, police, prison officers, civil servants, scientists, engineers and architects participated in the execution of the Holocaust. Not all participated knowingly or willingly, but the whole structure of National Socialism demanded the adherence of professional bodies and the application of their professional skills to the environment of racial domination.

The Holocaust Centre runs a series of development seminars for professionals from a variety of disciplines. The design of the training assists both personal and professional development for delegates.

The first principle behind the training is that the Holocaust should demand something of each of us individually. Using the exhibition

and dialogue with survivors, delegates are encouraged to confront the challenge the Holocaust presents to them as an individual.

Through a process of workshops and discussions, the issues the Holocaust raises for the delegates as professionals are addressed and discussed. The aim of the programme is for them to rethink their attitudes, policies and roles as professionals. In some instances, the seminars confirm that they are already using best practice. In many cases, adjustment to department policy is implemented as a direct result of visits to the Centre.

183

professional

"Monday was a very special day I'm sure I'll never forget. I have studied the Holocaust in much depth over the past 4-5 years, but I think being at The Holocaust Centre really brought home to me that the Holocaust happened to real people."

Emma Sutcliffe, RE Teacher

training
teacher

We knew it was important to provide space, time and expert support for teachers to develop their knowledge, skills and practice at the Centre. Seminars are scheduled on a regular basis on the teaching of the Holocaust in History, Religious Education, Citizenship, Primary Schools and for Holocaust Memorial Day.

Teaching seminars are structured to support current curriculum areas in which the Holocaust is taught. All seminars access the resources of the Centre in developing the fundamental historical knowledge necessary for teaching the subject in any discipline.

Staff and guest facilitators introduce a variety of pedagogical methodologies, better equipping teachers for classroom practice in a variety of curriculum areas under discussion.

185

professional

Teachers in Nazi Germany used the classroom to persecute Jewish children

"As one colleague put it, it was 'a very special and unique experience – challenging and emotive, current and relevant. This has enhanced and enriched my personal development.'"

Scott Harrison, HMI

Arek Hersh, Holocaust Survivor

Frank J. McDermott
Director of Schools, Diocese of Hallam

If you believe that the first responsibility of every teacher, no matter what subject they teach, is to nurture the human wholeness of the children in their charge, then The Holocaust Centre makes a significant contribution to teacher training and to their ongoing formation.

If you believe that true education has the capacity to transform lives; to help young people to be better brothers, better sisters, better mums, better dads, better friends, better neighbours, better citizens; to learn that who we are is more important than what we do; to accept that if I have rights, I also have responsibilities, then The Holocaust Centre has much to offer.

If you believe that education should focus on intellectual achievement where grades and levels are more important than human growth; where the position of the school in the league tables is more important than the human wholeness of the pupils, then The Holocaust Centre will offer you little.

For three years now, the Catholic Diocese of Hallam has visited the Centre as part of a programme for the professional development of teachers, chaplains, deputy heads and heads. Each year since 1994, every adult who comes to work in any of our 53 primary and secondary schools receives a letter of welcome from me as Director of Schools, together with a copy of those powerful words written by a survivor of Auschwitz:

Dear...
I am a survivor of a concentration camp.
My eyes have seen what no man should witness:
Gas chambers built by learned engineers,
Children poisoned by educated physicians,
Infants killed by trained nurses,
Women and babies shot and burned by high school
And college graduates.

So I am suspicious of education.
My request is:
Help your students become more human,
Your efforts must never produce learned monsters,
Skilled psychopaths, educated Eichmanns.
Reading, writing, arithmetic are important but only if they
Serve to make our children more human.

Each year we now conclude our induction programme for newly qualified teachers by having a day of reflection at the Centre. We remind our teachers that who they are is more important than what they teach, that not one child will have passed through their hands untouched by the person they are. Teachers, tired at the end of their first year, experience the impact of the exhibition and the gardens, hear the story of a survivor... and the challenges of their first year fall into perspective.

"Reading, writing and arithmetic are important but only if they serve to make our children more human."

In 2004 we brought our Religious Education Coordinators to the Centre and in the summer of 2005, deputy heads and head teachers from schools around the North East visited the Centre as part of a three-week sabbatical experience. Long-serving head teachers have found our visits to have a profound impact on them, both personally and professionally. In 2006, and in light of the work force reforms, two days have been booked to enable our classroom assistants to visit.

We believe that The Holocaust Centre provides a unique and profound experience for our staff. They return to school enriched and renewed with hope and enthusiasm for true education – education that transforms lives, education that nurtures human wholeness. May God bless you in your work.

"He who saves a single life saves the world entire."

"You have created the most amazing, very beautiful and thought-provoking memorial. The constant reminder of man's continuing cruelty towards his fellow man... begs the continuing question of what can we do, and how do we begin to change the prevailing view that 'we' can do little."

Joan Brown, Association of Head Teachers for Jewish Schools

"The sessions not only provided much needed extended knowledge on the issues surrounding the Shoah, but also advice on how to approach such issues within the classroom situation."

Nicola Halman, Student, University of Wolverhampton

Susanne Pearson
MBE, Teacher Trainer and Kindertransport Survivor

Several groups of teachers have opted recently to devote one of their curriculum days to considering the teaching of the Holocaust. Many of them did not have the opportunity to learn about this part of history, which is now a requirement at Key Stages 2 and 3.

The Holocaust Centre takes great care in planning sessions for their schools' particular needs. I have been most interested to participate in this, as it has given me the opportunity to draw on past skills as a Lecturer in Education.

My particular role in these sessions is to explain how I use my experience of coming to Britain on a *Kindertransport* as a lone child at the age of 11. I try to relate this to the history of that time.

I have found these groups most rewarding and interesting to work with, particularly during discussion when we usually explore the understanding of different age groups of the meaning of discrimination and loss.

Dorothy Fleming
Teacher Trainer and Kindertransport Survivor

The Holocaust Centre has an important role to play in the education of teachers, both at initial and in-service level. Because there are elements in both the primary and secondary national curriculum which touch on the history of the Second World War and the Holocaust, as well as related aspects of Personal and Social Development, the Humanities and Religious Education, the experiences offered by the Centre are pertinent and valuable for both new and experienced teachers.

The opportunities for educators to see the special exhibition on the Holocaust, to spend time in the Memorial Garden, to hear a survivor speaking and talk to them, and to have access to a great variety of useful educational materials, as well as opportunities for research, make this Centre exceptionally valuable and productive. Teachers also benefit from meeting and interacting with a variety of individuals with a wide range of experiences, both of the Holocaust itself and of telling and teaching about it. The informal, caring setting contributes to an atmosphere in which difficult and sensitive topics can be freely discussed and where moving and even upsetting experiences can be reacted to and integrated in discreet and professional ways.

The Holocaust Centre, Beth Shalom also provides teachers with many and novel ways to develop their area of curriculum, to create imaginative and practical lesson plans and to discover and experiment with new ways of integrating the topic of the Holocaust with other curriculum areas.

professional

professional

Motti Shalem
International School for Holocaust Studies, Yad Vashem

It is an honour for me to be a contributor in this special commemorative volume. Those familiar with the Hebrew language know that by reversing the words *Beth Shalom*, we get *Shalom Bayit*. *Shalom Bayit* is a term in Hebrew that refers to the importance of good relations among family members. Clearly, the Smith family is an excellent example of how one family can bring about educational change.

The founding of this Centre was inspired by a visit of the Smith family to Yad Vashem. As Stephen Smith notes in his book, *Making Memory*, "As we left Yad Vashem that day, we decided we would dedicate some of our time, energy and resources to assisting the British public in confronting the Holocaust and evaluating something of its meaning for their lives… We just knew we wanted to do something."

In the early 1990s, Stephen and James intensively studied for several weeks at Yad Vashem. They not only listened to lectures by many of the world's leading experts on the Holocaust, but also utilized the Yad Vashem information systems and established personal relationships with our staff.

In just ten years, The Holocaust Centre has succeeded in becoming a Centre specializing in teacher training on Holocaust education that is recognized and respected by international experts around the world.

The International School for Holocaust Studies at Yad Vashem and The Holocaust Centre, Beth Shalom have enjoyed close cooperation over the years. The publishing of joint publications as well as co-sponsoring teacher training seminars has enabled both of our institutions to strengthen our commitment to promoting Holocaust education and remembrance.

Throughout its existence, the Centre has demonstrated a clear commitment to creating change through teacher training. Ultimately, it is our hope that together, through an open exchange of educational experiences, we shall successfully build strong bridges for international cooperation to promote Holocaust education, remembrance and research around the globe.

Gillian Fisher

Education Officer, Jewish Museum, London

On my first visit to The Holocaust Centre, Beth Shalom – about two years after it opened –- I was greeted with a friendly hug by Marina Smith. I have since returned on many occasions and each time the warmth of that initial welcome has remained the same – even though the Centre itself has developed and changed somewhat. The gardens are now even more beautiful, providing a haven for quiet contemplation, reflection and a recharging of the spirit, away from the hurly-burly of London.

My next visit was to take part in the Graduate Training Seminar, an invaluable experience. My fellow participants were friendly and enthusiastic; the exceptionally high-quality lectures were thought-provoking and stimulating. We were encouraged to take a fresh look at our approaches to teaching the Holocaust and to delve more deeply into all the issues raised. We examined the contemporary relevance of these issues to the continuing racism and genocides of today, such as in Rwanda and Bosnia. We explored ways in which to make the lessons of the Holocaust more relevant and more accessible to our pupils, and were introduced to the Centre's extensive range of educational resources, to help us achieve these aims.

In my work with school groups at the Jewish Museum in Finchley, I make frequent use of these resources, especially videos such as *Wasted Lives*, which is a wonderful "springboard" for teenagers, and the excellent poster series. I also regularly recommend the resources to visiting teachers, PGCE students etc.

I have to admit that, at first, I was a little apprehensive about attending the Graduate Training Seminar – would everybody be more knowledgeable and experienced than myself, and would they be friendly? However, the genuine warmth created by Marina and the rest of her family gave me the confidence to also attend, at a later date, an International Seminar for Holocaust Educators at Yad Vashem in Jerusalem.

So "thank you" all at The Holocaust Centre and congratulations on reaching your 10th anniversary. May your important work in the field of Holocaust education continue to flourish and, as one of your visiting school pupils wrote – "Now I understand why you say that Beth Shalom is about people."

police
training

During the period of the Third Reich, reserve police units were drafted from police departments around Nazi Germany. Regular city policemen were turned into genocidal killers in a matter of days.

professional

Police forces in the United Kingdom were recently observed to have a worryingly high degree of 'institutional racism', in which structures and procedures appeared to cover for, and even facilitate, levels of discrimination that were widespread and severe.

Police training at The Holocaust Centre has begun with the local police force in Nottinghamshire. The setting of the museum and other resources at the Centre are a stark and undeniable reminder of the abuse of law enforcement.

The training seminars are designed to challenge police professionals as individuals to discuss their own personal attitudes and prejudices, and to build teams of police enforcers who are willing and able to challenge themselves before they challenge others.

Matthew McFarlane,
Chief Inspector (Operations), Nottinghamshire Constabulary

A key role of the police is to protect the vulnerable. When people turn to us for support, it is often because they have nowhere else to go. Victims of crime and harassment can feel afraid, isolated and vulnerable.

These feelings are even greater when crime is motivated by hate or prejudice. One of the challenges I face at work is to make an officer understand why verbal abuse that is racist or motivated by other prejudice is fundamentally different than other types of abusive behaviour. It is different because if it is not tackled, it grows and spreads. This is the lesson I saw in *Kristallnacht*. Mass murder

and genocide started with abuse and damage to property.

I wonder about the police in places where genocide has occurred. What choices faced the ordinary police officer in Nazi Germany, in Rwanda, in Bosnia? How could they allow the hatred to grow and be expressed in more and more violent forms? The role of the state in these situations is something which separates them from other horrific crimes, but it ultimately comes down to individuals and the choices they make.

I was particularly moved by a quote from a Rwandan survivor: "When

people say 'Never Again', what do they mean? Is it just a vain hope or are they prepared to do something about it?"

It is not simply a choice for the police to do everything possible to tackle crimes motivated by prejudice – it is our duty. It is these issues which The Holocaust Centre helps us to reflect upon. That is why we have recently worked with the Centre on providing training on hate crime to our Inspectors. The message is – if we allow hate to grow and flourish, this is where it can lead; what will you do to tackle it?

"A first-class day which took some hard thinking and will help me every day at work. Cannot fault it."

Ben Crane

"Excellent day, very impactful, useful points made by both speakers which are relevant to dealing with hate crime."

Sam Wilson

"The training seminars at The Holocaust Centre have opened up new perspectives for our officers on issues such as prejudice and hate crime. The Centre is a fantastic resource and the involvement of survivors is particularly significant."

Steve Green,
Chief Constable, Nottinghamshire Police

196

professional

prison
officer training

The first concentration camp in Nazi Germany was at Oranienberg prison near Berlin. It was a prison where the new Nazi hierarchy quickly interned political dissidents shortly after Hitler's accession to power in late January 1933. A tough regime of internment without trial, torture and abuse was introduced by the prison officers. It became the model on which later concentration camps such as Dachau would work.

Prison officers have a duty to uphold custodial sentences. They also have a duty of care toward inmates, as well as a training role as inmates prepare for rehabilitation into the community. Balancing the structures and relationships in order to create an environment of respect within the prison environment is difficult. Working in a place of

reform and preparation for integration back into the community, prison staff become significant role models for inmates.

The training programme for prison teams at the Centre encourages staff to confront the history of the Holocaust in a constructive way, to challenge the way in which they work as officers, and in particular the environment of respect they create for the benefit of the whole prison community.

197

professional

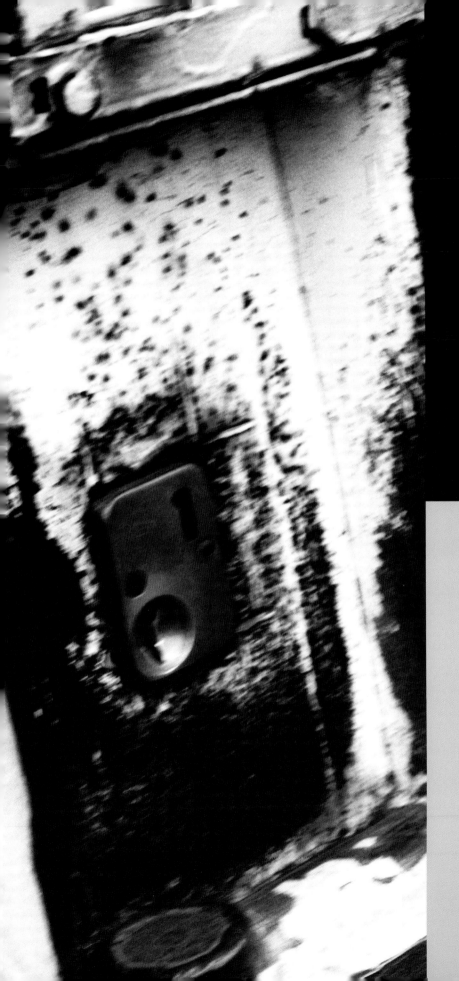

Simon Daly
Deputy Governor, HMPS Whatton

The Holocaust Centre, Beth Shalom designed a training package for HMP Whatton's Race Relations Management Team. The training was well constructed, expertly delivered and deeply thought-provoking, and has assisted the team to move forward in tackling Race Relations in a creative and reflective way.

I would thoroughly recommend using the Centre.

Jonathan Parry
Principal Officer, Race Relations Liaison Officer, HMPS Whatton

The Holocaust Centre, Beth Shalom is truly inspirational. Its images of the past and the survivor talks left me feeling very humble. The Centre and Aegis are not simply about the past; they are a beacon for the future. Their training is thought-provoking, practical and of the highest quality. Their staff are knowledgeable, friendly and of the highest integrity. The Holocaust Centre is an extremely valuable resource. I guarantee that you will never forget your visit.

198

professional

"I already had some knowledge of the theories about genocide, but personal accounts really deepened this. It brought home the thinness of our civilized veneer."

Ann Lewis, Library Assistant

"Heart-rending... moved to tears. What can I do to improve things?"

Prisoner, Race Relations Representative

"What was important to me was what can I do? I worry with all the horrible things in the world... but your theme 'He who saves a single life' is a good start and... gives courage and strength at the end to do something."

Seminar participant

Layla Thompson
HMPS Gartree

"As a diversity facilitator for the Prison
Service, I found it informative and
enlightening, enabling me to pass on
information and new knowledge through
training to staff and prisoners. Hopefully it
will lead to a spread in alerting people to the
issues that are current in the media and in
politics today."

John Stevens
HMPS Gartree

"Very interesting and stimulating day. The
personal reflections for me were the
highlights of the day. I would welcome more
information relating to the Gypsy and
traveller community. Ignorance is the
catalyst for discrimination."

Andy Findley
HMPS Gartree

"I do feel that the corner is being turned, but
only by the good work that people such as
those who spoke today are doing. I look
forward to those organisations working
closer with the Prison Service."

clergy training

During the Nazi period, the Christian Churches almost certainly secured their political and institutional survival at the expense of their moral, spiritual and theological credibility. There were instances where clergy spoke out and suffered because of their convictions. But such acts were surprisingly uncommon considering the fact that National Socialism was anti-Christian and diametrically opposed to Christianity in its social and ethical order.

The connivance of the Christian world to Nazi domination gives serious pause for thought for practising clergy today. The responsibility of moral and spiritual leadership is a heavy one, particularly in times of crisis, or when groups other than those who profess Christianity are under threat.

Seminars for practising clergy at the Centre address the long history of antisemitism in the Christian tradition and theology. They examine the role of Churches during the

Third Reich and the attitude of ordinary Christian people to the Jews being persecuted around them.

The seminars aim to give clergy time to evaluate their own leadership and to formulate how they might introduce issues arising out of the Holocaust for Christian people in their congregations and wider community.

Clergymen salute Hitler with high-ranking members of the Nazi hierarchy

201

professional

"I know from many of the conversations I had with people in the coach returning to Birmingham what a deep impression the museum and listening to the story of the survivors had on [the curates]... The Holocaust Memorial Centre is clearly making a unique contribution and I felt they were able to visit at an important time in their own ministerial development."

Marlene B. Parsons, Diocesan Director of Ordinands and Dean of Women's Ministry, Diocese of Birmingham

203

professional

Canon Ian E. Gooding
Rural Dean of Erewash, Diocese of Derby

A group of about 60 from my churches visited the Centre and the effect of the visit was quite dramatic, particularly on those born well after the end of the Second World War. Those born before or during the war were also visibly moved as things that had become memories were brought alive again. It would be true to say that folk were stunned, and if the sounds and images were not enough, the opportunity to hear and question actual survivors of the camps was utterly compelling and eye-opening and left no one in any doubt as to the reality of what happened. Some of our younger members needed to hear and see, and all were far better acquainted with the history and reasons for the existence of Israel.

The depiction of the Rwandan Genocide was equally effective and the determination, particularly on the part of the young, to ensure that such a thing did not happen again was almost tangible. Unashamed tears were shed.

Prayers in church for events in other lands have been far more real and urgent since our visit and there is a greater awareness of the potential for catastrophe around the world, and hence more informed prayer.

Prior to the churches' visit, I organised a visit for some 20 clergy. Some were a little cynical, some out for a day off, some knowing it all, having been to Yad Vashem. All left having been profoundly moved and deeply aware of the processes that can so easily lead to genocide.

The educative value for churches is immeasurable and if it was left to me, a visit for all within reach would be compulsory.

Right Reverend Richard Harries

The Bishop of Oxford, speaking at the Centre, 25 January 2001

We sometimes say of another person that they have been traumatised and by that we mean that they have experienced something so horrendous that they have been changed for good. The Christian Church ought to be traumatised by the Holocaust. It has not yet been traumatised enough; and yet it has begun to be changed. First of all by an awareness that what happened, happened in the most cultured country in the world and one which was extensively Christian. Secondly, the fact that the long history of what has been called the "teaching of contempt" prepared the ground for the noxious weed of antisemitism to grow in the nineteenth and twentieth centuries. The long history of disparagement of Judaism shaped people's hearts and minds in a particular way which allowed poison eventually to spoil the whole system.

The Christian Church has begun to wake up to the fact that even in the New Testament there are difficulties, because the New Testament was written up after the split between church and synagogue. The documents reflect the hostility which was then growing and many of the things which were said there are utterly unacceptable by today's standards.

Yet the good news is that people are now beginning to take this seriously and here one would pay tribute to the Vatican, and not only the Vatican Council but perhaps especially those who have worked in Rome to produce documents like "The Right Presentation of Christianity in relation to Judaism", so that Christianity can be taught in such a way that Judaism is respected and honoured; so that the New Testament can be interpreted in such a way that Judaism cannot be simply set up as a foil for Christianity. But I do believe there is still a very long way to go, and the work of educating the Christian Church has to be done afresh in every generation.

The Council of Christians and Jews, which I have the honour to chair, was founded in the dark days of 1942 by the then Chief Rabbi and the then Archbishop of Canterbury. I suppose its first task was to try and make the world a safer place for Jews and Judaism. And it then moved on to try to bring about greater understanding between these two religions. My hope is that there might be a third stage of Jewish-Christian relations, and that is that Jews and Christians stand together, not simply praying that God's just rule might come on earth, but that they might stand in solidarity, confronting injustice and cruelty wherever it might be.

It has of course been deeply moving to listen to many of the stories today. The Christian Church needs to continue the hear these stories in order that a new, very different kind of relationship might be built between the two religions.

Participants in the Clergy Conference, 2000

professional

Canon Andrew White
Foundation for Reconciliation in the Middle East

My daily life has made me a witness to the horror of war, and at times even the terror of genocide. As I travel around the world, I visit many different Holocaust museums, centres and memorials; in the streets of Jerusalem I regularly hear the cry "Never again!" But one place for me is different. It is called Beth Shalom – the House of Peace – and that is what it is.

Nestled in the Nottinghamshire countryside, it is a place where the words "Never again" are put into practice. The work is not just about echoes of the past, it is about the present and the future. The *Shoah* is remembered, but it is the Centre's commitment to examining contemporary genocide and doing all in its power to prevent further such tragedies that makes it a continually relevant living memorial. It is about people and ensuring that the evils of antisemitism are not renewed or transferred.

Sadly, I see daily how important the work here is, and how much there is still to do as The Holocaust Centre strives to bring healing to a broken world.

Revd. Canon Valerie Rampton

I was Vicar of the Church of St. Michael the Archangel, Laxton, from 1993 to 2002. Early in my time there, I was invited to visit The Holocaust Centre, Beth Shalom. I was shown the existing buildings and gardens, I learned the plans for The Holocaust Centre. The vision was remarkable, and surprising for an isolated set of buildings outside a small Nottinghamshire village of 250 people, known mainly for its continued use of the three-field medieval system of strip-farming. Laxton people had seen the buildings go from a farmhouse to the home of the retreat centre, and wondered what this new development would bring. Some welcomed the proposals, but there were also anxieties, mainly about the increased volume of traffic on the narrow roads in and around the village and the possibility of antisemitic attacks on the Centre with violence spilling over into the village. The issues were explored with the Smith family.

When the Centre was completed, Laxton people were invited to visit, and those who did so were very impressed. As the work of the Centre has expanded, people have come to value its presence within the parish.

I grew up in North London knowing many Jewish people, so it has meant a great deal to me that Beth Shalom, founded by a Christian family, is a place where Jewish and Christian people can come together in penitence and reconciliation. When I visit, I am always humbled and inspired by people met and insights gained. My life and ministry have been greatly enriched.

"The whole reflective environment you have created is a real contribution to thoughtfulness. I felt that the museum was particularly clearly presented in a way which enabled me to sort out various elements in the appalling story in a consecutive way. It really was an excellent opportunity not only to be a bit more informed about facts..., but also to talk over the sets of circumstances which can create the dangers of such extreme responses to racial fear as the Holocaust did."

The Venerable John Duncan,
former Archdeacon of Birmingham

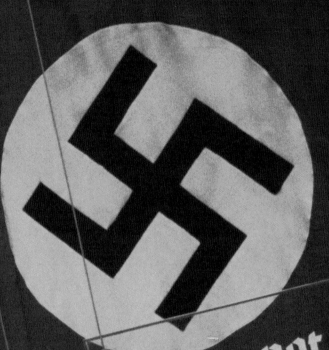

Juden
sind hier nicht
erwünscht

Jews
are not wanted

We do not want
Jews. see
our misfortu

religion & ethics

"If there is any religion in the world, this is how it is supposed to be..."

Suzanne Damazar

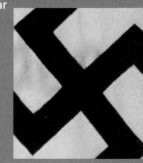

the place of
ethics

The Nazis had their own warped form of ethical principles. They executed an ethics of exclusion, hatred, power and race supremacy. Their ethics allowed for the persecution of those deemed less than human. It demanded the mass murder of the Jews in pursuit of their ethics of supremacy through genocide.

The fact that an ethical system could be so distorted, bringing about untold destruction and the mass murder of families without mercy, shows how tenuous our ethics can be. It highlights the extent to which we need to continue to examine the application of our own modes of behaviour.

We are concerned that two generations later, so much closer attention still needs to be paid to the ethics we subscribe to and

defend. It seems there is still an urgent need to scrutinise our behaviour and the principles behind our actions. Through the Centre's programme of lectures and seminars, the ethics of stable societies are a regular discussion point.

John K. Roth

Edward J. Sexton, Professor of Philosophy; Director, Center for the Study of the Holocaust, Genocide and Human Rights, Claremont McKenna College, USA

The Holocaust Centre at Beth Shalom shows at least two crucial features about ethics.

First, the Holocaust history documented there reveals how much the Holocaust damaged ethics. The Third Reich's assault on the Jewish people and its traditions, which include the Sixth Commandment, "You shall not murder," aimed at their utter destruction. Nazi Germany's genocidal antisemitism and racism did not fully prevail, but it came much too close for comfort. The effectiveness of ethical teachings and traditions remains in question after Auschwitz.

Second, the Centre provides a strong moral response to the *Shoah*. Now a decade on, the ongoing work of the Centre shows that neither the Holocaust nor any other genocide is fated to take place. Such murderous activity can be prevented or checked if people make the right decisions, if people choose not to stand by while atrocities occur, but stand up against powers that disrespect human life. Countless lives have been touched for the better through the Holocaust Centre at Beth Shalom. By keeping alive the memory of all that was lost in the Holocaust, its work ignites courage and determination to mend the world and to restore respect for ethics at its best.

theology
and the Holocaust

Theological dilemmas after the Holocaust are extensive and demanding for Jews, for Christians and for people of other faiths who believe in the goodness and power of deity. The implication is that if God is good and God is powerful, and the Jews are God's people of covenant, then the Holocaust should not have happened to the Jews. Alternatively, God chooses not to protect the Jews.

All theological options prove either impossibly difficult to rationalise or morally accept.

The theological challenge of the Holocaust is one Jewish thinkers have been grappling with for more than two generations, indeed from within the Holocaust itself. Christian theologians have been somewhat slower to respond, but have finally begun to question the efficacy of the Christian Church and its theology after such a cataclysm in 'Christian' Europe.

Most other faiths still struggle to apply directly the challenge and consequences of the Holocaust for belief generally, choosing instead to look at moral and ethical imperatives to emerge from its history.

The challenge to theology is a complex one, which the Centre addresses on a regular basis. Through its undergraduate seminars and lecture series, theological issues are raised, both in relation to the past and in relation to the future, too.

"The Holocaust Centre, Beth Shalom, has performed an important role in educating a new generation to the memory of the Holocaust and all that implies for the fight for freedom, tolerance and mutual respect. I congratulate them on the work of their first ten years - may their activities grow and continue to inspire."

The Chief Rabbi, Sir Jonathan Sacks

Richard L. Rubenstein

President Emeritus and Distinguished Professor of Religion at the University of Bridgeport, USA, and Lawton Distinguished Professor Emeritus of Religion at Florida State University

In the 1999 lecture at The Holocaust Centre, Beth Shalom, I shared some of my thoughts on the meaning of the *Shoah* for contemporary religion, society and international affairs, a subject of fundamental concern to me in my vocation as a rabbi and theologian. Yet, if one examines the works of some of the most influential Jewish thinkers of the second half of the twentieth century, such as Martin Buber, Gershom Scholem, Joseph B. Soloveitchik, as well as my teachers, Abraham Joshua Heschel and Mordecai M. Kaplan, it is clear that none confronted directly the central issue of Jewish theology in our times, the question of God and the Holocaust.

When, for example, as a student I would raise the issue with Dr Heschel, he would always reply, "Richard, study more deeply and you will understand." That, of course, was not an answer. His response implied that there was some failing in me, a deficit of religious learning that, once corrected, would cause the issue to disappear. In reality, Heschel and the other great Jewish thinkers knew there was a problem, but saw no adequate way of resolving it without

somehow implicating God, as did the ultra-Orthodox thinkers. They seem to have regarded avoidance of the issue as the prudent course. The world into which they had been born and in which they had acquired their knowledge of the sources of Jewish tradition had been irretrievably smashed. They had more than enough on their hands in making the tradition available to the first post-Holocaust generation without exploring the painful and disturbing problem of God and the Holocaust.

The question of God and the Holocaust was unavoidable for me. I was nine years old when Adolf Hitler came to power and fifteen when the Second World War began. I had no close European relatives, but I was deeply affected by the events taking place in Europe. As I entered the serious study of the Jewish tradition, I was keenly aware of how little I knew in comparison with the twentieth century's great Jewish thinkers. As someone who came late to Judaism, I had to make up in experience and reflection on the texts I had studied for my insights. My Harvard doctoral dissertation, later published as *The Religious Imagination*, was a multi-year exploration of the rabbinic responses to the Jewish catastrophe of ancient times, the Fall of Jerusalem and the destruction of the Temple in 70 C.E. In effect, I attempted to gain insight from the classical rabbinic responses to catastrophe in order to understand the

catastrophe of modern times. Reluctantly, I came to see that, as horrific as was the earlier Jewish defeat, it was in no way comparable to the *Shoah*. The Romans never sought to exterminate the Jews. They sought to assert their power over them. With very few exceptions, the Germans did seek to exterminate them root and branch. Since the ancient situation from which Jewish thinkers have traditionally drawn their responses to catastrophe was not comparable to the *Shoah*, any attempt to respond as if the two situations were comparable was bound to lack credibility. One could, for example, speak of God as chastising Israel in order to show the people the right path in response to the Fall of Jerusalem in 70 C.E., but not in a situation of outright genocide such as the *Shoah*.

I saw the difficulty long before I wrote about it. I was constrained by the example of my teachers, especially by Dr Heschel's admonition to study more, and I kept silent until an unforgettable incident in Berlin the week the Wall went up in August 1961 that I have often retold. Speaking with heartfelt conviction, a German Lutheran clergyman, who had risked his life to save Jews, told me that he believed it was God's will to punish the Jews at Auschwitz. Given the time, place and circumstance of our encounter, I could no longer keep my germinating views to myself. I knew that I had to make them publicly available.[1]

It was that *experience*, not the texts I studied or my dissertation, that changed my life and led to my so-called "death of God" theology which was never atheism. (The last chapter of the revised edition of *After Auschwitz* has the title "God after the Death of God.") Since coming to know them, I have had a strong sense of spiritual kinship with Stephen and James Smith. To the best of my knowledge, it was their *experience* in Israel and at Yad Vashem that changed their lives and, with the support of Ed and Marina, resulted in The Holocaust Centre, Beth Shalom and the Aegis Trust. Our paths converged because we were not content with conventional wisdom and were not afraid to rely on experience to understand our world. We also possessed a shared commitment to *Tikkun Olam*, the repair and restoration of a broken world.

In reflecting on the tenth anniversary of the Centre, I rejoice in its very genuine accomplishments. I am grateful to have been able to share in a small way in its work.

The Centre was a surprise to me when I first visited it on Sunday, 5 September 1999. I came to lecture on my theological response to the *Shoah*. I had come to know it through work on the Executive Committee of Remembering for the Future 2000 under the leadership of Dr Elisabeth Maxwell. I had heard of the Centre at our meetings, but could not imagine what sort of memorial institution to the *Shoah* could be located in Nottinghamshire. When I finally saw for myself what was taking place there, I was impressed with the library, the research facilities, the physical facilities and the spirit and competence of the leadership and staff. I was also pleasantly surprised by the size of the audience that came for the lecture, many from London.

As I came to know the Smith family, I understood the intelligence, devotion, ecumenical spirit and sheer dynamism that had created The Holocaust Centre. I began a fruitful relationship that continues to this day. I felt especially honoured when I was asked to conduct the wedding of James and Beatha. Of especial importance to me is that my Beth Shalom affiliation has enabled me to work in a spirit of cooperation and trust with a group of like-minded Jews and Christians of exceptional ability, whose life and vocation has, like mine, been deeply influenced by the *Shoah*.

1. The response can be found in Richard L. Rubenstein, *After Auschwitz: History, Theology and Contemporary Judaism*, 2nd ed. revised and enlarged (Baltimore: Johns Hopkins University Press, 1992); Richard L. Rubenstein and John K. Roth, *Approaches to Auschwitz: The Holocaust and its Legacy*, rev. ed., Louisville, KY: Westminster/John Knox, 2003; *La Perfidie de l'Histoire* (Paris: Éditions Les Provinciales and Les Éditions du Cerf, 2005).

"On Thursday we abandoned our RE lesson and spent the 50 minutes talking about what they had learned. They also feel that in the light of what they have heard, they cannot stand by and watch the events in Kosovo... The day had immeasurable value – not just for their examinations, but also for the whole of their lives."

Mrs C. Acheson, Head of Religious Studies,
William Lovell School

"In the next teaching session following our day with you, the thoughtfulness and depth of reflection of the pupils was impressive. They are not a group accustomed to such depth of thought and so their responses make me feel both thankful and hopeful."

Chris Mayo, Head of Religious Education,
Pool Hayes Community School

Margaret Brearley
Writer and Lecturer

The Holocaust Centre, Beth Shalom is an inspired vision transformed into an astonishing, dynamic reality. The Smith family recognised a void, the gaping absence of any major Holocaust memorial in Britain, and set about filling it with passion, dedication and great entrepreneurial skill. They created a small but powerful museum, embraced hundreds of Holocaust survivors and enfolded them into their family, kindling serene beauty – statues, the rose garden, stained glass windows, fine buildings – to memorialise the horrors of the *Shoah*.

My own visits with Jewish groups and as a participant in several academic conferences on genocide, have always resulted in inspiring encounters: with Stephen, James and Marina themselves, committed and eloquent; with survivors of the *Shoah* and of later genocides; with men such as General Romeo Dallaire or Philippe Gaillard of the Red Cross, both heroes within the Rwandan genocide; with academics committed to full-time research – itself heroic – into Holocaust

and genocide. The Centre's high ethical standards are matched by its high standards in books and other publications; I was delighted with their format for the Holocaust Memorial Day Pack for Churches, which I produced when honorary advisor on the Holocaust to the Archbishops' Council.

Two men and one woman, all remarkable, have created Beth Shalom and Aegis. With their team of colleagues, they have had a national and international impact on thousands of lives and tens of thousands of minds. May they and their creative vision go from strength to strength, empowered by their urgent message of the need to mend the world, a mending which itself takes place at the Centre.

religion & ethics

"The Urban Theology Unit group was left asking many questions: How does the Holocaust affect our understanding of God? How do we relate our understanding of a God who answers prayer, with the six million whose prayers it seems were not heard?"

Revd Christine Jones, Urban Theology Unit, Sheffield

relations
Jewish-Christian

The presence of Christian antisemitism was not sufficient to cause the Holocaust. But the long history of enmity between Christians and Jews, evidenced by a cultural milieu saturated in precedents of hatred, was arguably a necessary precondition. The ingrained notions of Jews became the feeding ground of *Der Stürmer*, the antisemitic Nazi weekly. It drew on previous stereotypes, prejudices, myths and cartoons week after week for years, hardly needing to introduce new Nazi ideas for its readers.

Much of this divisive culture had been driven by the Christian Church for centuries, harbouring theological, spiritual and ethnic hatred deep within its texts, liturgy and preaching. Whatever the link between Christianity and the Holocaust, it is certain that the relationship between Jews and Christians was sufficiently poor for good Christian people to go to church to pray, while their Jewish neighbours were deported.

The issue of Christian-Jewish relations is particularly pertinent at the Centre, and we see it as a practical action, avoiding superficial dialogue in favour of facts on the ground. Through its continued existence and the absence of institutional and religious barriers, the Centre will continue to play a facilitating role in bringing Jews and Christians closer together in the wake of a difficult past.

religion & ethics

ZIEMIA
JASIELSKA

ontinuing tension within Jewish-Christian relations was well illustrated over the Auschwitz convent controversy

Elisabeth Maxwell

**President Emeritus of
Remembering for the Future**

After the Allies liberated Nazi death and concentration camps in 1945, much work had to be done to rehabilitate the Christian Churches in the eyes of the world, following their appalling, "resounding silence" when six million Jews were burnt in the crematoria of Germany and Poland. It took true Christians of the calibre of Bonhoeffer or James Parkes, Roy Eckardt or Franklin Littell, or the late Popes John XXIII and John Paul III, to realise how over 2,000 years, Christian teaching of contempt had prepared the terrain in which Jews were no longer considered the neighbours whom Jesus directed us to love and help in danger, but as sub-humans, a vermin to be eradicated from the surface of the earth.

More recently, in our country, a family with a Methodist Christian background took up the challenge, following in the footsteps of those great visionaries, dedicating their lives to reinstating a meaningful relationship between Christians and Jews. Humble and modest when faced with this immense task, they had no qualms in asking questions of those already engaged in Jewish-Christian dialogue. Far from reinventing the wheel, they brought a new, enthusiastic approach by creating strong emotional relations between survivors and the youngsters they were trying to teach. They were not too proud to invite some of their elders and well-known Holocaust scholars to sit on The Holocaust Centre's Executive Board and guide them in their first steps of atonement and dedication to this mission of renewal with the tradition of our older brothers in religion.

In fact, the two young men who direct the Centre have brought to their mission of 'rapprochement' a missionary zeal inherited from their parents, and they have extended a friendly hand to erstwhile antisemitic countries like Poland and Lithuania. Sitting in the Centre's lecture hall, you should not be surprised to find alongside you a young man or woman listening with great intensity in order to go and preach the 'good news' to their students, back in their own country.

religion & ethics

Edward Kessler

Founder and Executive Director, Centre for the Study of Jewish-Christian Relations, Cambridge

I am delighted to contribute to this volume since, like countless others, I have the deepest admiration for the Smith family and for the Beth Shalom Holocaust Centre.

I started taking my students to the Centre soon after its inception in 1995. It was clear to me at the time that university students, particularly theology students and most particularly Christian Ordinands, needed to reflect on the Holocaust. The Holocaust Centre provided not only an educational centre and an oasis of calm, but also a positive Christian response to the horrors of 1933-45.

Today's encounter between Judaism and Christianity takes place in a turbulent and increasingly threatening world. Developing a positive relationship is dependent upon tackling difficult topics as well as the easier ones, and none can be more difficult than the Holocaust.

Ten years ago, we talked about the 'window of opportunity'; that it was essential for our generation to build quickly on the work of pioneers in the study and teaching of the Holocaust. We worried then about how long the 'window of opportunity' would remain open. The worry has increased... and there are times when the window seems to be on the verge of closing and the interfaith outlook seems gloomy.

The rabbis say, "You are not free to complete the task but neither are you free to desist from it." We have begun the task but there is a long way to go.

The Holocaust Centre has contributed greatly to this God-given task and I hope will contribute for many years to come. The Centre for the Study of Jewish-Christian Relations is proud to be a partner on a journey of *tikkum olam*, to heal this world. This, I believe, should be the common purpose of Judaism and Christianity.

"I do feel that if more Christian organisations came to grips with understanding to a small degree the Jewish religion and its teachings, then the antisemitism, often unintentional, spread by the Church would be negated. I think that as well as children need educating, often their parents and grandparents need the same, and a visit to your organisation could only do good."

Jack Davis

Geoffrey Wigoder

Former Professor of Jewish Studies, Hebrew University, Jerusalem; Editor in Chief, *Encyclopaedia Judaica*; Academic Advisor, The Holocaust Centre, Beth Shalom

The Holocaust brought difficult questions to the Churches. This coincided with the new openness of the post-war era, the ecumenical movement and in the Catholic Church with the revolution inaugurated by the Vatican Council which radically changed so many aspects of that Church, in theology and practice. Churches now began to realise and acknowledge that their liturgies, catechisms, textbooks and teachings still enshrined anti-Jewish prejudices and stereotypes, some to a lesser degree, some to a greater. But all had contributed to relegating the Jew to a position of inferiority, and this in turn had led to the varying degrees of acceptance of the fate of the Jews in World War II...

[The Churches] had to face the facts of the active collaboration with the Nazis and pro-Nazis of clerics in many parts of Europe, including a Catholic priest serving as head of a state – namely Slovakia – during the cruellest period of anti-Jewish action (and he is still the object of adulation in Slovakia where his statue was recently put up). Fortunately, there was another side and there were many examples to the contrary in which Churches, clerics and individual Christians risked their lives to save Jews; and the Church played a major role in saving the Jews of Bulgaria and the greater part of the Jews of Italy. But these did not obscure the fundamental problem.

Geoffrey Wigoder was Advisor to The Holocaust Centre's founders from 1992. He played a significant role in supporting the concept and gave the opening address on 17 September 1995.

Lisa Vincent
Kindertransport Survivor

Personally I would say Beth Shalom has become my church, my synagogue, my second home.

It's had a tremendous effect on me. I've rethought things. So in more ways than just in an emotional way, it's kept me going, physically and mentally.

Sir Sigmund Sternberg
KCSG

I was delighted to propose that Stephen Smith should receive the Interfaith Gold Medallion of the International Council of Christians and Jews in June 2000. This award has been presented to monarchs, statesmen, religious leaders and other distinguished individuals – most recently to the late Pope John Paul II earlier this year – who have contributed to the making of a world which, learning from the past, reaches out for a better future.

Stephen's award reflected his achievements as a scholar and pioneer, not only of Holocaust education in this country but also of Jewish-Christian relations internationally. In so many fields he has shown himself to be a brilliant communicator and leader who could unite groups with diverse interests to break new ground in making progress toward the valuable goals of common acceptance of, and responsibility towards, every individual and group with whom we share our world.

Combining his role as co-founder of both Beth Shalom, Britain's first Holocaust Centre, and Aegis, the world's first genocide prevention initiative, Stephen was not only advisor to the British and other European governments in his capacity as a member of the International Task Force on Holocaust Education; he even found time to continue running his family business.

In recognition of his unique contribution to developing dialogue, understanding and respect between Christians and Jews through his work in the creation of Beth Shalom, I felt deeply privileged to present the Interfaith Gold Medallion. In so doing, I felt confident that he qualified for this award under each of the criteria that the judges took into account in reaching their decision on a truly worthy recipient for the year of the Millennium.

"We thought Beth Shalom a marvellous place with a power and assertiveness alongside a peace and awesome reflectiveness with yourselves and participants. You seemed to achieve a difficult and admirable balance between past, present and future, for all of us... The terrible challenge to me was, I think, about the failure of Christianity, a very cutting and essential charge... I did write to our Rabbi some years ago to apologise for the appallingly offensive words in the Christian scriptures. We've been friends ever since with joint meetings between our congregations."
Revd. Richard Tetlow, 2000

"As a Quaker of Jewish lineage, it made sure that I was put on the spot – where I will remain, I dare say so long as I live...The essential message that got to me... is the one on the plaque as one enters the basement: each illustration is of an individual person. No one is a statistic..."
Henry Rose

"I personally was impressed with the fact that this Centre was conceived by those without a Jewish background and who felt it was essential for the younger generation to know what occurred. This is particularly true at present when the tabloid press is inciting anti-Muslim beliefs in a similar racist fashion."
Jean Osborne, '50' Club

"...heartfelt thanks for your kind provision and wonderful hospitality to our Young Leaders' weekend participants. We have received feedback which was all extremely positive and included 'wonderful place to stay, food excellent, gardens beautiful', 'the peace, tranquillity and special atmosphere of the Centre and the extraordinary family have made it so memorable', and many more in the same vein... Thank you so much for all that you do."
Jane Clements, Council of Christians and Jews

"It is always a moving but wonderful experience to come to The Holocaust Centre... It was, in hindsight, a God-given experience which is enabling the Smith family to help to change the world, after 2,000 years of antisemitism and the Holocaust..."
Sister Kathleen Harmon, The McGuinness Training and Resource Centre

"Numerous lessons must be learned from that horrific event and this can only be done by the use of education in fostering understanding between peoples. In the words of the great teacher Hillel, when asked about life, he replied 'What is hateful to you, don't do to others – the rest is commentary.'"
Victor Huglin, Liverpool

"What was new and unexpected was the sincerity and devotion by a Christian family in trying to right a wrong of many hundreds of years' standing. We are aware that since the end of the Second World War, but very slowly, Christian theologians are beginning to reconsider the interpretations put on the New Testament in order to denigrate Jews. It is a painfully slow but welcome development. Your family is the trail-blazer!"
Woolf Abrahams

"I find it difficult to give adequate expression to the extraordinary experience you afforded us at Beth Shalom... Out of the goodness of your hearts and your deep concern for the victims of the Holocaust who were largely forsaken by the free world, you have created a project which is not only a beautiful and emotional tribute to their memory, but in a brilliantly skilful manner provides information on the background and tragedy of the Holocaust to the masses of visitors who come to the Centre with very vague, if any, knowledge of the genocide of six million Jews as well as many others, and who are bound to go home fully aware of a bloodstained chapter in recent history, coupled with the message it carries for the future."
Revd. Gabriel Brodie, Manchester Great & New Synagogue (Stenecourt)

learning

"The Holocaust should keep stalking our souls..."   John K. Roth

learning
the place of

Our understanding of the Holocaust is still developing. Research, archival findings, publications and new perspectives on the causes and consequences of the mass murder of European Jewry continue to emerge apace. We felt it should be part of the Centre's role to bring significant scholarship to our membership through a programme of annual lectures and seminars.

The nature of National Socialism, the psychology of perpetration, religious and philosophical implications, the Righteous among the Nations, historiographical developments, the deployment of genocidal policy in various countries across Nazi-occupied territory have all been covered by leading academics at the Centre.

The Centre is committed to remembering the past and teaching its fundamentals to a younger generation. This chapter quotes some of the scholars who have contributed to the life and thinking of the Centre through our lecture series.

227

learning

Geoffrey Wigoder
Inaugural Address

We were all shocked by the recent survey which concluded that over 60 per cent of children between 11 and 14 had never heard of the Holocaust and one wonders what they know of Jews and Judaism. The educational problem is apparently universal.

The need to teach the Holocaust is self-evident, especially as it fades from living memory. The obscenity of Holocaust denial would be inconceivable were it not a fact. As time goes on, the great lie will be the more credible and it will become growingly essential to counteract it. Moreover, the Holocaust must be seen as something more than an episode in Jewish, European or world history. It has a universal message. Its occurrence in the 20th century in what was considered one of the most civilised countries in the world shows that in some form, racism in its most barbarous form could reappear anytime, anywhere.

At the same time, Holocaust education must be conducted in perspective. In some cities of the United States, teaching of the Holocaust has been introduced into general school education and there are many universities where it has entered the curriculum. It has been reported that the latter are the most attended Jewish courses by Jewish students. There is, however, the danger that a student – Jew or non-Jew – whose knowledge of the Jews and Judaism is confined to the Holocaust, is going to get a distorted view. For a young Jew, it means he is constructing a negative Jewish identity which, without the positive side of Judaism, will not be a value to be handed down over the generations. The non-Jew will come away with an exclusive picture of the Jew as a victim without an awareness of the positive aspects and of Jewish culture, and also perhaps of seeing the Holocaust as an episode and not as the culmination of a millennium of Christian antisemitism.

If the Jew disappears from educational horizons with the end of the Bible period and does not appear again until the Holocaust, where is the Jew? Where does the average schoolchild or student learn of what the Jew stands for, what are his values, what is his self-understanding? The Holocaust cannot be taught in a vacuum. The realisation of this problem here is one of the many very positive aspects of The Holocaust Centre, Beth Shalom. When Stephen Smith said to me, "We cannot go right into the Holocaust but must have an introductory section on where the Jews came from," I knew he was on the right track. This should be the rule for all Holocaust museums and educational programmes. To present the Holocaust without the perspectives of Jewish history – including the full implications of the aftermath of the Holocaust – will leave the visitor and student with inadequate knowledge.

Here we reach the especial significance of this Centre which is being inaugurated today. I have had the privilege of following its fortunes since it was originally conceived and must pay a very special tribute to Stephen Smith, to his family and to the community which has backed them. Knowing the Smith family has been a very special experience. They exemplify what the morality of religion should mean. Undertaking this project was for them the most natural thing in the world. It was simply something that had to be done and no questions asked. Their outlook has constantly reminded me of the Protestant village of Le Chambon in France which saved thousands of Jews during the war. The villagers, under the leadership of their pastor, did not have any doubts or arguments; they were just doing what any good Christian should do. And the Smiths approach this ideal in the same way. While others in Britain have discussed and argued and got lost in planning and financing, they have simply gone ahead and done it. It has been accomplished with love and instinctive understanding of what should be done and how to do it. Not a sterile memorial but an educational centre, already making plans with schools in the region. Now visiting here, I find it even exceeds my expectations and I must pay a special tribute to Stephen for his knowledge and understanding – and to the insight and work

of James and their parents. They have got it right
– both in the exhibition and in their idea of how
to utilise it to teach the Holocaust and its broadest
implications. It is an inspired concept and I feel
privileged to participate in its inauguration.

learning

Opening address at The Holocaust Centre, Beth Shalom, 17 September 1995

Geoffrey Wigoder, Former Professor of Jewish
Studies, Hebrew University, Jerusalem; Editor in
Chief, *Encyclopaedia Judaica*; Academic Advisor,
The Holocaust Centre, Beth Shalom

Martin Gilbert
The Righteous

learning

Those Christians who acted to save Jews – whom Yad Vashem in Jerusalem has recognised after legal, notarised testimony, some 20,000 of them – were people of infinite bravery. Brave certainly, yet every one of those whom I met in the course of writing my book *The Righteous* insisted that they were just ordinary people doing the decent thing, behaving (although under great pressure) in the way in which they thought every human being would behave if the opportunity were offered to them to do so...

In the course of my research, I found many individuals and groups who had never made any claims about themselves to have been rescuers or helpers. I found many Germans who had risked their lives and saved Jews, not only in Germany but in Berlin itself. I found that every Christian religious group was represented in the pantheon of the Righteous. I found evidence of Baptists who lived in villages in what between the wars was the far eastern region of Poland and is today the Ukraine, who were themselves isolated and surrounded by hostile neighbours. They believed that if a Jewish person came to their door – and

one has to picture that this coming to their door meant arriving bleeding, broken, perhaps the only survivor of the massacre of a family or a community – that the appearance of this person was a sign of God testing their faith as Christians; and that to take that Jew in and hide him, feed him, protect him, not only from the Germans but from the other neighbours who would be keen to betray them all, was their Christian duty... Then I found another group that never sought recognition – the Muslims of Bosnia and Albania... These Muslims had no problem with saving a Jew, in fact the reverse: they felt that as the joint descendants of Abraham, sharing the same origins, they do must what they could to hide and save Jews as the decent and human thing to do...

The story of the Righteous is not only the story of individuals; it is also the story of collective acts of rescue and national acts of rescue... In Denmark the story was remarkable. A German official, a member of the Nazi Party, Georg Duckwitz, who was in charge of German shipping interests in Denmark, learned a week in advance that all the Jews in Denmark, more than 7,000, were to be taken to Germany and murdered in the camps. He immediately travelled to Sweden and prevailed on the Swedish authorities to agree – although Sweden was playing a major part in enabling the German war effort to continue – to take in any Jew who could get to the borders of Sweden. Duckwitz then went to Copenhagen, where he alerted the Jewish community and the Danish resistance. As a result of his initiative, virtually

every one of those 7,000 Jews was saved. Although Duckwitz had signed up to the Nazi Party's goals, he had not signed up to mass murder.

In Italy, in October 1943, after the Germans occupied the country from Rome to the Alps, they tried to begin the deportation of Jews. But the mass of the Italian populace, instructed by its Church leaders and also acting according to individual conscience, made such a successful effort that two-thirds of the Italian Jews who could have been deported to the camps were found sanctuary in homes, churches, monasteries and nunneries. When the SS moved into Rome and produced a list of 5,731 Jews to be deported from the city to Auschwitz, on the Pope's instructions hiding places were found overnight – for 4,238 Jews, 477 of them in the Vatican itself.

...That brings me to look at the initiatives, ingenuity and inventiveness of many of the rescuers. In thousands of cases, what was required and what happened was that the person opened their door to someone pleading to be admitted and hidden. But even after this spontaneous act, many things had to be done, over the months and years ahead, sometimes for two or three years, to hide this person or family or group, and in many cases we know that twenty, thirty or forty Jews were hidden. It involved providing food when you yourself – the rescuer – were under the severe ration system of occupation. It meant if possible some form of light, some form of fresh air, if possible some ten or twenty minutes per day of exercise, getting rid of waste, avoiding noise, avoiding tell-tale signs. In many cases, it also involved hiding those who were being hidden from your neighbours, from the people who saw you every day, who knew your habits. If you were taking in too much bread, or even too much water from your well, they might wonder what was it for...

... Many people in the world, most people perhaps, Christians, Jews, Muslims, bear some sort of affiliation, some sort of badge, of religious affinity, but do we know what our Christian, Jewish or Muslim principles are? This lay at the bottom of the response of those who saved Jews; they may not have known it consciously, but they had some instinct of the principles of the Judaeo-Christian tradition, or the Abrahamic tradition, and they acted upon them.

Extract from a lecture given at the Centre, 2003

Martin Gilbert is the biographer of Winston Churchill and a historian of the twentieth century. He has written eight books on Holocaust themes and has also pioneered a series of historical atlases, including *Atlas of the Holocaust*. He has taught both at Oxford University and University College, London, and lectures widely. The full range of his books and forthcoming lectures may be seen on his website: www.martingilbert.com

"Beth Shalom has impressed me by its strength of purpose and the skill of its presentation. It is a haven of knowledge and contemplation for scholars, educators, teachers and students alike."

Martin Gilbert

learning

Professor Yehuda Bauer
Jews for Sale?

It's a great honour to be here today on the second anniversary of an institution that I had only heard about and with which I am tremendously impressed. And I hope to transmit these messages to others whom I happen to meet and where I work, because what you do here not only has an impact and not only is of the greatest importance, but also is endowed with an unusual amount of tremendously good taste...

I want to talk today about a book I have published on Nazi-Jewish negotiations between 1933 and 1945... What if anything, were the intentions of the Nazis in all this? What did they want? Was it meant seriously? Or was it an attempt to mislead the Jews in some way, to calm them down? Was it morally justified, from the Jewish point of view, to negotiate with the Germans at all?... Ultimately, there is a major issue involved: were these ways in which more Jews could have been saved from the Holocaust? And, if so, why wasn't it done? and, if so, who was responsible? ...

Now, what was the attitude of the Allies? Were they aware of it? Were they aware of the tragedy?

Could they have done something and didn't do it? Not just things that that are very important in themselves, of course, like the bombing of Auschwitz or the Bermuda conference, refugees and so on and so forth, but these negotiations, these practical things. Or were they practical? Ultimately it boils down to the question: Was the Final Solution final? Because, if the Nazis were prepared, under some conditions, to release Jews, even if only some Jews, then the finality of the Final Solution isn't final...

... What were the results of these negotiations? When you look at it carefully, I think you must reach the conclusion that these negotiations should not have led to anything. The fact that they led to something – a little bit – is really quite amazing... The Jews were in a trap, you see. They had no power. They could appeal only to the feelings of pity of the Western powers... And so the Zionist leadership did the only thing it could do. It suggested – very intelligently, I think – to the British and then to the Americans: "Negotiate for the sake of negotiations, in order to drag the thing out until the war is won. And make a condition – that the Nazis shall stop the murder while they negotiate." But the British rejected it and then the Americans rejected it.

..."The Jewish heroes [who negotiated] were no knights in shining armour. Rabbi Weissmandel was a fanatic ultra orthodox opponent of Zionism. Joel Brandt was an adventurer, a drinker and a person whose devotion to the truth was not the

most prominent mark of his character. Kasztner was an ambitious, overweening and authoritarian personality, guilty of rescuing Nazis from post war justice to satisfy his honour and power....Yet, heroes they all are. Their attempts to save Jews involved a tremendous self-sacrifice, courage and devotion... They remind us that our heroes were ordinary humans, perhaps more gifted with insight and courage than the rest of us. They did the correct thing at the right time. Given the circumstances, they could not succeed. That they did in part is a wonderment. In any case, they should be judged, not by their success or failure, but by the answer to a basic moral question: Did they try? And try they did.

... We now have the documentation to show that Ben Gurion was quite different from what was previously thought. He was emotionally tremendously involved and he tried. How? Not through the official Zionist organisation. That was useless, it was a debating club. He had a small group of activists who tried to rescue. They really had no chances of success, but they tried. Nobody put it better than Ben Gurion himself:

"What have you done to us, you freedom-loving peoples, guardians of justice, defenders of the high principles of democracy and of the brotherhood of man? What have you allowed to be perpetrated against the defenceless people?... Why do you profane our pain and wrath with empty expressions of sympathy which ring like a mockery in the ears of millions of the damned in the torture houses of Nazi

Europe? Why have you not even supplied arms to our ghetto rebels as you have done for the partisan and underground fighters of other nations?... If, instead of Jews, thousands of English, American or Russian women, children and aged, had been tortured every day, burnt to death, asphyxiated in gas chambers, would you have acted in the same way?"

Extract from a given lecture at the Centre, 1997

Yehuda Bauer, born in Prague in 1926, is a Professor of Holocaust Studies (Emeritus) at Hebrew University, Jerusalem; Founding Chair of the Sassoon Center for Studies of Antisemitism at Hebrew University; Academic Adviser to Yad Vashem; Academic Adviser to the International Task Force for Holocaust Education, Remembrance and Research; Member of the Israeli Academy of Science, and recipient of the Israel Prize (1998).

"The moment I met the Smith family, the Centre caught my imagination and my full support. The Holocaust Centre, Beth Shalom is a unique Holocaust memorial and education facility, led and organized with tremendous devotion. The spirit is undoubtedly to teach about the Holocaust, the paradigmatic genocide, and cause people to realize that this was a turning point in our contemporary civilization and must be turned into a warning, with practical, topical results."

Yehuda Bauer

learning

Richard L. Rubenstein
A Twentieth-Century Journey

I have known Stephen Smith for a number of years, and wanted to visit The Holocaust Centre, Beth Shalom, but did not dream what an excellent place this is: I am truly astounded... Let me start this brief personal and theological memoir by explaining what I have been trying to do throughout my life. When my first book, *After Auschwitz*, came out, it was the object of a great deal of controversy. As a theologian, I was trying to make sense out of a horrible world, in terms that were quite different from traditional theological discourse. Nevertheless, strange as my writings may have seemed at first, they were innocent in comparison with the world that I was attempting to understand and explain. And I don't have to tell you what I mean by that...

... I especially remember one phrase in the older version of the Reform Jewish Prayer Book – "And now that we live in pleasanter times and pleasanter places." The night before Rosh Hashanah, 1944, news came out that the Russians had come upon Majdanek concentration camp and discovered 600,000 ownerless shoes. The image of 600,000 ownerless shoes has stuck in my

mind ever since. That evening, I asked myself, "How can I recite, 'Now that we live in pleasanter times and pleasanter places' with Majdanek?" The Russians hadn't come to Auschwitz yet. Majdanek was enough. Some of my professors at the Hebrew Union College were saying things like, "When the war is over, Jews can go back to the countries from which they were expelled and help to build up democracy." That was nonsense. We know what happened in Kielce, where they came back and were slaughtered.

... I became very interested in Europe and visited Germany in August 1961. On 13th August, when I woke up, I heard on the radio that the Wall had just been put up in Berlin. I arrived there several days later. The atmosphere was apocalyptic. I was invited to meet with Dean Heinrich Grüber, the only German to testify against Adolf Eichmann at the trial held earlier that year. As we were talking, American tanks were going down his street every 90 seconds. It was that kind of tense atmosphere. His church was in East Berlin; he lived in West Berlin. He spent three years in Sachsenhausen for opposing the Nazis... He said to me, "Herr Doctor Rubenstein, we Germans are being punished. We made people refugees, and now we are refugees. We made people homeless, now we are homeless. We destroyed churches and synagogues, now our churches are being destroyed." He got carried away with himself, and said, "Herr Doctor Rubenstein, it was God's will to send Adolf Hitler to punish the Jews at Auschwitz." That was probably the most important theological moment in my life...

I realised that Dean Grüber was taking biblical covenant theology and applying it to Auschwitz. My immediate reaction was, "I'd rather be an atheist than believe in such a God." To which he said, "Herr Doctor Rubenstein, how can you be a rabbi if you don't believe in such things?" I said, "Dean Grüber, I need one thing more than God to be a rabbi." And he said, "What is that?" I replied, "A few live Jews. By your logic, we could end up praising God for eliminating all of them."

...Now I was in a very simple dilemma. When I confronted the Holocaust theologically, I found no models in the writings of contemporary Jewish thinkers. I didn't say to myself: "Let's eliminate the traditional doctrines of covenant and election." I said: "Recognise that we cannot accept this intellectually, but also recognise that Jewish liturgy has its own integrity which we cannot ignore." I was known as the Jewish Death of God theologian, but notice what I was saying: *I never said that God was dead.* I said – very carefully – "We live in the *time of the death of God.*" It was impossible for me to look at genocide and see evidence of the presence of God in human existence; nor could I accept the idea of God purposefully guiding Jewish history. Maybe I was wrong; I don't think so. At the time, the great Jewish theologians were writing as if Auschwitz never happened. I didn't want to follow their example and I was not about to write anything that would in any way hint that the Jewish people deserved what happened to them or that God was involved in it.

...There is a tradition in Jewish mysticism that speaks of God as that which has no limit (*Ayn sof*). It is a very simple conception of God. God is the ocean; we are the waves. Each wave has its moment when it has its identifiable existence, never totally separate from the ocean; and eventually it returns to the ocean from whence it came. If there is eternal life, it is the eternal life out of which we come; into which we return. That, in essence, is my way of seeing God. It shocked some of my teachers and it shocked some of my colleagues. Nevertheless, I was trying to make sense out of what seemed to me a senseless world.

Extract from a lecture given at the Centre, 1999

Richard L. Rubenstein is President Emeritus and Distinguished Professor of Religion at the University of Bridgeport, USA, and Lawton Distinguished Professor Emeritus of Religion at Florida State University. Rubenstein's first book, *After Auschwitz*, (Bobbs-Merrill: 1966) initiated the contemporary debate on the meaning of the Holocaust in religious thought, both Jewish and Christian. His other books include *The Cunning of History* (Harper and Row: 1975) and *Approaches to Auschwitz* (Westminster/John Knox: 2003), co-authored with John K. Roth. Rubenstein's latest book, *La Perfidie de l'Histoire* (Paris: Éditions du Cerf and Les Provinciales), was published in Paris January 2005.

"My involvement with The Holocaust Centre, Beth Shalom, began when I was invited to deliver a lecture at the Centre. I was enormously impressed by the quality, comprehensiveness and impact of its programme and its resources. When Aegis was established, I considered it an honour that I was invited to serve on the Advisory Boards of Beth Shalom and Aegis. The work of the two institutions complement each other. I consider both among the world's best in their respective, though related, fields."

Richard L. Rubenstein

236

learning

John K. Roth

How is the Holocaust Best Remembered? Reflections on the Ethics of Memory

Memory is not purely or simply good. It can be a source of great evil. Antisemitism, racism and hate are impossible without memory in general, and without specific memories in particular. Memory was a condition for the Holocaust itself; if memory had been wiped out before the Holocaust took place, there could have been no Auschwitz... Holocaust survivor Primo Levi... reminds us that "human memory is a marvellous but fallacious instrument." Memories...can blur and decay. They can become selective, stylized, embellished and influenced by later experiences and information. In addition, memories can be repressed, denied and falsified. Nevertheless, memories can also be as accurate as they are painful, as clear as they are irrepressible. They can be sharpened, recorded, intensified, documented and even corrected so that they bear witness to the truth with penetrating insight...

At the very time when attention to the Holocaust is more prominent and unavoidable than ever, the Holocaust – sooner or later – may also be destined for low-intensity, inconsequential remembrance, if

not to being largely forgotten. At the beginning of the twenty-first century, nagging doubts remain about the future of Holocaust memories... Unquestionably, the vast outpouring of resources to document the Holocaust has been fuelled by awareness that the generation of eyewitnesses, especially Holocaust survivors, is dying out. Institutionalization of the Holocaust cannot guarantee deep memory about it. Soon the survivor generation will be gone. The intensity of concern about the Holocaust may diminish once that generation disappears...

...Post-Holocaust encounters with the Holocaust should keep stalking our souls... In particular, encounters with the Holocaust should make us remember how deadly it can be for racial thinking and racism to reassert themselves, for hate and violence to continue their destructive work, for the insidious perceptions to exist that wealth or class determines justice and that might makes right. If such inquiry into the Holocaust does not have a high priority in contemporary life, then not only will the Holocaust be forgotten more quickly, but also the quality of human life may be endangered even more in the twenty-first century than it has been in the bloody twentieth century...

So, believing as I do, that good memories are crucial, here, very briefly stated, are ten good-memory lessons that Holocaust education and the ethics of memory should teach, for the world can ill afford to forget them.

Remember that the Holocaust targeted a particular people, the Jews, first and foremost. Consequently, the preciousness of all human life and the homes it requires, the highest qualities of goodness and even God were assaulted as well.

Remember the Holocaust as a warning. Do not overestimate the degree to which the Holocaust gave antisemitism and racism a bad name. Do not forget where prejudice, hate, antisemitism and racism can lead.

Remember that there were people who risked everything to perpetrate genocide.

Remember not to be a perpetrator, a victim or a bystander.

Remember to give Hitler no posthumous victories.

Remember that there were people who risked everything to help others. Do not allow indifference to forget or abandon them; instead, try to follow their example.

Remember the fatal interdependence of all human actions; take responsibility for one another.

Remember that the devil is in the details, but also that commitment, force of will, sensitivity and healing are in the details as well. Do not overlook the fact that even small deeds and modest actions can be life-saving.

Remember not to despair but to build within the ruins of memory in ways that can mend the world.

Remember to take nothing good for granted.

...So quickly, and in such devastating ways, the Holocaust swept away good things – basic ones that every person needs, such as a home, safe and secure – that too often are taken for granted. Holocaust education and the ethics of memory needed to support it take place at memory's edge. That edge is at the border between honest loss of memory and forgetting, on the one hand, and the distortion, falsification, and even denial of memory, on the other. Memory's edge must be kept sharp, clear, keen, alert, and true. To teach about the Holocaust and to learn from it is the responsibility that the ethics of memory puts upon us.

Extract from a lecture given at the Centre, 2001

John K. Roth is the Edward J. Sexton Professor of Philosophy and the Director of the Center for the Study of the Holocaust, Genocide and Human Rights at Claremont McKenna College, where he has taught since 1966. He is the author or editor of more than 40 books, including *Approaches to Auschwitz: The Holocaust and its Legacy* (with Richard L. Rubenstein).

"My work at The Holocaust Centre, Beth Shalom has given me inspiring contact with amazing people who have survived the Holocaust and other genocides, with distinguished scholars and educators and with outstanding leaders such as Stephen and James Smith, who dedicate themselves to mending the world. The Centre's commitment to enhance learning about and from the Holocaust provides important encouragement in a needy world."

John K. Roth

learning

David Cesarani
The Making of Adolf Eichmann, genocidaire

learning

Adolf Eichmann had a normal childhood. There were no signs of abnormal behaviour in his youth. He was socialised and politicised in a politically right-wing and antisemitic milieu, but this was the norm for thousands of other Austrians and Germans who did not end up as practitioners of genocide. In any case, Eichmann didn't join the Austrian Nazi Party or the SS just because he hated the Jews. There were plenty of other groups that didn't like Jews that he could have aligned with. He joined the Nazis because they were gaining status and attracting people he respected. He liked their nationalism and strenuous opposition to the socialists. And he thought it was befitting his standing to join this rising party.

When Eichmann left Austria and enrolled in the Austrian Legion of the SS (after the Austrian Nazis were suppressed by the government), he did so anticipating a speedy return to Austria, not a career persecuting Jews in Germany. He trained in the SS and no doubt was indoctrinated in certain forms of antisemitism. However, when he opted to join the SD, the Nazi party security service, this was not because he wanted to persecute Jews.

When he joined the SD, it had no role in the 'Jewish Question' and didn't even have a Jewish department.

However, once he was a member of the SD Head Office in Berlin, Eichmann came under the influence of men with sophisticated 'scientific' ideas about the Jewish 'enemy'. He experienced sustained political education and indoctrination on Jewish questions. By 1937, he had a developed doctrine about Jews. He characterised the Jews as a dangerous, powerful racial enemy that was waging war against the Aryan/ German people. Jews could not be tolerated in the Reich and all Jewish policy had to be devoted to removing them as speedily and efficiently as possible to places where they could not threaten German interests.

Elements of this doctrine were rational, such as fostering Jewish emigration and working with Zionist groups to achieve this end. But other parts were fantastic and ominous, notably the notion that Jews formed an immensely powerful, worldwide network, and that an individual Jew – no matter how innocuous they might appear – was somehow connected to influential and threatening Jews in other countries, be they capitalist America or Communist Russia.

Once he was a part of the SS and SD, Eichmann was also taught the qualities of ruthless efficiency and decisiveness. The only ethical criteria that would influence conduct pertained to the welfare of the Aryan people, the good of the Nazi Party and the interests of the German state. Except on pragmatic grounds, the civil and human rights of non-Aryan Germans were simply not a factor to be taken into account when making or implementing policy. To the fully indoctrinated Eichmann, the Jews had no intrinsic claim to life. Even more radically, according to his doctrinaire views of the Jews as the enemy, they had to be destroyed. Jews and Aryans were engaged in a war to the death. He was willing to play a part in that war, although it was more like a campaign against an epidemic.

During the war, Eichmann saw himself engaged in a scientific, if sometimes distressingly messy, operation to eliminate a racial biological threat to the Aryan people. And this threat was inherent in every Jew, no matter how feeble they seemed. The capacity to do what he did was not inborn. Eichmann was not hardwired to become an accomplice to atrocities. He was taught to hate. He learned how to become a perpetrator of genocide and he chose to become one. The key, I think, to understanding Adolf Eichmann lies not in the man, but in the ideas that possessed him, the society in which they flowed freely, the political system that pervaded them and the circumstances that made them acceptable.

What Eichmann did was made possible by the dehumanisation of the Jews, the construction of the Jewish people as an abstract racial, biological threat and a political enemy, and the disabling of inhibitions against killing. Anyone subject to these processes might have behaved in the same way, be it in a totalitarian state or a democracy, and that is why institutions such as The Holocaust Centre, Beth Shalom are so vital because they warn against the past and they teach ways to avoid a repetition of such atrocities.

Extract from a lecture given at the Centre, 2004

David Cesarani is research professor in History at Royal Holloway College, University of London. He has advised the Home Office unit responsible for Holocaust Memorial Day and the Foreign and Commonwealth Office delegation to the Intergovernmental Taskforce for International Cooperation on Holocaust Education, Remembrance and Research. He has written and edited over a dozen books including (ed.) *After Eichmann: Collective Memory and the Holocaust since 1961* (2005); *Eichmann. His Life and Crimes* (2004); *The Jews and the Left/ The Left and the Jews* (2004); *Justice Delayed. How Britain became a Refuge for Nazi War Criminals* (1992). He has appeared in and been a consultant to numerous TV, radio and film documentaries.

"I have had the pleasure of addressing audiences at conferences and seminars at The Holocaust Centre on several occasions and I have always found them to be committed and well-informed listeners. The mix of survivors, academics and school students at these events is challenging and stimulating. The Holocaust Centre creates a unique atmosphere in which people with very different backgrounds and interests can come together and reflect on some of the most disturbing and urgent questions of our time."

David Cesarani

learning

Carol Rittner, R.S.M.
The Holocaust and the Christian World

The Holocaust and the Christian world. There is something obscenely incongruous about the juxtaposition of these two phrases. How can they exist together? When I say "Christian", I think of love, understanding, acceptance, respect, graciousness, friendship, generosity unto death – everything that for me exemplifies that extraordinary Jewish man Jesus, whom I accept as the Christ of God. But when I say "Holocaust", I think of evil, terror, horror, absoluteness, absurdity, godlessness – everything that for me exemplifies a descent into what was a terrifying spiritual abyss that contradicts entirely my understanding of "Christian". And yet, I have to face the fact that the Holocaust... was carried out not by disembodied demons but by human beings, almost all of whom were baptized Christians like myself...

...The number "six million" has become familiar, perhaps all too familiar. In any consideration of the Holocaust, such quantification of evil can have a numbing effect on our minds and hearts. It can even make us more accepting of "lesser" evils such as what happened in Cambodia in the 1970s, what happened in former Yugoslavia and Rwanda

in the 1990s, and perhaps even what is happening today in Zaire and Sierra Leone. We are numbed by horror. We get into the habit of saying things like, "Well, less than a million were killed. Or, less than a thousand. Or, less than a hundred." And thus the evil that was the Holocaust – the *Shoah* – continues to cast its long shadow over these past 55 years since the end of World War II and the liberation of the Nazi death camps...

What interests me personally are ethical and moral questions, as well as questions about human behaviour. Hundreds of books have been written about the Holocaust, but they have not diminished what Primo Levi called "the grey zone", that region of haunting questions about human behaviour that cannot be answered with certainty. True, we know a great deal about *what happened* during the Holocaust, about who was responsible, and who was victimized. What we don't know, however, is why so many Germans and their collaborators in every country in Nazi-occupied Europe so enthusiastically became one of Hitler's "willing executioners", to borrow Daniel Goldhagen's phrase.

How could ordinary human beings, people presumably raised to distinguish right from wrong, people with families of their own, participate in the vicious slaughter of powerless men, women and children? True, most Germans and others in Nazi-German occupied countries did not directly participate in the murder of the Jews of Europe. Many were not members of *Einsatzgruppen*, nor

were they death camp doctors, concentration camp guards, or collaborating police who rounded up Jewish men, women and children throughout occupied Europe and stuffed them into trains bound for Auschwitz, Treblinka, Sobibor, Birkenau and Chelmno.

Most were bystanders, people who were immediately present, actual witnesses even, those for whom involvement was an option, but who chose instead to simply go about their daily lives during one of the ghastliest dictatorships the world has even known. They continued to work and raise their children, to make love and to make money. They did not necessarily want to kill Jews, but neither did they want to become involved – at some risk to themselves – in trying to alleviate the suffering of others. What they wanted to do, as far as possible, was to maintain, more or less, the normal rhythms of their lives. As a result, the round-ups and deportations went on with horrifying regularity, as Jews unrelentingly disappeared from the cities, towns, villages, hamlets and streets all over Nazi Germany and, later, occupied Europe. And the smokestacks of Auschwitz continued to spew their ashes on the wings of the wind...

...We Christians in particular used to talk about BC and AC – "Before Christ" and "After Christ" – but perhaps what we really should talk about is BR and AR – "Before Rwanda" and "After Rwanda", not to mention a host of other "befores" and "afters", including Bosnia, Cambodia and Auschwitz,

learning

among others. One could say that the ashes of Auschwitz are everywhere, and they are still floating on the wings of the wind, 55 years "after Auschwitz", depositing their awesome fragments here, there and everywhere, polluting the ecosystem of our common humanity.

Throughout Nazi-dominated Europe, there were thousands of concentration and death camps, scattered, one might say, all over the place. The structure worked because millions of ordinary people simply did their jobs. Someone signed the forms, another filed them, another drew up lists, another worked in the chemical factory, another laid down railway lines, another drove the trains. Cumulatively these people contributed to an evil of great consequence. At the same time, all over Europe, in villages and towns close to the camps, or far distant from them, people continued to go to church each Sunday and Holy Day of Obligation, most oblivious to the fate of their Jewish "neighbours" who once lived in their midst, but now were absent from the markets, shops and offices these same Christians – Catholic, Protestant and Orthodox Christian alike – frequented. Such obliviousness is not without its consequence.

The Holocaust is part of our shared remembrance of human failure and the capacity that exists for the destruction of human life and dignity. If we are to be liberated to hope, we must confront this nightmare of genocide in such a way that we come to understand that human beings are responsible for their actions, that no act is inconsequential. The rabbis of old taught that "whoever saves one life, it is as though they had saved the whole world." Our task today is to remember that goodness is not measured in numbers. That what each of us does is of consequence. That even one person can make a difference. That while we may never finish the task of reweaving the moral fabric that holds our world together, neither are we free to desist from engaging in that never-ending task.

Extract from a lecture given at the Centre, 2000

Dr. Carol Rittner, R.S.M. is Distinguished Professor of Holocaust and Genocide Studies at The Richard Stockton College of New Jersey (USA), where she has taught since 1994. She is the author, editor or coeditor of numerous publications, including *The Courage to Care* (New York University Press), *Different Voices: Women and the Holocaust* (Paragon House), and *The Holocaust and the Christian World* (Continuum Press). Dr. Rittner's most recent book is *Genocide in Rwanda: The Complicity of the Churches?* (Paragon House: 2004).

learning

"Several years ago, I was invited to be on the Executive Committee for Beth Shalom Holocaust Centre and Aegis. I was appointed Editor of both **Perspectives** *and* **The Aegis Review on Genocide** *and have served in that capacity for the past three years. It has been a pleasure to serve as editor on two Aegis joint publications with Paragon House:* **Will Genocide Ever End?** *(2002) and* **Genocide in Rwanda: Complicity of the Churches?** *(2004)."*

Carol Rittner, R.S.M.

Dr Elisabeth Maxwell
A Gentile Reflects on the Holocaust

Whilst preparing this lecture, I transported myself back in time to 1938 when, although I am a French Protestant, I lived in the part of Paris mostly inhabited by Jews. From our home in the south of France, my father's job took him to Paris, and we had to move. In the late 1930s, it was very difficult to find accommodation in the capital because hardly any new apartment blocks had been built following the world financial crisis. But, through a friend, my parents were offered the top floor flat of a fairly modern building at a reasonable price. It was conveniently situated in the heart of Paris, not far from the Town Hall, the National Library and the celebrated Place des Vosges, and a few steps away from the French *lycée* where I studied. It was also the former Jewish ghetto of Paris, although we were not aware of that when we moved in. It was only years later after we had moved again that we realised why we had been so lucky – we had purchased our apartment not just from people from Alsace Lorraine, as they had told us, but from Jews who were obviously in a hurry to sell, and had the good sense to leave Paris, and hopefully France, ahead of the German invasion.

Most of my classmates at school were Jewish, yet it had no significance for me then. Religion was never discussed at school. Being Huguenots, my family was not antisemitic, yet there was no osmosis at all with my friends' families. I was not invited to their homes and they would not accept my invitation to mine. I was upset, but didn't know then that they couldn't eat in a Christian home; besides that, they were afraid and did not trust any Christians at the time. I have purposely recalled these particular memories because they show how my own cultured, well educated family was unaware of what was happening to Europe's Jews up to1939.

I was deeply ignorant of the existence of a Jewish world outside my own Christian one until I saw yellow stars appearing on people's clothing in our flats in late 1941. I knew even less about the fate of Europe's Jews until the liberation of Paris in September 1944. Nowadays, with the internet and especially in an environment like Beth Shalom, this seems an incredible statement, yet it is the truth, and it troubles me deeply.

...I well remember the summer of 1959 when my husband first took me to Auschwitz, where he had lost almost 500 members of his family. I was shocked and almost incredulous that this had happened in my youth and I had not known about it. Few people visited the death camps in these early days. We walked the road to death taken by those millions of victims. Not only did I feel bereft of any normal human warmth but it

was almost as if Nature herself had abandoned me. Endless grey clouds seemed to hang over the row of remaining wooden huts where prisoners were once herded. It was as if the smoke from all those millions of charred corpses still hovered between heaven and earth, refusing to disappear lest the world forget. We walked from one crematorium to another, then followed overgrown tracks leading to a woodland pond. A dilapidated metal structure still stood there, above the level of the water. A rusty wheelbarrow had long since tipped its last cargo of ash into the murky depths. We knelt beside the dull grey waters and my husband plunged his hands into the mire, pulling out a handful of greyish mud full of charred, pulverised bones...

Since then I have returned to Auschwitz several times and the feelings I first experienced there have been transformed into anger and a fierce determination never to allow mankind to forget the horrors it is capable of committing. It was after that first trip that I took the solemn decision that I would never say anything about the Jews that I could not say with the thought of burning children in Auschwitz in front of my eyes, and I would find out about the role of Christianity when all these crimes were being enacted. These were the impulses that guided me towards the first Remembering for the Future conference.

... Auschwitz primarily symbolises what may be done by one nation to any number of other nations. Given the prerequisites of ideology and culture, technology and power, any nation may develop along the lines of modern Germany and fall into the hands of a powerful ideology coupled with a bureaucratic-enabling technology which will develop into a death camp mentality. And, through education, we all need to be aware of this... Teaching and education of the Holocaust must have a solid historical base which cannot be replaced by fiction or films.

It was the French writer Charles Péguy who said that for every man and every event there is a precise moment in time when the bell tolls to signify that reality has frozen into history. Once history has taken over from memory, there may be no way of correcting any detail in the accepted record that has been falsified... If our generation can ensure that as much of the story is preserved as possible within our century, then we will have fulfilled our belated duty... Nothing in my view is more important and more urgent than to gather the testimonies of Holocaust survivors who have not yet been interviewed, as well as to facilitate for all scholars and students the easy location of existing written or oral testimonies... In the words of Elie Wiesel, speaking of those who perished, "They knew they would not return but they wanted to be remembered."

Extract from a lecture given at the Centre, 2004

Elisabeth Maxwell is President Emeritus of *Remembering for the Future*, a charitable organisation responsible for major international conferences on Holocaust Studies in Britain. She was the first woman elected as Vice-President of the International Council of Christians and Jews. Her memoirs are entitled *A Mind of My Own*, published in 1994.

"Although I am now becoming an old lady, I cannot, and will not, desist from my involvement in remembering the Holocaust and through its history, the important lessons derived from it. For this reason I like to remain involved with The Holocaust Centre, Beth Shalom, where I find an echo of my own thinking, friends on the same wavelength and kindred spirits trying to leave the world a better place than they found it."

Elisabeth Maxwell

learning

Hubert Locke
The Role of the Churches during the Holocau

The *Shoah*, or the annihilation of European Jewry, was an event of such shattering proportions a half century ago that the whole of human existence must be reshaped and redefined by its occurrence. In large measure, the English-speaking world is a bystander to that event. The destruction of the ghettos, the operation of the extermination camps, the death marches and all the other unimaginable horrors that occurred between 1939 and 1945 took place upon European soil and under the auspices of nations and peoples with whom we were locked in mortal combat. Yet, as bystanders, our nations are as much under the shadow of the *Shoah* as are those nations which were its perpetrators and accomplices...

...It is likely of little comfort to our Jewish colleagues, but at least the Churches have been willing, in the shadow of the *Shoah*, to examine themselves, to examine their teachings, their behaviour, and most of all, their silence during the fateful years 1933 to 1945. And while this may seem a woefully inadequate and obviously belated response, let it be noted that the self-examination of the Churches is far more than any other institutional or organisational segment of the western world has been willing to do. No single government, no civil service system, no judiciary, no medical association, no cluster of universities, nor any nation's military, has asked of itself "Where did our counterparts in Germany go awry? What might we, who were outside the borders in which the annihilation occurred, have done to halt the horror? How do we reconsider our professional roles and our institutional responsibilities in the light of the *Shoah*? How do we train and instruct present and future generations of accountants, lawyers, journalists, geneticists, judges, university professors and teachers, as well as clergy, so as to ensure that our societies are led by professionals who would never think of contributing to such madness as their professional counterparts in Germany did a half century ago?"

The Churches, I believe, have learned essentially two things in their self-examination and in their dialogue with their Jewish confreres: one is the terrible costs of delay in responding to racialist ideology, of which antisemitism is the most virulent form. The second is the tragic consequences that occur when the Churches, in the midst of a major national crisis, occupy themselves only with their own internal situation... Both German Catholic and Protestant clergy concerned themselves principally with the political and institutional battles they had to wage with the Nazi government. To their immense shame, they did not stop to concern themselves with the deteriorating circumstances of Germany's Jewish citizens...

...It is quite proper and appropriate to censor the German Churches and their clergy for their failure to come to the defence of Germany's half million Jewish citizens in those critical years of 1933 to 1939, before the systematic annihilation began and while the German Jews were being subjected to all sorts of discriminations, boycotts, personal indignities and other oppressions. It was in *this* crucial period that the voice of the Churches might have made a difference. It was in *this* crucial period that the voice of the Churches needed to be heard... The lesson, it seems to me, is clear and obvious: never again must the Churches be silent but, equally important, never again must the Churches be tardy in recognising the plight of the oppressed. And never again, even when religious institutions find themselves under assault, as the Churches of Germany did, must they fail to recognise and respond to the plight of those who are outside their fold...

... As we stand at the eve of a new century and a new millennium, I believe, I fervently hope, that we are ready for a new era in Jewish-Christian relations. That era is one which must be based firmly on an acknowledgement of the past history of the Jewish-Christian encounter, and especially on a recognition and acceptance of responsibility on the part of Christians for how much of that history has been shrouded for Jews in pain, suffering and tragedy. But I also believe that the new era and relations between our two faiths is not one which can continue to be predicated on accusations of blame or expressions of guilt. On the part of the Jewish community, there needs, it seems to me, to be a recognition that as we prepare for the century and the millennium before us, what is needed most from Christians are not more confessions of guilt over the past... What is needed is a firm Christian resolve to join with its Jewish colleagues in an unremitting endeavour to stamp out the evil of antisemitism, to see that evil as not just another in a long chain of regrettable ethnic, racial or religious attitudes but rather as the mother of all prejudices which has bequeathed, not just to the Jewish people but to the entire world, nothing but tragedy and sorrow. On the part of the Christian community, there needs to be a reassessment of the relationship of Christianity to Judaism and the Jewish heritage...

...Would that all Christians might realise that our faith is a child of Judaism, a branch of that tree that is the faith of Abraham, Isaac, Jacob, Moses and their descendants. Children may well go on to achieve great things in life, but they never triumph over their parents. They always, whatever their accomplishments, however great their numbers and however lofty their vision, they always stand not on the shoulders (as metaphorically it is so often put) but in the shadow of those who brought them into being, who taught and nurtured and imparted to them those basic insights and ideals on which they build their own separate existence. And parents, though they may sometimes view their offspring with sorrow or regret, sometimes as hopelessly rebellious or as thankless renegades, parents never reject their offspring. Such is, and must always be, in my small view, the relationship between Christianity and Judaism.

Extract from a lecture given at the Centre, 1996

Hubert G. Locke is Professor and Dean Emeritus, the Graduate School of Public Affairs, University of Washington. In 2004, he was Arnold Visiting Professor of Religion, Whitman College and in 2005-6 he is Distinguished Visiting Fellow, Antioch University.

"Over the course of more than a half-century, I've enjoyed a number of pleasant and personally rewarding associations with institutions, groups and organizations on both sides of the Atlantic. None have been as meaningful, nor have I had a higher regard for the work being done, than my years spent with Beth Shalom. It stands as an international model for what one family can do to make an impact of significance, not only in the United Kingdom but – in the centres that have been modelled after Beth Shalom – around the world!"

Hubert Locke

learning

Jonathan Webber
Creating a Culture of Healing

No one who was not present during those terrible times can say what it was like. So let me start with a question; what precisely is remembered, or ought to be remembered, about the Holocaust? What precisely should Holocaust remembrance consist of? Too much happened during the Holocaust for anyone to be able to remember it all. And the Holocaust certainly covered a range of events far wider than the concentration camps alone, far wider than Auschwitz on its own.

So to return to my question, then: How to go about choosing a set of memories, or a set of remembrances, that will represent somehow the entirety of the Holocaust? It's not at all self-evident. And what does one concentrate on? The universal aspects? The particular Jewish aspects? The failings of the Germans then? The failings of us now? The need for forgiveness and reconciliation? While one starts thinking about all this, one wonders how much we have achieved so far. Are we getting the right messages across? Have we got enough of all the different elements, including rescue, for example? Are we, in short, getting the balance right?...

... What you've got in the Auschwitz museum, for example the broken-down remains of those eye-glasses, those Jewish prayer shawls, those dilapidated suitcases, could be taken as banal and misleading. Because what you can't show... is, of course, what the Jews left behind, in their own homes. You can't show the vibrant Jewish culture that was destroyed. There are hundreds of towns and villages across eastern Europe where there are abandoned synagogues, abandoned Jewish cemeteries, former Jewish schools and hospitals, theatre buildings – all of them demonstrating by their very presence the systematic manner in which the Jews were uprooted from their native setting and so rapidly brought to an end. So we have to think, it seems to me, very globally about Holocaust remembrance.

I should just say that in Poland a great deal has been done. The Auschwitz museum has started programmes for school teachers, a Polish university centre for Holocaust studies has been founded, and in Oswiecim, the last surviving synagogue was recently restored. Auschwitz is now not only a place of mourning and not only a tourist destination, it is also a place of encounter. I think it's incredible what's been happening...

... But we also need more information. Do you know that 55 years after the defeat of Nazi Germany, we still do not know where the Jews were actually murdered? Forget about their actual names; that's another question. We don't even know where they were murdered. Of course, we've got the Auschwitz museum, we've got the Majdanek museum, we've got a few concentration camp museums in Germany, Austria and elsewhere, but we've done almost nothing for the two million Jews who were shot. We haven't marked the mass graves, often deep in the countryside; we haven't made sure that these mass hangings, which we have seen photographs of, have got proper commemorative plaques. We have not even got, in fact, a database just giving a simple list of these sites, let alone telling you more details. The remembrance of these historical locations of mass murder has been random, uncoordinated, either too personal or else too impersonal, done without a fully inclusive approach to the subject...

Hence, at the Stockholm International Forum on the Holocaust, convened by the Prime Minister of Sweden in January 2000, I made the proposal that we should have a European Holocaust Commission. I don't need to say to a British audience that this phrase and this concept should be modelled on the Commonwealth War Graves Commission. We want to make sure that these graves are properly marked, that local people are taught about the history, that it enters the local schoolbooks and so on. But the challenge isn't just at a local level; the challenge is to establish a culture of remembrance at a European level – to remind people that genocide happens in the midst of civilised populations, and that its consequences are not only local, but thoroughly international as well...

Finally, what I am arguing for, in more general terms, is the importance of giving attention to the need for cultural healing. We must get away from the atmosphere of accusation and counter-accusation that have characterised the argument over the convent at Auschwitz and other related issues there, such as the crosses or most recently the discotheque. The role of The Holocaust Centre, Beth Shalom in both participating in this debate and also sponsoring major new activities to stimulate and promote cultural healing and reconciliation is unbelievable and unique...

Extract from a lecture given at the Centre, 2000

"Since The Holocaust Centre, Beth Shalom has been in existence, it has gained a completely justified international reputation as an extraordinary institution to launch and see through crucial new initiatives. Long may these continue."

Jonathan Webber

Professor Jonathan Webber holds the UNESCO Chair in Jewish and Interfaith Studies at the University of Birmingham. He is the author of the forthcoming *Time, Memory and Historical Consciousness* and *Traces of Memory: the Ruins of Jewish Civilization in Polish Galicia* (Littman).

conferences

The tranquil, reflective space at The Holocaust Centre serves as an ideal setting for small, focussed conferences and seminars.

Using the Holocaust as a departure point, many conferences are training days for hearts and minds, designed to inspire professionals about the need to take responsibility for anti-racism and diversity efforts.

Other conferences bring colleagues together from local authorities or schools to examine good practice, as for example in relation to the delivery of Holocaust Memorial Day in the education sector or local community.

Sixth-form conferences are held each year on Holocaust themes for students at the upper end of high school.

Some conferences draw significant experts together to network and develop new perspectives, the aim being to advance the field in relation to Holocaust education, citizenship or genocide prevention – for example, the joint Foreign and Commonwealth Office/Aegis Conference on Genocide Prevention held at the Holocaust Centre in January 2002.

249

learning

"It seemed to me that the first step in genocide prevention was getting the right people in the room together to think about what we need to do, to even have the smallest chance of success. That is why we convened the 2002 conference on genocide prevention with the Foreign Office."

James M Smith

251

learning

Aegis/Foreign and Commonwealth Office Conference on Genocide Prevention

Two succinct comments by conference participants make a good point of departure for a summary of the conference: "The beast of genocide," said Gregory H. Stanton, director of the International Campaign to End Genocide, "lurks in the dark." Romeo Dallaire, the Canadian general who headed the UN Assistance Mission in Rwanda, made a counterpoint when he urged that "the need is to stop the disconnect between the experiential and the intellectual." The conference shed light in and on the darkness that Stanton identified. With participants from government, the military, non-governmental organizations, and universities, as well as genocide survivors, it also reconnected the experiential and the intellectual.

At least five overarching themes found repeated expression. First, the discussions showed that genocide prevention is a goal that exceeds any single person's expertise, any discipline's methodology, or any government's reach. Genocide prevention requires working together at every point. Second, no automatic link exists between intellectual analysis of genocide and the action that is needed to prevent it. That connection can be made only through political will. How to muster and sustain that political will is among the most important questions raised by the continuing threat of genocide in our world.

Third, governments, even if they are alert and activated, will not – indeed cannot – do everything that is necessary to prevent, stop or heal the wounds that genocide inflicts. That fact leaves us to mobilize other agencies that may be able to lend a hand in that crucial work.

Fourth, at times there is no substitute for military intervention, which is essential to maintain stability and security. Military intervention, however, is not enough to meet the needs that genocidal threats present. We need political, economic and educational aid... to defuse potentially genocidal situations. Fifth, prevention of and intervention in genocide are long-term commitments, otherwise genocide prevention will remain ineffective. The long-term commitments must involve all sorts of institutions, and not least of all the media, which have the power to alert, inform and urge the need for action.

The beast of genocide does lurk in the dark, but the dark is not only the darkness of murderous ignorance, lethal discrimination and bloodthirsty arrogance. Instead, genocide lurks largely in the darkness of irresponsibility and non-accountability. In that genocide-related darkness, too little is prevented and intervention comes too late. General Dallaire got it right: the disconnection between the experiential and the intellectual must be stopped. If it is stopped, then genocide may end. We have no right to regard striving for that objective as hopeless.

John K Roth

"Thank you for asking me to the Genocide Prevention Conference. It was truly ground-breaking and of historical importance. I am sure that I will refer to it often in my future work. I congratulate you."

Linda Melvern
Honorary Professor, Department of International
Politics, University of Wales, Aberystwyth

"Congratulations for the initiative of your conference on Genocide Prevention. Please be assured of my support and my real desire to participate in the continuity of your work."

Romeo Dallaire
UN Commander in Rwanda, April-July 1994

Philippe Gaillard, former Head of Red Cross, Rwanda, 1994 at the Aegis Conference

Gregory Stanton
President, Genocide Watch; Founder, The International Campaign to End Genocide

This conference brought together genocide survivors, academics, journalists, military personnel, government policy makers and advisers and NGO specialists to consider concrete steps that should be taken to prevent genocide. In our discussions we focused on the hard questions. We confronted why the world has thus far failed to prevent genocide. And we planned ways to build the institutions and political will for prevention. The personal networking at the conference was vital because the world is still, and always will be, personal. In considering the crime that is the ultimate expression of de-personalization, the personal connections built at the conference have already had a lasting impact. The ground was laid for the Stockholm Forum on Genocide Prevention in 2004, which brought 55 governments and hundreds of policy makers and experts together to broaden the consideration of the issues raised at the Aegis/FCO conference. The International Campaign to End Genocide (ICEG) gained new member organizations and in 2002 first proposed the appointment of a Special Adviser to the UN Secretary-General on the Prevention of Genocide. In perhaps the most moving personal moment for me, on the eve of the conference, General Romeo Dallaire and Dr Philippe Gaillard met again for the first time since the Rwandan genocide. Their tearful reunion reaffirmed the reality that heroes walk among us, that they are as human as we are, and that, yes, we can change the world.

Agneta Bohman
Ambassador, Ministry for Foreign Affairs, Sweden

learning

After a week I have not yet digested the rich impressions from the conference... I think it represented a 'unique premiere' with the mix of scholars and activists that was for me, professionally and intellectually, so stimulating. It was also a very inspiring encounter with courageous and impressive persons that opened new perspectives. The meeting was an incitement to reflect on how I can better use my professional and personal life.

I was deeply impressed by your work. The scope and education was even broader than I could imagine.

For me the Aegis conference marked an inspiring starting point for further activities in the fields of genocide prevention and

transitional justice. After the work with the Stockholm conference on "Truth, Justice and Reconciliation" in 2002, initiated by the Swedish Prime Minister's office, and the "Genocide Prevention" conference in 2004, I worked with different initiatives at the Ministry of Foreign Affairs: reconciliation projects in the Western Balkans within the framework of the Stability Pact for south-eastern Europe; initiatives in the fight against impunity in the former Yugoslavia; several papers about the role of war crimes tribunals in post-conflict situations and in preventing genocide; and most recently, an article ten years after Srebrenica in a Swedish daily, *Svenska Dagbladet*.

It has been a privilege to follow the work and networks of Aegis and to develop contacts with Stephen and James Smith. Aegis' work is a unique combination of deep knowledge, compassionate idealism, concrete projects and realistic political advocacy. Its work is marked by a fundamental respect for the victims of genocide and of mass atrocities, in which "never again" is a powerful driving force for preventive efforts and not an empty catchword.

Eric Markusen
Danish Institute for International Studies

In an emerging, interdisciplinary field like genocide studies, researchers tend to be spread out over the world. Therefore, conferences and seminars are a valuable source of information, ideas and mutual support. Aegis Trust has organized a number of conferences on diverse aspects of genocide. I have attended three, including the Genocide Prevention conference, 22-25 January 2002; the seminar on Nationalism, 19-20 November 2002; and the seminar on Genocidal Mentalities, 21-24 March 2003.

These have all been rewarding experiences. The seminar on Genocidal Mentalities brought together a small group of scholars for several days of intense discussion. The unprecedented opportunity to present my work and get detailed feedback from colleagues from different fields, and to hear about their work and thinking, helped me advance my own thinking about this concept, which I have been working on since 1990 when Robert Jay Lifton and I published

The Genocidal Mentality: Nazi Holocaust and Nuclear Threat. The seminar also generated a special issue of the *Aegis Review on Genocide* devoted to the concept of genocidal mentality.

The Genocide Prevention conference was an important milestone in the struggle to prevent genocide. For three days, approximately two dozen women and men from around the world debated and discussed theoretical and practical aspects of defining, anticipating, preventing and punishing genocide. The conference began with short statements by survivors of the Holocaust and the Bosnian and Rwandan genocides. In addition to providing for the exchange of information and perspectives, the duration of the conference allowed ample time for individual and small group discussions and networking. Many of the participants at this conference played key roles in the 2004 Stockholm International Forum: "Preventing Genocide: Threats and Responsibilities".

254

learning

Sweden and the Holocaust

Beth Shalom's sixth anniversary was marked by a conference entitled "Sweden: Then and Now", involving the participation of Stephen Feinberg of the US Holocaust Memorial Museum, Christer Mattsson of Sweden's Living History Project, Professor Per Thullberg, Vice-Chancellor of Södertörns Högskola University, Paul Levine of Uppsala University and Stephen Smith.

The panel discussion opened with an outline of the role Sweden is currently playing in Holocaust education through the work of the Living History Project, the International Task Force and the Stockholm Forum – all of which are a great source of inspiration. Both Britain and Sweden have similar issues, in many respects. Now, for both countries, it is not about whether we remember the past, but how, and toward what end.

Examining why we should teach the Holocaust, Christer Mattsson explained that it was not "a breakdown of civilisation; it was the dark side of civilisation." The real challenge, he added, was how to interpret the impact of the Holocaust on the post-war world, the meaning of the Holocaust in our own time, how to move from dead artefacts to living history. As he concluded, "We need the artefacts, we need the memory, we need the memorial sites to get a framework. But the framework must come to life, and that is our duty as educators."

The day was also marked by the Opening of the "Gateway of the Righteous" by His Excellency Mr. Mats Bergquist, Ambassador of Sweden, who commented on Sweden's role during the Holocaust. "I am immensely proud to be a member of the same [diplomatic] service as Raoul Wallenberg was, and Per Anger as well, who saved

thousands or perhaps tens of thousands of Jews in Hungary in 1944 and 1945... We did too little as a nation, but we did a little, and the little we did we should be proud of. And the rest that we didn't do we should remember for the future."

The day's proceedings concluded with the UK première of the award-winning film *Stateless, Arrogant and Lunatic*, introduced by Mr. Marcus Storch. The film tells the little-known story of the efforts of Gilel Storch, a Latvian Jewish refugee in Sweden, whose activities were central to the exploits of Raoul Wallenberg, who saved tens of thousands of Jewish lives during the closing months of the war.

Lithuania and the Holocaust

In October 2001, Beth Shalom welcomed representatives from Lithuania for a conference focussing on the work of Museums and Holocaust Education in Lithuania and the UK. Lithuanian Government representatives included Ina Marciulionyte, Vice Minister of Culture, and Alfonsas Eidintas from the Ministry of Foreign Affairs; and the museum sector was represented by Rachel Kostanian from the Jewish State Museum, Emanuelis Zingeris from the Jewish Cultural Society, and participants from the House of Memory, the Centre for Tolerance and the IX Fort, Kaunas. James Kidner and Naoual Margoum represented the UK's Foreign and Commonwealth Office.

Conference workshops and discussions centred on Working in Education, Britain and the Holocaust, Project Work at Beth Shalom and Issues in Lithuania, and the visit was also enhanced by further sessions at the Imperial War Museum in London, examining the educational facilities offered at the museum, the rationale for the Holocaust Exhibition, its ongoing care, arts fund-raising and the planned new museum on the life of Sir Winston Churchill. The visit concluded with a final day of discussion at the Foreign Office.

As Rimantas Zirgulis, Director of Kedainiai Regional Museum wrote, echoing the general reaction of the participants, "I'm sending you my heartfelt thanks for the possibility to visit Great Britain and to see the impressive and unique activity of your Holocaust Centre, Beth Shalom. All this left an indelible impression upon me."

Irena Veisate
Holocaust Survivor and Founder of the House of Memory, Lithuania

The Holocaust Centre, Beth Shalom is a unique place, a unique institution with unique people, who have played a very important role in introducing Holocaust education in Lithuania. It is a very controversial and painful topic in our country. On the one hand, the country was occupied by Nazi Germany from 1941 to 1944 and became a testing ground for the Holocaust. On the other hand, Lithuania's in fact powerless temporary government proclaimed the country's independence on 23 June 1941, but never protested against the persecution and killings of its Jewish citizens; and, unfortunately, some Lithuanians became auxiliaries of the Nazis and participated actively in the execution of Jews. How should the Holocaust be introduced to young people in such a complicated situation?

Being myself the Chair of the Open Society Fund, Lithuania and also a Holocaust survivor, I invited Stephen Smith to start with seminars for Lithuanian history teachers. It was a hard job to do, but Stephen was brilliant. After several visits to Vilnius, Stephen invited a Lithuanian delegation to the UK to celebrate the third anniversary of Beth Shalom. As a result of our collaboration, and maybe indirectly as a result of this visit, a group of Lithuanian intellectuals and teachers decided to establish a non-governmental organisation called "The House of Memory", which took a very active, even a leading position, in introducing Holocaust education into our high schools. One especially successful project was the competition for high schools, already held four times, to write an essay on the topic "Who were the Jewish neighbours of my grandparents and great-grandparents?" Almost 200 schools got involved in this competition. A vanished world in Lithuania was discovered and the best essays are published in two volumes.

It is hard to overestimate what The Holocaust Centre, Beth Shalom has done, and not only in England. In a world where we feel the lack of moral values, of tolerance, of goodness, the Centre and the whole Smith family are standing up for a better world of justice and love.

I hope very much that in the future our collaboration will be even closer, to the benefit of all.

Reporting in an Age of Mass Death

The conference "Reporting in an Age of Mass Death" brought together an impressive gathering of scholars and journalists to debate issues relating to media reporting of the Holocaust and genocide. As Stephen Smith outlined in his introduction, "The shadow of the Holocaust and the tragic persistence of mass death today means that all of us in some way will write, record, watch or read about the wasted lives of our fellow human beings. The least we can do is stop and think for a few moments. How *are* we to convey the import of their lives and the folly of their deaths? How should we inform, provoke and perhaps awaken the conscience of our all-too-often, all-too-distanced lives?"

Professor David Cesarani's opening lecture outlined how the Holocaust has been reported over the decades, and this was followed by a panel session, "Holocaust Fatigue", involving contributions from James Smith, Ned Temko, Jon Silverman and Frank Furedi. It focussed on the challenges of presenting the story of the Holocaust, on problems with newspaper editors, the reasons for the current appetite for Holocaust stories, and its negative consequences.

Journalist Fergal Keane opened the subsequent session with a lecture on "Genocide in the 20th Century: Uses and Abuses of the Holocaust". He examined the role of the media, both in fomenting hatred and in reporting its consequences, and the collective failure of journalists to pay adequate attention to areas where genocide may erupt or is being committed.

The following panel session, including contributions from Mark Levene, Jonathan Charles, Liz Leonard and Jake Lynch, explored "The Media in a World of Genocide: News and the Public Conscience". Speakers focussed on society's attitude to genocide, the element of 'them and us', the importance of showing graphic evidence of atrocities to make people think and react, the problem of news fatigue and the responsibility of journalists.

Liz Leonard
Senior Producer, BBC Religion and Ethics

We have a moral responsibility as journalists to report accurately and not to sanitise; we have a responsibility to allow the victims of a genocide to tell their own stories; we have a responsibility to encourage debate in a way which promotes tolerance and respect of other people's opinions; above all we have a responsibility to ask questions... Words matter and they are powerful. They fuel hatred, fear and prejudice. In the wrong hands they can be used to incite nationalism and take away the identity of the person being prosecuted. But they can also be used to expose the truth... Journalism at its very best does not simply report; it also has the potential to change attitudes and even thought processes.

BBC journalists Liz Leonard and Jonathan Charles at the conference

Sculpture donated by Mark Pope on the occasion of the Germany and the Holocaust Seminar

Germany and the Holocaust

Yom Ha Sho'ah was marked at The Holocaust Centre in April 1999 by a lecture and panel discussion on Germany and the Holocaust.

The keynote lecture was given by Professor Karl Schleunes, author of the seminal text *The Twisted Road to Auschwitz*. In a fascinating and wide-ranging lecture, he considered the impact of the Holocaust on modern society and culture, looking at its implications for us today.

Going on to review the history of antisemitism which led to the Holocaust, Professor Schleunes set the event in its context and showed how the bases of European and western society, both secular and religious, were implicated by the catastrophe. He concluded that it was not, of course, religious concepts or secular ideas from the so-called Enlightenment that were responsible

for the Holocaust. Rather, it resulted from the decisions of individual people. Yet to understand how those decisions came to be made, they could not be viewed in a vacuum, and it was for this reason that we needed to consider their historical context.

Following the lecture, a panel of six eminent participants from Germany and Austria gave presentations on "Education and Memorials in Germany Today". They included Dr Tom Freudenheim, Deputy Director of the Berlin Jewish Museum; Annegret Ehmann, Director of Education, Memorial House of the Wannsee Conference; Prof. Hanns-Fred Rathenow, Director of the Institute for Social Studies at the Technische University, Berlin; Gisela Blume, founder of the Fürth Memorial; Marta Halpert, Director of the Anti-Defamation League, Vienna; and Dr Edith

Raim of the Dachau Concentration Camp Memorial.

The programme also included the unveiling of a new sculpture by Holocaust survivor Naomi Blake, a six-branched candelabrum in the form of a figure with raised hands, which will be lit each year on Yom Ha Sho'ah, and an exhibition of the paintings of Stanislaw Brunstein, an artist who suffered under both Stalin and Hitler and lost his family in the Holocaust.

remembering for the future

In 1988 Elisabeth Maxwell created the first conference in this country to bring together scholars of Holocaust studies as an interdisciplinary, international field. Hosted by her late husband Robert Maxwell, over 500 scholars from around the world gathered in Oxford for the first "Remembering for the Future" conference. The event was repeated in 1994 in Berlin and again in 2000 in Oxford. It has resulted in the publication of hundreds of academic papers in its published volumes.

In 2000 Elisabeth Maxwell invited The Holocaust Centre to take over responsibility for Remembering for the Future and develop its potential over years to come. The project has some 500 scholars associated with it.

In 2005 the Centre announced that Remembering for the Future will maintain the leadership role it has played for two decades with the launch of an academic digest of the latest scholarship in Holocaust and Genocide studies, entitled, "Remembering for the Future", from 2006.

Elisabeth Maxwell

President Emeritus, Remembering for the Future

As the former Executive Chairman of Remembering for the Future (RFTF), I recall with pleasure our close association with The Holocaust Centre, from my first meeting with its Director, Stephen Smith. He was then a young man in his twenties with a string of achievements behind him. I was impressed, but even more so when he said he had read all three RFTF 1988 volumes from cover to cover, and wanted to discuss the 'future of remembering'. On a visit to Beth Shalom, I then met his brother, James, and their parents and discovered what had already been accomplished in just over one year. The hall was built, the rose garden in progress, the offices teeming with eager, young helpers; and survivors were already speaking to students. The Holocaust Centre, Beth Shalom was the only Holocaust memorial centre in this country, five years before the Imperial War Museum's exhibit opened in July 2000. From that first visit, I witnessed with amazement its growth, vitality and importance as a powerful educational tool to remember the Holocaust.

When RFTF staged a large conference in Oxford and London in 2000, including a gathering of over 1,000 survivors, Stephen played an important role in organising the Education section. So in 2002, when I decided to relinquish my Chairmanship, it was a natural step to pass on the torch to The Holocaust Centre. RFTF thus became its academic arm, ensuring that RFTF's original aims would be respected and adding a further dimension to the Centre. And RFTF's work now continues in annual lectures and a database project focussing on Holocaust survivor testimony.

We at RFTF and The Holocaust Centre have greatly helped to place the Holocaust at the centre of our collective consciousness. Holocaust teaching and education must have a solid historical base so that we can teach our children to avoid the pitfalls of complacency and learn to detect danger signs.

> "Don't forget the survivors…. Don't condemn them to a second death… listen to them; they are our teachers…
>
> Don't forget the forgotten… they were raped in the streets, thrown in the gutter, beaten, hacked,…. shot, gassed, burned… and they have only us.
>
> And if you must remember anything… Remember for the future."

Stephen Smith's words, delivered at the Stockholm Forum in January 2004, should convince anyone that in ensuring RFTF's continued life with The Holocaust Centre, we have placed it in good hands.

THE JOURNAL OF HOLOCAUST EDUCATION   Volume 5 Number 1 Summer 1996

JOURNAL OF GENOCIDE RESEARCH   VOLUME 2 NUMBER 3 NOVEMBER 2000

Holocaust and Genocide Studies   Volume 7, Number 1, Spring 1993   Oxford University Press

David Patterson

CBE; Emeritus President of the Oxford Centre for Hebrew and Jewish Studies and Emeritus Fellow of St Cross College, Oxford

I first met Stephen Smith when he came to the Oxford Centre for Hebrew and Jewish Studies as a graduate student on our one-year programme. I was immediately deeply impressed by this young man who had built a substantial business in confectionery, but was at the same time passionately engaged in all aspects of the Holocaust. Subsequently, we were involved together in the wonderful conference entitled "Remembering for the Future", and later I was able to visit the most impressive institution called Beth Shalom and meet the other members of the remarkable Smith family. Since then I have been an enthusiastic admirer both of the family and the extraordinary development of Beth Shalom as a Centre for spreading the knowledge of the horrors of the Holocaust to a growing public, and particularly in the education of the young. I cannot speak too highly of its accomplishments and the admirable devotion of the Smith family to what can only be described as an inspirational Centre for education. May it go from strength to strength, and may the second decade be even more successful than the first.

John T. Pawlikowski OSM

Professor of Social Ethics and Director, Catholic-Jewish Studies Program, Catholic Theological Union, Chicago; Chair, Church Relations Committee, USHMM, Washington, DC

The two major "Remembering for the Future" conferences in the UK played a central role in expanding and solidifying the study of the Holocaust. Through these conferences the perception was clearly established that understanding the Holocaust is not only critical for historical knowledge of the twentieth century, but central as well to addressing many of our current political, social and medical questions.

Holocaust education is currently on the rise in universities in the United States and elsewhere. Many of the professors now teaching these courses deepened their interest in the Holocaust through participation in the "Remembering for the Future" conferences. As a Professor of Social Ethics, I know that the 2000 gathering in particular created a permanent place for the Holocaust in ethical studies. I am pleased that The Holocaust Centre, Beth Shalom continues the ground-breaking work begun at these conferences.

Yael Danieli

Director, Group Project for Holocaust Survivors and their Children; Co-President, International Network for Holocaust and Genocide Survivors and their Friends, New York, NY, USA

I recall quite vividly the excitement generated by the first "Remembering for the Future" conference, not the least by the genius of its title. It was one of the most dignified gatherings, and since everyone was there, it created a forum for crucial multidisciplinary networking and dialogues that poured into the Oxford nights, and on to numerous future professional and commemorative events, ongoing contacts and concepts for fruitful interventions and contributions to and around the world. Its most memorable recent legacy was our mutual work in Rwanda, which Stephen and James, with their unique gifts, extended to healing a nation.

Dr Alice L. Eckardt

Emerita Professor, Lehigh
University, Bethlehem, PA., USA

"Remembering for the Future", Britain's first international conference on the Holocaust and its continuing significance was held in 1988 in Oxford and London under the sponsorship of Mr Robert and Dr Elisabeth Maxwell. Approximately 560 scholars from many countries participated, producing three large volumes of papers. A second conference, held in Berlin in 1994, resulted in a paperback in both German and English; and a third, returning to Oxford and London in 2000, yielded another three volumes. The conferences revealed the powerful impact of the Holocaust on large numbers of people, on many fields of endeavour, particularly on Christian theology. "Remembering for the Future" met the imperative need felt by many Christians for its faith to radically alter its view and presentation of Judaism and its people. Theological revisions were proposed by many. In 2000, considerable changes in Christian thought and in education were evident, along with widespread impact in the various arts.

At the 1994 gathering, Dr Stephen Smith presented a paper dealing with Holocaust education in Britain, which led to his serving on the Executive Committee in 2000 and heading the education section. Furthermore, the Beth Shalom Holocaust Centre became a sponsor. Subsequently, "Remembering for the Future" was transferred to The Holocaust Centre for future use since its educational programmes and museum focus on similar matters, and hence it plays a significant role in fostering continuing work.

intern
programme

University students who have studied the Holocaust, or are about to, have become a regular feature of The Holocaust Centre's transient staffing complement. Intern and gap-year students have been applying to spend time at the Centre and in its overseas field operations.

263

learning

There are up to five places each year for interns, who have come from as close as Nottingham and as far away as California. In coming years, the Centre intends to develop facilities to create a rolling intern programme, to facilitate greater numbers of students wishing to gain professional experience in the field of Holocaust and genocide studies in practice, during their student years.

Below are reflections from a few interns who have been part of the Centre and its life in recent years.

Susi Kim, Claremont Mckenna College, Aegis Intern 2005

Colin Hunter

Aegis Intern, Claremont McKenna College, 2003

In May of 2003, I boarded a flight from the western United States to Birmingham, UK, and shortly thereafter arrived at The Holocaust Centre, where I was introduced in earnest to the work of both the Centre and the Aegis Trust. My internship that summer would take me to Kigali, Rwanda, where I wrote a report on the prospects for filming Rwanda's ongoing *gacaca* genocide trials and edited proposals for genocide memorials to be established throughout the country. First, though, I spent several days at The Holocaust Centre, where I pored over videos, books and photo collections documenting the Centre's contributions to Holocaust and genocide remembrance over the previous decade. My internship was, from beginning to end, remarkably educational; it afforded me opportunities to learn firsthand what most can only learn through books or the media – that genocide destroys peoples, societies and the human bonds that hold these together.

I travelled to Kigali with little idea of what to expect. I knew I was to work on a report on the *gacaca* filming project, but had little idea what that would entail. I now consider myself privileged to have worked on this project, which afforded me the opportunity to work with an international team of academics, to view firsthand a *gacaca* trial,

to meet Rwandan Government officials and politicians, and to test my own abilities in a challenging environment. Friends and family are still awed at stories from my time there – the time we met with the mayor of Kigali, for instance, and helped him to write a grant proposal for the main genocide memorial in Kigali.

That summer, I was the only intern in Kigali and one of only a few working for Aegis or The Holocaust Centre. The internship programme is by no means vast, but it is by any measure extraordinarily valuable. Looking back, I cannot imagine what my university years would have looked like had I not interned for Aegis that summer. I saw firsthand everything that I had read about – and more – and I worked as a full member of the Aegis team in Rwanda. Neither of these experiences is usual, and so long as Aegis and The Holocaust Centre continue to offer such in-depth internships, they will be doing a great service for both the interns and for academia itself.

Brandi Hoffine

Aegis Intern, Claremont McKenna College, 2005

Working for Aegis at Beth Shalom has been one of the most rewarding experiences I've had as a student. Aegis is able to reach its goal of policy change without losing sight of what is really important in this kind of work – the survivors. Having the opportunity to meet so many incredible individuals who survived such atrocities, and yet still have the strength to tell their stories, is what gives me the strength and determination to continue working towards achieving that change. I know that wherever life takes me, the lessons I've learned and the people I've met during my time at Aegis have forever changed who I am and what I value.

265

learning

Sophia Pickles
Aegis Intern, Durham University, 2004

Below me, the apparently infinite orange of the Sahara; above, the heat of an African sun shielded by metal plane circumference and ahead, six months in Rwanda – an internship for Aegis.

The 8th October 2004 marked the beginning of my amazing six Rwandan months; an opportunity to work for Aegis, a chance to begin to know Africa, and specifically Rwanda. Working on an Education Programme to begin presently at Kigali Memorial Centre, those short six months wove new cultures, ideas, people, histories into something incredible; a new horizon.

There were challenges and difficult moments, but these were rewarded; Odette invited me into her family so that now, they are my second, and African, family; and there is the 'Aegis family' – those Rwandans who worked at Kigali Memorial Centre, guiding me through a maze of streets, bargaining skills, weddings, memorials and their own histories.

Working for Aegis, driving towards such incredible and meaningful goals with them for six months, was a privilege, and a challenging, inspiring and rewarding one. My horizon has changed, and there is a small part of me left, still there in Rwanda, waiting... soon I will return to join it.

Richard Newell
Work Experience Intern, 2005

Working for Aegis over the past year has been an immeasurable privilege. In terms of personal development, there were many areas where I developed skills, learning to work in a professional environment.

Academically, working alongside the founders of Aegis, has broadened my horizons and given me an understanding of world affairs, particularly with regard to the prevention of genocide, that I could not hope to find anywhere else.

Personally, this year has been highly beneficial. The opportunity to work with such people, toward such an ideal, has inspired me to pursue international law at university. I cannot thank Aegis enough for this opportunity so early in life.

learning

Preparing bones for burial at Kigali Memorial Centre

Cyanne Loyle

PhD candidate, University of Maryland
Aegis Intern, Jan-Aug 2004

Kigali Memorial Centre, 7 April 2004

I looked around and thought about all the sleepless nights. The 5 a.m. mornings when I pulled myself out of my bed to meet journalists who would never show up. The midnights moving bones that would turn into the dawns sorting mass grave remains. I was looking for artefacts and trying to ignore the toe bones still in their socks that told more stories than any rosaries or key chains I would pull up. I choked on my cigarette and imagined that I could still feel the dust in my lungs; Rwandan dust from being on site during the dry season, from pushing around the dirt, now half skin and half blood.

Forever there is a place that I can go to in my mind. A vision where my eyes get glassy and my lips turn into the expression of sucking on something sour, something foul that I want to spit out of my mouth. And I fill in the spaces between the socks and the toe bones, between the faded, stringy underwear and the cracked pelvises. I add dark brown extensions to the skulls that I moved around the room. My dreams become filled with the blood that I never saw and the screams that I never heard.

And you could have put me on a plane. You could have sent me back a failure. But instead you kept me around and you took me through that. I came back to the States and tried for months to be a real American, to sink back into the apathy and idealism that had defined my relationships and my goals. But instead, I wake up from my nightmares, explain away comments about my glassy expression and choke on dust that has long since dissolved from my lungs. I am here, but I remember Rwanda and the faces that thanked me for my presence.

publishing

"No matter how much one reads… there's always something new and shocking."
Tom Conti

publishing

The publishing programme of the Centre is an important means of reaching wider audiences for a number of years. The in-house editorial and design team have produced high quality publications – including survivor testimony, general history texts, digests, multimedia tools and educational resources – to take the Centre's content to a wide readership. As well as the Centre's own list, we have completed several joint publications with publishing houses such as Paragon House, Continuum and Hodder Murray.

The publishing programme has been divided into a number of discrete areas:

The Survivor Memoir List is linked to the speakers at the Centre. Victoria Vincent, Arek Hersh, Paul Oppenheimer, Waldemar Ginsburg, John Chillag amongst others published by the Centre are, or have been, regular contributors to the Centre. We have always tried to ensure that the publishing programme makes the life stories of survivors more accessible, and in particular gives students reading material to complement their visit. The Centre sells in the region of 5,000 survivor testimonies each year.

The Education Resources List includes CD-ROMs, posters, websites, workbooks and education packs. These are developed for curriculum-specific areas and distributed nationally to fit history, religious education or citizenship work. Resources such as posters and films are distributed in connection with specific events, such as Holocaust Memorial Day, for use in informal as well as formal educational settings.

The General List includes Holocaust poetry, reference works, edited volumes on Holocaust and genocide, as well as texts for use in the Higher Education setting.

The Digest List contains the two regular digest publications of the Centre: *Perspectives* and *The Aegis Review on Genocide*.

Examples of some of the Centre's publications are detailed in the following pages, to illustrate the breadth and considerable depth of the titles currently in print.

Survival

One of the more recent publications in the series, *Survival* details short introductions to the whole team of survivor speakers at the Centre.

Each chapter of several pages describes one life, one family, one community. Each describes a survivor's own Holocaust, the Holocaust they saw and experienced, the one which tore their life and family apart, the one which lingers in their own memory two generations on. This book illustrates how diverse, how singular and yet how all-encompassing the Nazi intent to wipe out all the Jews of Europe was. From countries right across the European continent, these individuals eventually made their way to England, either as refugees prior to the war, or as survivors of ghettos and camps afterwards. Their collective voice is testament to their individuality, a memorial to their families and an inspiration to the thousands of younger readers who purchase the book each year.

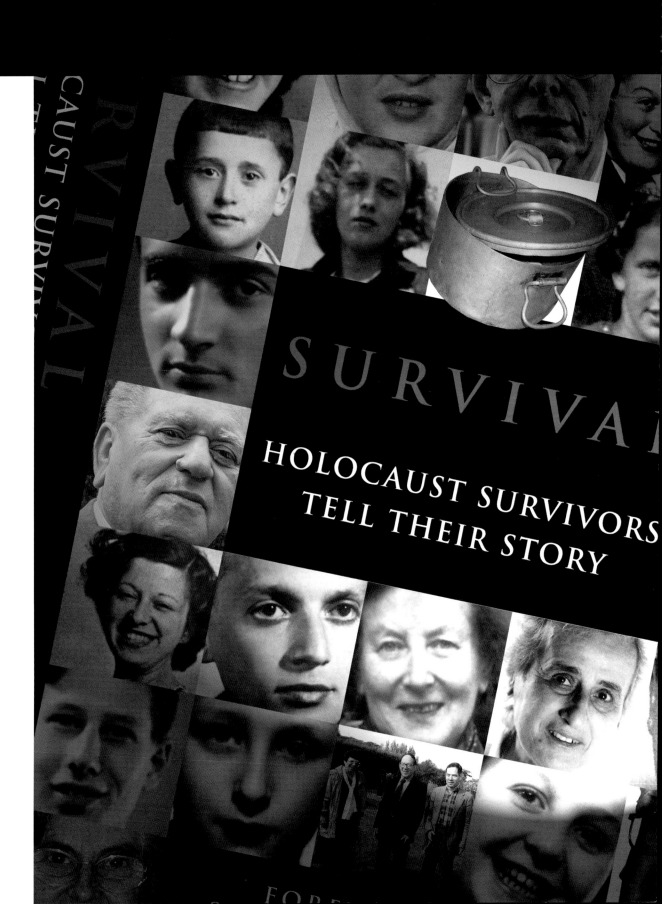

SURVIVAL

HOLOCAUST SURVIVORS TELL THEIR STORY

A Detail of History

Arek Hersh
Holocaust Survivor

I first decided to write a book about my life and experiences during the dark days of the Holocaust about 12 years ago, determined to tell as wide an audience as possible about what had happened to me, and the lessons to be learned from the experiences of a little boy, growing up all too quickly in the ghettos and camps of Nazi Germany. I owe The Holocaust Centre, Beth Shalom a great debt of gratitude for publishing this book, opening many new horizons where I meet people, tell them my story and challenge them to consider the lessons to be learned from what happened in those intensely tragic days, now over 60 years ago.

I take copies of my book to all my talks, so that it has now been read by schoolchildren and their teachers, university students, staff and inmates of prisons, police officers, Rotary Clubs and members of the public in all sorts of other contexts. I have spoken in Germany, in Ireland and recently to members of the National Security Agency at the Pentagon in Washington DC, making available copies of *A Detail of History* on every occasion.

As I wrote the book, I was able to reflect more deeply and in more detail on what happened and how I managed to build a new life from nothing. As a result, I am now able to speak more effectively, understand more clearly the relevance of those events to what is happening in the world today, and discuss the challenges we all face.

Thank you for all your support, friendship and for the opportunities you have given me to speak to young people, in particular during the past ten years, and to fulfil a promise I made to myself in the camps – to let the world know what happened to me and the relevance of my story to the future of the world in which we live.

273

publishing

Let One Go Free

Ruth March
Daughter of Hannah Hickman;
Senior Principal Scientist, AstraZeneca

My mother, Hannah Hickman, once said of *Let One Go Free*, "I hope it will speak to a general readership. It is not an academic book, but it is meant to describe the events of the Holocaust as they affected my family and myself, in simple terms." Her great hope was that this inspiring story of an ordinary German-Jewish family could help people understand the triumph of tolerance over racism and war.

This 'family book' was intensely painful for my mother to research and write. In her family home town of Würzburg, she was shown the listing of her mother, brother and sister, on a train to Auschwitz on 17 June 1943. No records were ever made of the arrival of this train, and so she could never be truly certain of her family's fate.

It was not easy to find a publisher for this unique story, and it was some years before my mother contacted The Holocaust Centre, Beth Shalom. By this stage she was in the last years of her battle with cancer. At one

stage, the book was nearly completed when she collapsed and temporarily lost her memory. After this, she insisted on annotating the photos of her family from her hospital bed, as we realised how close we had come to not being able to complete her story.

The launch of *Let One Go Free* was a triumph for my mother and the staff of The Holocaust Centre, who had enabled her to fulfil her deep wish to let her family's story be heard. She was interviewed in many newspapers, on television, and was especially glad to be able to tell her story to schoolchildren. Many ordinary people, with no knowledge of history, have been moved by this story and inspired by its positive message of hope and reconciliation.

publishing

Edith Hofmann
Holocaust Survivor, Artist and Author

At the age of fourteen, I was deported with my parents from Prague to the Lodz ghetto. Within a year my parents and all my relatives were dead. Auschwitz, labour camp, death march and Belsen followed. Mentally bruised, with the memories of the last four years and the pleading of the older inmates, "You are young, don't let the world forget us," haunting me, I knew I had to let the world know what happened.

Back in Prague, I bought an exercise book and filled it with detailed accounts of everything I could remember – one day I was going to write a book. The absence of my family and friends made me decide to join my sister in England. It didn't take long to realize that I was alone with my memories, nobody wanted to know. After two years in this country, I decided to have a go at writing that book. With my limited knowledge of English, I set about telling in a simple way the story of those strange years as experienced by an adolescent girl and people around her. It was satisfying on various levels: it had to be told if only for future generations. Secondly, I

hoped that once it was on paper, I could let go of the nightmares, get it out of my system and move forward. Not least of all, being close to my family, bringing them back to life was a rewarding, comforting experience. I had it typed out and sent it to several publishers. They didn't want to know; people had had enough of war.

It lay in a box in a drawer for almost 50 years until it found its way to The Holocaust Centre, Beth Shalom. On 25 January 2001, to mark the 56th anniversary of the liberation of Auschwitz, the beautifully produced book, *Unshed Tears*, was placed before me.

.. Judith got hold of some paper and a pencil.
She found it in the canteen cellar when she
went to exchange her spade... Here was an
opportunity to exercise her mind which she
believed was going stale, and at the same time
an account of the happenings in camp might
stand her in good stead one day. Cheered by
the novelty of the idea, she screwed up a pile of
papers and the pencil and hid them under a
sack near the exit door, in case she was
searched on reporting back. A little while later
when the girls drank their coffee and the
supervisor's attention was turned on a group
of girls having a quarrel, Judith slid back and
recovered her treasure.

For the rest of the day she worked on her idea
of writing a diary...

"I must not fall, not today anyway, perhaps
tomorrow a miracle will happen," Judith kept
telling herself every morning. Afterwards it
was all right. She could lie down and sleep in
peace except for the lice which had made her
body almost raw. Prisoners stumbling over her
and a kick from a Capo from time to time did
not bother her. Everything around was like a
dream and through that dream she knew that
there was only one thing that really mattered.
"Keep on going, keep on just for a little longer,
don't give in, don't give in!"

Extract from *Unshed Tears*, an autobiographical
novel written in 1948.

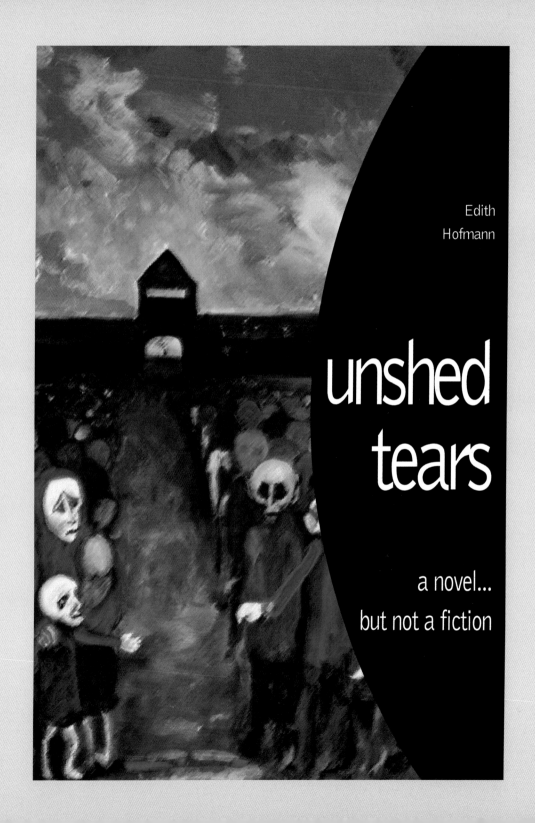

Edith
Hofmann

unshed
tears

a novel...
but not a fiction

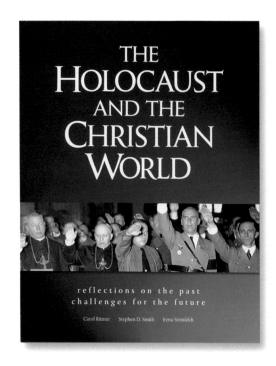

Carol Rittner R.S.M.

Distinguished Professor of Holocaust and Genocide Studies, The Richard Stockton College of New Jersey, USA

The Holocaust and the Christian World, prepared for the March 2000 historic visit of Pope John Paul II to Yad Vashem in Jerusalem, contains high quality, short essays by well-known Christian and Jewish scholars from Europe, Israel and North America on Christian-Jewish Relations and the Holocaust. In addition to the essays, there are documents issued on these topics over the years by the various Christian Churches – Roman Catholic, Protestant and Orthodox – video and web resources, as well as an extensive bibliography and chronology. That the book has been well received by both Jews and Christians is evident from the fact that in the Fall 2005, it will have its third printing in an up-dated edition.

This book is a small but important part of the ongoing work at the Centre that I am pleased and privileged to be part of in our efforts to remember the Holocaust for the sake of the future.

"The Holocaust represents one of the darkest episodes in the history of humankind and raises fundamental issues that go to the very heart of Christianity. Such disturbing questions are a serious challenge to Christians in every generation and of all traditions, and so I warmly commend The Holocaust and the Christian World. *It is a book which will raise more questions than provide answers, but in the nature of the case, that is its important, indeed unique, contribution."*

The Rt. Revd. Dr. James Mehaffey, retired Bishop of Derry and Raphoe, Church of Ireland, Londonderry, Northern Ireland

Irena Steinfeldt

**Executive Assistant to the Chairman of
the Yad Vashem Directorate**

It was only natural for Yad Vashem to choose
The Holocaust Centre, Beth Shalom as
partner in the publication of *The Holocaust
and the Christian World*. Our joint goal was to
commemorate the historic visit of the late
Pope John Paul II to Yad Vashem in March
2000, and to publish a book that would
provide readers with an opportunity to
confront the role of Christianity during the
Nazi period and to deal with the challenges
the Holocaust continues to pose in the
present era. Work on this book with Stephen
Smith and Carol Rittner brought together
people from three continents, three

religions/denominations and three
nationalities, but at the same time it revealed
how much it is we actually share. Mostly, it
was an extremely enriching experience and
dialogue. With The Holocaust Centre and Yad
Vashem's joining forces, we enjoyed the
cooperation of the most prominent
researchers and scholars.

As editors, we sought to create a balanced
and accessible picture of these very complex
issues. The guidelines that underpinned this
effort were to explore and probe the
questions by demonstrating to the reader the
wide range of responses that existed; to
avoid the pitfalls of self-righteous value
judgements; to encourage a genuine
discussion that is firmly rooted in a
fundamental understanding of the historical
reality; and to put particular emphasis on the
use of case study, personal experience and
documents.

The result is not a definitive text. It does not
provide all the answers, but rather gives rise
to more questions. Hopefully, it will stimulate
further discussion, research and dialogue.

opy of *The Holocaust and the Christian World* **was given
ardinal Kasper during his visit to Yad Vashem.**

Learning about the Holocaust is a brief history of the

Holocaust for 13-16 year olds. With the assistance of the Leo Baeck Lodge of B'Nai Brith and the Association of Jewish Refugees, this has been distributed to in excess of 60,000 young people across the country who have visited the Centre.

279

publishing

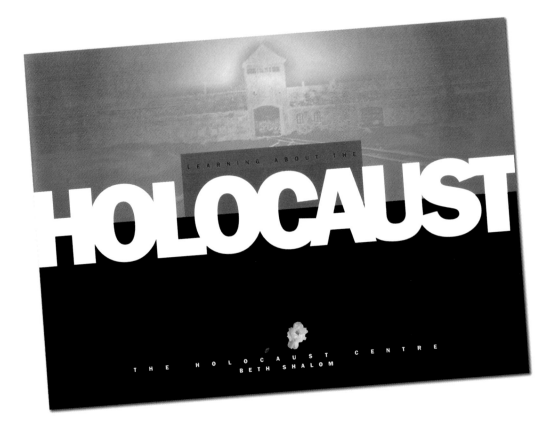

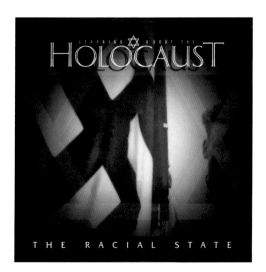

The Racial State

This CD-ROM is a multimedia resource detailing the emergence of National Socialism and its steady development of antisemitic policy during the 1930s. The resource was aimed at high-level students, particularly those working on Advanced Level history studies. It has been purchased by over 1,000 schools teaching about the origins of antisemitism in the Third Reich.

"This is – quite simply – an excellent resource. User-friendly and well-presented, this interactive multi-media package contains a wealth of material not just on the background to the Holocaust, but also on Nazi Germany... The material includes a splendid range of sources, including short film extracts, 'sound bites', photographs (which are of excellent quality), newspaper reports, eyewitness accounts and documentary evidence. These sources are accompanied by a straightforward text; a good glossary; and a variety of tasks ranging from factual multi-choice to open-ended questions..."

Alan Farmer, *History Review*, March 2000

Educational Publications

The Holocaust and Genocide: Why Does it Happen?

This resource is a joint multimedia publication of the Centre and Hodder Murray. It is a cross-curricular resource aimed at 13-16 year olds. It details the history of events during the Holocaust, in Rwanda and in Bosnia in three units. It also asks cross-cutting questions about the moral and philosophical questions such histories raise. This resource is distributed to schools nationally as a CD-ROM and through selected schools' broadband consortia as an internet-based learning resource.

Steve Connolly

**Digital and ICT Publisher,
Hodder Murray**

Hodder Murray and The Holocaust Centre first met to discuss the development of an interactive product to support teaching and learning of the Holocaust and genocide in May 2003. Following a series of meetings, it was clear to us that the wealth of educational experience and survivor testimony that the Centre had at its disposal could be put to good practice within an interactive resource designed for both whole-class teaching and individualised learning. The result has been the very successful publication of *The Holocaust and Genocide – Why Does it Happen?* CD-ROM.

This remarkable educational software allows teachers and learners to bring survivors into the classroom to share their experiences of genocide during distinct phases – origins, events, aftermath and impact in the longer term. Many department heads within UK secondary schools have lauded the approach of the content, which aims not only to explain what happened, but to encourage students to explore for themselves and reach their own conclusions. Whilst the material was written to one of the scheme of work units for history at Key Stage 3 (11-14 age range), it is also being used within RE and citizenship lessons, promoting effective cross-curricular teaching of the subject. It is no coincidence that the CD-ROM was Hodder Murray's best-selling stand-alone interactive resource in 2004 and continues to be adopted by schools across the UK.

"This resource, aimed at Key Stage 3 History, RE or Citizenship classes, draws upon a wealth of source material to present students with a study of the Holocaust, comparing it with genocide in Rwanda and the Balkans. The resource promotes meaningful historical investigation, the realisation of the relevance of history to modern life, and the study of human rights..."

Review by Schoolzone

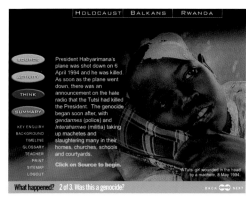

publishing

"An excellent resource... I really like the fact that the students can work through the activity task sheets by finding out the information, listening to real people and their experiences, looking at video, photo and written sources. I haven't seen anything as good because it is designed with young people in mind. The History, RE and PSHE departments are all looking at the resource. We are going to be falling out over who is going to use this first!"

Cheryl Zanker, The Dukeries College, Nottinghamshire

Genocide

Through the work of Aegis, we included in our publishing programme the development of texts related to the understanding of genocide. Along with colleagues on the Aegis advisory team, Carol Rittner RSM and John K. Roth, Aegis established a publishing partnership with Paragon House in the publication of texts on genocide issues.

283

publishing

We also established *The Aegis Review*, a new journal on genocide prevention. This digest is intended for practitioners grappling with the difficult role of genocide prevention in practice. *The Aegis Review on Genocide* covers topics such as legal issues, policy papers, practical issues, conference reports and book reviews.

Gordon L. Anderson
Executive Director, Paragon House Publishers, St. Paul, Minnesota, USA

Paragon House has partnered with Aegis on the publication of two books, *Will Genocide Ever End?* (2002) and *Genocide in Rwanda: Complicity of the Churches?* (2004). Knowledge about how an evil like genocide can develop in a civil and religious society is the first step toward prevention of future occurrences, and these books provide just such insight.

Both books are of high quality and well-edited under the leadership of Professors Carol Rittner at Richard Stockton College and John K. Roth at Claremont McKenna College.

Through a selection of well-organized and focused essays by leading specialists in genocide studies, readers of *Will Genocide Ever End?* will understand the history and causes of genocide as well as strategies to combat it. In *Genocide in Rwanda*, a provocative anthology on the role of Christians and Churches in the Rwandan genocide, contributors provide a clear presentation about the political and cultural dynamics that turned a peaceful society into a bloodbath.

Both books have received endorsements by many scholars who use them in classroom teaching, and both have been "highly recommended for all levels" by *Choice*, a magazine for the American Library Association. Bringing together contributors for the conferences that produced these books was invaluable. This kind of candour, commitment to social justice and call for social responsibility is desperately needed in our world today. The Aegis Trust is to be commended for its role in producing these texts, and we have been proud to include them in our Genocide and Holocaust Series.

Each year the Centre produces a poster series covering one area of Holocaust and genocide studies for a general education audience. These are designed for use in classrooms, libraries and other public buildings.

"Holocaust Issues" is one of three series of posters for in-school learning or public venue display. This particular set of 12 posters looks at the conditions that create the possibility of mass violence and genocide occurring. Each poster highlights a single issue such as "Racism", "Prejudice" or "Persecution", and shows how these actions were deployed during the Third Reich, and continue to be issues to understand today.

Marie McCann
Mayor's Secretary, London Borough of Merton

The Mayor's Office of the London Borough of Merton has worked closely with the representative from Wimbledon Synagogue since the very first National Holocaust Memorial Day in 2002. The Commemoration is attended by the Mayor, civic representatives and many faith groups and each year it attracts a larger number of people.

In order to open up the Commemoration to all members of the community in our Borough, the venue chosen each year does not have an affiliation to any faith group. It has always been held in a hall close to one of the municipal parks where the Mayor plants a rose tree. The planting is followed readings, singing by the Wimbledon Synagogue Choir and talks, often by survivors of the Holocaust.

In order to contemplate on the significance of the Day, an exhibition of The Holocaust Centre's posters is displayed around the hall, and in the past many people have commented that the strong images portrayed bring home to them the reason why we must continue to be part of Holocaust Memorial Day so that the world will never forget.

285

learning

Perspectives is the Holocaust Centre's digest of views, personal stories and reflection on the Holocaust, written by members and associates of the organisation. The journal was established to ensure that current issues around the Holocaust were represented through regular publication. Perspectives includes articles by survivors who may have travelled back home recently, book reviews of recent publications, responses of young people to the Centre, edited versions of recent lectures, among other topics.

We never intended Perspectives to be a newsletter, but rather it is a digest of current Holocaust education issues, debates and reflections on recent developments in the field and it is just as relevant in the United States or Australia as in Nottinghamshire, England.

"Please accept our heartfelt congratulations on the wonderful production of the current issue of Perspectives. It is not just the printed articles, but the manner of their presentation which impressed us deeply."

Felix and Hedy Franks, 2004

"Many congratulations on an excellent and very interesting edition of Perspectives."

Gillian Walnes, Executive Director, The Anne Frank Trust, 1998

"Thank you very much for publishing my article "From Memory to Peace" in Perspectives. You did a marvellous job of presenting it. Wonderful graphics gave it added depth."

Ester Golan, 2004

film

"For so many without a known resting-place, film is above all their lasting memorial"   David Nelson

the place of
film

In an age of visual images, we decided early in the life of the Centre to use the medium of film to portray history and engage wider audiences. Visual images allow us to construct new narratives, exploring the Holocaust from a variety of perspectives. Representing the Holocaust through documentary film can unlock a great deal about specific people, places, issues and complexes that are not the preserve of a museum.

This is why the Centre decided to set up its own film unit to archive audio-visual testimony, produce historical documentaries and teaching resources. The film unit has created a series of documentaries and a number of film-based educational resources and has also developed a film archive.

This is now extended to establishing an audio-visual documentation programme in Rwanda. Aside from documenting survivor testimony, twelve teams of videographers are collecting and archiving the *gacaca* genocide courts for the Government of Rwanda.

Gacaca court hears genocide suspect in Rwanda. Aegis has twelve full-time film crews documenting this unique process of justice.

David Nelson
Television Producer and Media Consultant

As mainstream cinema rediscovers Holocaust themes, it is an inescapable fact that with approaching old age, many survivors feel a pressing need to document their stories. There is nothing more compelling than eyewitness evidence and film is an immediate and accessible way of recording it.

As I have found working with The Holocaust Centre, placing survivors in the physical context of their stories, even though places change, adds a dimension impossible in audio or text.

The film-maker has responsibilities. Striking a balance between telling the story and keeping an audience interested is the main one, especially within the time constraints of a documentary. Editing testimony poses similar challenges – a dramatic soundbite is more tempting than a rambling tale. Using archive also poses questions. We have all seen film compilations telling the Second World War "for the first time" in colour. While an admirable exercise to update a

previously monochrome war, there were, however, no colour cameras at Auschwitz, so the existence of this camp goes unreported. However, the raising by US Marines of the Stars and Stripes at Iwo Jima does appear, for this event was re-enacted for the newsreels. This is just one problem of using film as witness – like any evidence, it can be manipulated. I am no great fan of the "reconstruction"; it's prone to crude stereotyping and often looks staged – did every Nazi meeting really take place in a smoke-filled room lit by a single overhead lamp?

The key to the best use of film as witness is perceptive programmes and accurate archiving. In this The Holocaust Centre is playing a key role.

And perhaps we should not forget that for so many people without a known resting-place, the place of film is, above all, their lasting memorial.

film

Claudine Baker
Radio Journalist

I spent ten eventful weeks working with Stephen and James in summer 2000, making the documentary *Wasted Lives*. It aimed to explain genocide to schoolchildren, previous incidences of genocide and the steps that can be taken to prevent it. None of us had any real experience in putting together a film but Stephen and James's attitude – as is always the case – was quite simply that it *could* be done. It was the first project of what was later to become the Centre's film department.

They gave me certain starting points – contact names or numbers of organisations that might lead us to a survivor of the Rwandan or Bosnian genocides... Holocaust survivors were easier to find. And it was through our combined research that the Smiths were introduced to Apollon Kabahizi from Rwanda and Kemal Pervanic from Bosnia, with whom they still work very closely.

Things seemed to progress very quickly – overnight an almost coherent script was written. I felt that the brothers often went with their instincts but without jumping on the bandwagon. If a narrator or a price or an editing suite seemed like a good option, their attitude was "Let's do it and be done with it." They were always very decisive:

"Yes, I like that photographic still – that works... let's have it."

Within weeks, interviewees, film crews, editors and a producer, Alan Kassel, were discovered, interviews done, other images – stills – gathered, background music and a narrator chosen and *voilà*! – a 15-minute film emerged. It was yet another worthy project completed in Mary Poppins style by the Smiths – done with near-superhuman efficiency, but extreme sensitivity to the content material.

"I was married in 1985. When the genocide in Rwanda happened, I had four children, two boys and two daughters. I've now two daughters and I lost my two boys in the genocide... In a country like mine in central Africa,... in a small country, it's a crime against humanity."

Ancilla Mukarubuga, Rwandan Survivor

film

"All my relatives, all our relatives, all my aunts, uncles and so on, they were deported to the Azores and they were massacred there in the Azores. Every other night almost, there's a nightmare of those things that happened... I could point to the place where I saw people hanged."

Haroutune Aivazian, Armenia

death march

Kitty Hart-Moxon made her first trip back to Auschwitz with a film crew from Yorkshire Television in 1978. The result was the award-winning *Kitty: Return to Auschwitz*, a documentary about her two years incarcerated in the camp, and how she rediscovered the Auschwitz-Birkenau site 35 years after she first arrived there.

Kitty had long wanted to return to central Europe, to re-walk the route of her death march in the winter of 1944-45 and make a second film, this time about her journey after Auschwitz. *Death March: A Survivor's Story* documents the journey of Kitty and Stephen Smith, who travelled the route of her death march together at the same time of year as Kitty originally walked it. The film, produced by David Nelson, was screened several times on BBC 2.

film

Kitty Hart-Moxon

OBE, Educator and Survivor of Auschwitz

It was in 2001 at The Holocaust Centre's sixth anniversary that David Nelson of BBC Midlands said he would try to persuade the BBC to allocate some funding for a documentary film recording my experiences in the last six months of the war – after I was evacuated in November 1944 from Auschwitz, where I had survived for two years.

The death march had never been documented in a film, though I had recorded the event in my book.

The BBC undertook extensive research. I had learned a great deal these past 55 years that I didn't know at the time. For example, why was it that, together with 200 other girls, I was transported some 1,000 miles across Germany in open coal trucks, without food or water for eight days? To start our journey, we were on the death march and had to climb the Sudeten mountain range into Czechoslovakia for about two weeks.

Needless to say, only a small number had survived the whole journey. Our destination was an underground electronics plant in Porta Westfalica. We did not know then that it was Albert Speer, Hitler's Armaments Minister himself, who had sent an urgent telegram to the *Gauleiter* of Silesia ordering him to transfer a group of 200 women working in the electronics factory in Telefunken in Silesia to the subterranean electronics factory in Porta Westfalica – some 1,000 miles away. The reason was that he believed these women were highly skilled workers and were urgently required at the Phillips Plant.

However, Albert Speer was mistaken because the original 200 skilled women had been deported to Auschwitz from the Phillips Plant in Holland and were murdered there. We, the group of 200 women, were in fact totally unskilled slave labourers! The few who had survived the journey began work in the underground Phillips Plant, but work was soon suspended as much of the equipment had failed to arrive due to the Allied invasion of Holland.

Stephen and I learned a great deal during the filming. We discovered many historical details previously unknown – the importance of the whole region to the war effort, with its numerous caves where thousands of slave labourers worked and lost their lives. We discovered giant quarries where 40,000 prisoners had excavated granite; others were constructing the new Hitler Headquarters, some working on Panzer tanks. There were German scientists engaged in highly secret developments of 'anti gravity' flying objects.

I was convinced that The Holocaust Centre needed to be involved in making this important historical documentary film. I knew that Stephen would be the right person to join me in the project because of his incredible insight and understanding of the events that had taken place. I also hoped that the film would become an addition to the Centre's extensive archives, where it could possibly be used as a teaching aid for visiting students.

I would like to thank David Nelson and the BBC for allowing us to make this film. It is something I had wanted to do for a very long time.

296

film

void ^{the}

Pinchas Gutter arrived at Majdanek one day in May 1943, having left the burning ghetto of Warsaw behind the previous day. He was just 12 years old when he stood awaiting selection with his twin sister and parents. Like thousands of other families, they were split, men one way, women the other.

As his twin was sent running to the gas chambers, all he remembers is her golden plait disappearing into the distance. To this day, he does not remember her face.

In *The Void*, Pinchas travels back to Poland with his family for the first time. He visits places in search of a memory lost in time and relays to his family how the experiences occurred and how they have shaped his identity.

Pinchas stands by the mausoleum at Majdanek, where soil, ash and bone are piled in memorial to the victims. Surrounded by his family, he sings *"El Mole Rachamim"* and prays Kaddish. His lone cantor's voice floats across the barren landscape of empty barracks.

The journey is complete.

Pinchas

Going to Poland helped clarify many of my feelings and fears. Much of my ambiguity about the country was put to rest. Particularly, visiting Majdanek, the last resting place of my parents and twin sister, saying prayers over their remains, left me with a kind of peace which is almost physical.

Being surrounded and supported by my wife and children, for the first time I felt really able to connect emotionally with my family and fully experience the bond between us.

Dorothy

We did it! After so many years of irresolution, obsessing, worry, anxiety we finally went to Poland. All of us. For eight intense days, we went through a welter of emotions from laughter, nostalgia, grief and horror. For me, what underlay the experience was a strong sense of relief that all of us, very much together, saw it through.

Whether verbalized or not, the Holocaust is part of the everyday transactions of every Holocaust survivor's family. Whatever the support and understanding, blocks, barriers and inhibitions linger. Experiencing Poland together, especially mourning in Majdanek together, shook the kaleidoscope of the family relationships into a more stable, more beautiful pattern. To a small but critical extent, we were no longer only listeners, but became, in the process of that week, part of Pinchas' story. It took all of us months to calm down and it is a wonderful opportunity to be able to look back three years later and acknowledge the lasting and profound effect on all of us.

Tanya

This was a chance to meet my grandparents and aunt, my father's twin sister. In the last place they saw, the only place still standing that they had inhabited, I was able to say hello and attempt to say goodbye. I feel so sad that I never knew them – other than through Papai who gives me a sense of what kind of people they must have been.

When Papai took us with him on that journey back to Poland and made the terror real for us, it helped all of us understand more deeply who he was. It helped him too, I hope, to know that we understood him better than before. That opened a door to reveal much love that had remained hidden, because for a long time no one knew how to unblock the channels that connected us. Tentatively at first, but with increasing confidence, questions could be asked, discussions could be had in a much more open and healthy way. The missing pieces of the jigsaw puzzle that made up our family were found in Poland.

Jan

Our trip to Poland made the experiences my father had spoken about over the years real for the first time. Through his emotional reaction to many of the places we visited, we got a glimpse into both the joy and the horror of his early years. We saw repressed emotions liberated. The sense of loss became very real for all of us.

Listening to my father say Kaddish for his parents and twin sister at Majdanek, the very place where he had last seen them alive almost 60 years ago, was an experience of indescribable emotion that brings tears to my eyes as I write these words. It was a pivotal moment in our relationship that drew the two of us closer together.

Lauren

I have been married to Jan for 20 years and so it was very special to be included by the family for this emotional and personal journey. I gained an even greater respect for Pinchas.

It brought the family together and it moved me very much to see the family share so much and demonstrate so much emotion and affection.

Rumi

The trip was a liberating experience for me. In spite of being the daughter of a survivor and going to a Jewish Day School, my knowledge of this part of our history was rather general and abstract. I always felt a sense of detachment from these events and the experiences of my father. The visit to Poland afforded me access to that past in a very real and tangible way so that, gaining a better understanding of my own relationship to this terribly complicated and tormenting part of history, I no longer sought to evade or deny this part of our history. Since the trip, studying the Holocaust has become very important to me and I am now willingly able to engage with the material of the Holocaust. My goals in life now include teaching others about the Holocaust and helping to break down the barriers erected by racism all over the world.

During the trip, our family developed a greater closeness and mutual respect for one another. Since the trip, we have continued to gain a deeper sense of appreciation for our individual differences and the bond that unites us as a family.

the power of
goodness

Genia Rapaport was an eight-year-old child when living in the Radom ghetto. One day, her father asked her to say goodbye to her mother. He passed her through a window, where a pair of hands were waiting to receive her on the outside of the ghetto. She spent the next few years of her life in hiding in a Polish Catholic home in Warsaw. She became a runner for the resistance and watched as the family of her rescuer, Sophia Grudzinska, was destroyed by the Nazis.

The Power of Goodness traces the journey of Genia, now Gina Schwarzmann, to Poland to meet the family of her rescuer in the places of her childhood memories. Her rescuer's family were due to receive the "Righteous Among the Nations" award, with which she had been honoured posthumously.

Gina Schwarzmann
Holocaust Survivor

"The journey back to Poland with my family was important on several levels. Firstly, to honour the woman who saved my life. Secondly, to show my children what happened to me, where I lived, how my life was saved. Thirdly, to bring our families together, because we have a bond which is deep and real because of the goodness of Sophia Grudzinska. Finally, to make this story available to many other people through the film. I want people everywhere to know that goodness is a powerful weapon against evil. I know that more than anyone; without the goodness of one brave woman, I would not be alive today."

"To realise that such bravery existed amongst such hatred is unbelievable."

Rachelle Schwarzmann

"I don't think we really appreciated the links that we had with Poland.. I've felt a whole raft of emotions over the last few days from slight despair going back to Radom, to a lot of hope and a good feeling about the fact that... we were all there, they didn't manage the Final Solution and the whole family was there... We really have made a deep connection to a lot of very important people... I would not be here if it hadn't been for this family."

Nimrod Schwarzmann

302

film

britain
and the holocaust

This short documentary explores the role of Britain in the run-up to the Second World War and during the Holocaust. It is a 30-minute historical analysis of how Britain responded to the persecution and murder of the Jews and asks demanding questions, many of which remain unsatisfactorily answered. Historians David Cesarani, Jo Reilly and Bill Williams grapple with the issues. Survivors and liberators reflect on the effect of British Foreign Policy on their lives and its long-term impact.

303

film

BRITAIN AND THE HOLOCAUST

Tony Kushner
Southampton University

"And what we see in 1938-9 is a grassroots movement to *do* something. The *Kindertransport* is probably the best example of that – that many, many thousands of ordinary people in Britain, Jews and non-Jews, were appalled at what was happening and wanted to do something to help, and did something very, very practical..."

"Racism, rather than having been removed as a stigma, has continued and blights the experience of minorities today."

Bill Williams
Manchester University

"There should have been sufficient awareness within government circles to have actually relaxed immigration policy more fully and more completely, and earlier..."

"I am implicated in the way that individuals live out their lives in every part of the world and every part of this country. Until I take that on board, change isn't going to happen."

David Cesarani
London University

"And the very high echelons of the political and military authorities in Britain had access to the Ultra documents. These are the documents of highly secret radio transmissions from German military and police units in Russia back to Berlin, that were being cracked by the Enigma machine and the team at Bletchley Park. The Russian Government of course was learning about these murders, the Polish underground was sending information back to London, to the Polish Government in Exile..."

"This is part of our history, it's a part of our heritage, and what's more, the kind of atrocity perpetrated during the Holocaust, the massive violation of civil rights, the violation of human rights, the descent into barbarity and mass slaughter, the acquiescence of populations, these kinds of things are going on still today."

Major Dick Williams
British Army 8 Corps

"All one could see around was just the bodies or bundles in their horrible striped uniform, some sitting, some lying, some just curled on the ground, hanging on the barbed wire. There were a lot of huts there; each one had its own barbed wire round it. My estimate when I went back to see the Brigadier was that there were thousands to feed and thousands to bury, how many thousands, no idea at all. I'd never seen so much carnage in my life."

Extracts from Britain and the Holocaust

arts

"Here all things scream silently...."   Yevgeny Yevtushenko

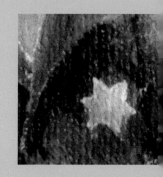

the place of
art

Art forms in all their different modes and media have become increasingly visible to describe the Holocaust and grapple with its meaning.

Creating, performing and showing cultural representations about the Holocaust are fraught with all sorts of tension. How can such events be portrayed in words, images and actions? Is silence really an alternative? If silence is not sufficient to say what needs to be said, what sort of representation is appropriate without trivialising the events and their meaning, or meaninglessness?

During the Holocaust itself, Jewish artists struggled with their own experience in music, art and literature. Some of the most profound artistic representations of the Holocaust were created by those doomed by National Socialism's sweeping power. The poet Izaak Katzenelson and painter Charlotte Salomon, to name but two creative forces

caught up in the maelstrom, led the way for fellow creative artists to respond to the Holocaust with the creativity of their trade.

Survivors have gone on to create a whole genre of art linked to the Holocaust experience. Artistic representations created by survivors have won Nobel Literature prizes, Israel Prizes and the Prix Médicis. Elie Wiesel, Primo Levi, Charlotte Delbo, Aharon Appelfeld and Samuel Bak have all set demanding standards for our cultural responses.

The Holocaust Centre facilitates artists from performing and visual arts through its cultural programme. In order to explore the boundaries of cultural representations, performances, commissioned works, temporary exhibitions and book launches all contribute at the Centre to representing a trauma which defies representation.

Skeaping

Roman Halter

visual

art

The art displayed at The Holocaust Centre has almost exclusively been created by survivors and eyewitnesses. Works such as the stained glass windows were commissioned. Other temporary exhibitions have been invited to the Centre to facilitate survivors' own representations of their experience.

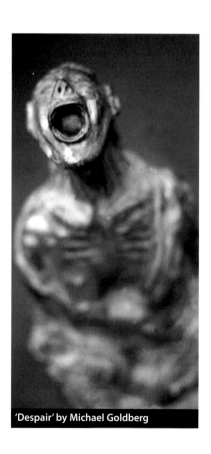

'Despair' by Michael Goldberg

Painting by Edith Hofmann

Aviva Halter
Watercolour Artist, Stained Glass Designer and Maker

The work for The Holocaust Centre's stained glass windows started in the 1990s. Roman Halter, my father, and I designed every window with care and precision. Some were haunting memories, some commissions that we were asked to work towards for the patrons of the windows, who wanted their own memories to be recorded.

We worked on four different stained glass window designs. A mother hugging her child close, in reds, purples and blues. Another window depicting the forest partisans. The third showing the star of Bergen-Belsen concentration camp. The last window, a grandmother and her grandchildren walking to their death in Auschwitz-Birkenau. The designs were drawn and redrawn countless times to get a balance and flow; this was the first time that

we had designed windows to fit into a circular shape.

The window that we both felt took on its own soul was the grandmother and her grandchildren walking alongside the railway to the gas chamber to be gassed – the stoop of the old woman, the children unaware, the subject always makes me weep. The image before the glass was inlaid was incredibly strong. We discussed that the colours must be respectful, but then the light blues must always sing out the song that throughout life and death there is always hope.

With stained glass the mood is created by the colours; they can be very healing for the viewer, the colours, cut deep, stamping their presence into the core of the onlooker, as strong ,vibrant, unforgettable images.

This particular unique stained glass window method was invented by my father, casting aluminium as a whole. It differs greatly from the stained glass method of the past where the glass is held together with lead and does not allow for a true continuity of the image.

I was incredibly proud to be involved in this project, to work with my father, Roman, making The Holocaust Centre's windows. I feel they make a statement that befits the subject of the Holocaus. They have a power and presence that will continue throughout time.

R. Stephen Rubin
OBE, Chairman, The Pentland Group; President, The Holocaust Educational Trust

In 1999, my family were delighted to donate a painting by British landscape artist Ken Hancock to The Holocaust Centre, Beth Shalom. The painting portrays two children standing in the foreground whilst around them stretches a bleak, snow-covered plain. Behind, people disembark from a cattle train; guards march them towards the distant gate of Auschwitz, its chimneys staining an overcast sky. As a soldier with the British army, the artist Hancock saw the aftermath of the Holocaust in the concentration camps and was deeply affected.

As the President of the Holocaust Educational Trust, I know the importance of educating our future generations about the Holocaust. Unfortunately, whilst some do not want to know and others will never learn, The Holocaust Centre, Beth Shalom provides the opportunity for people of all ages to visit the fascinating exhibition and realise what actually happened. Many pay their respects, or contemplate the lessons of the past, in the memorial garden.

312

arts

"The work of The Holocaust Centre, Beth Shalom has inspired me as a sculptor to give expression to my feelings regarding the horrors of the Holocaust. I find that through my art, my aspirations and those of Beth Shalom converge."

Mark Pope
Sculptor

One of a series of paintings by Refugee Survivor Hans Jackson displayed at The Holocaust Centre

Helen Aronson
Lodz Ghetto Survivor

In October 2004, together with my daughter, I attended a presentation of a book called the *Lodz Ghetto Album* at The Holocaust Centre. This book features photographs taken by Henryk Ross, the official ghetto photographer, many of which had never before been published. As a Lodz Ghetto survivor myself, I was, of course, very interested to see this book.

During the on-screen presentation of the photos, I was pleased to see several pictures of friends I had known during my five difficult years in the ghetto. Then it came to the very last photo in the book. It showed a group of people at a party in the concentration camp, which was formed with the sole purpose of exterminating the remaining few hundred people left in the ghetto at the end. This party took place on the actual day the Russians liberated the camp. As I looked up at the screen, I realised that I recognised the man in the centre of the shot, playing the accordion. "That man was my boyfriend, Shlomo Vysocki. He emigrated to Israel after the war," I said.

But suddenly, my daughter turned to me and said, "But Mum, that girl next to him in the photo is you!" She was right – there I was in a photo that I had never before seen, taken 60 years ago, on the day that five years of hell had ended for me. It was an incredibly strange and emotional feeling – I didn't know whether to laugh or cry. But in the end, I just did both!

Edith Hofmann
Holocaust Survivor, Painter and Author

I came to this country in 1946. As soon as I could speak English, I wrote a book based on my wartime experiences. It wasn't published until 50 years later. Meanwhile the memories of the squalor of the Lodz ghetto, the chimneys and red skies of Auschwitz, the struggle through the snow of the death march and the walking corpses of Belsen never left me.

In the 1970s I was doing an A-Level course in History of Modern Art. Suddenly it came to me that I could interpret those vivid memories in a visual way. I joined an A-Level course in Fine Art in order to learn to paint. Eventually, after much deliberation, I evolved a pictorial language which enabled me to put my visions onto canvas. It wasn't so

much the cruelty or the physical suffering that I wanted to record. Most of all, I wanted to show what it was like, what it felt like to be a human being encased in the starved, emaciated, strange-looking body, forever being separated from loved ones. Above all, I wanted to pay tribute to all those who so innocently went to their death, and leave behind some evidence for future generations.

I was very excited in 1997 to be given the opportunity to exhibit the paintings for a length of time at The Holocaust Centre.

literature

Since Tadeusz Borowski's first bold literary depictions of his incarceration in Auschwitz in the late 1940s, authors have explored their experiences through short stories, novels and poetry, in a variety of literary styles.

The literature of the Holocaust would now fill a library of volumes. We understand the need to facilitate these representations, hence the library collection, the literary volumes we publish and events we run profiling specific new works of Holocaust literature.

315

arts

Hadassa Ben-Itto
Former Supreme Court Judge, Author

I have something in common with the Smith family because we both hold onto the belief that each and every one of us can do something. There is not one of us who cannot do something, however small.

When I was a judge I was very often on loan from all kinds of other jobs. I was twice a member of a delegation to the UN, and so on. I was often confronted by the blood libel issue and the *Protocols of the Elders of Zion* and didn't use my right of reply. The Jews had ignored the *Protocols* for 100 years and that's a fact. To this day, there is no Hebrew translation. I wanted to know more about it and being a judge, I would go to the trials relating to the *Protocols*, for my own curiosity as it were. I realised that the truth had been told before, but the books were all written in academic style. There wasn't one aimed at the general public, written in simple direct style, so I decided I was going to do it. For this, I retired from the court because the subject burned within me. I thought it would take a year or two. It took six.

Why did I decide to tell this story? Why did I research it? I wrote it because I believe there is an open-minded public. We have sinned by ignoring this whole story for a whole century. We have ignored it and allowed it to grow. The only way to fight a libel is to tell the true facts, not to say simply, "It's a lie." We have to make the truth known and accessible to the public in order to combat this.

Hadassa Ben-Itto's book, *The Lie That Wouldn't Die*, is published by Valentine Mitchell, and was presented at the Centre by the author, in conjunction with Jewish Book Week.

Theo Richmond
Author of *Konin: A Quest*

Sadly, only a few of the survivors remain, yet when the last has gone, their voices will still be heard, not only literally on cassette and film but on the page – in testimonies recorded by others, in books they have written themselves, and in works written about them.

In my own quest for a once-flourishing community on the River Warta in Poland, I attempted to resurrect that small Jewish world and its people. Scholars trying to achieve – perhaps in vain – fact-based "objectivity," have brought historical perspective to the understanding of the Jewish tragedy under Nazism. Not least, novels, plays and poems – the stuff of "literature" – have drawn on artistic creativity to probe the hearts and minds of perpetrators as well as victims, to explore the human darkness that leads to genocide. Although they are products of the imagination, they can contribute their own important truths.

Searching for the lost inhabitants of Konin heightened my awareness of the different means by which their voices could be saved from oblivion. The Holocaust Centre, Beth Shalom demonstrates yet another, treading its own special path. Reinforcing its acts of remembrance and commemoration, it works tirelessly and selflessly in the cause of educating today's younger generations, alerting them to the evils of genocide in all its manifestations. I can think of no more valuable way of ensuring that those voices do not fade.

Shemá

You who live secure
In your warm houses,
Who return at evening to find
Hot food and friendly faces:

Consider whether this is a man,
Who labours in the mud
Who knows no peace
Who fights for a crust of bread
Who dies at a yes or a no.
Consider whether this is a woman,
Without hair or name
With no more strength to remember
Eyes empty and womb cold
As a frog in winter.

Consider that this has been:
I commend these words to you.
Engrave them on your hearts
When you are in your house, when you walk on your way,
When you go to bed, when you rise.
Repeat them to your children.
Or may your house crumble,
Disease render you powerless,
Your offspring avert their faces from you.

Primo Levi

Shemá (translated by Ruth Feldman and Brian Swann) from *Holocaust Poetry*, ed. Hilda Schiff, published by Quill Press, the imprint of The Holocaust Centre. This poem is based on the principal Jewish prayer, "Hear. [Shemá] O Israel, the Lord our God, the Lord is One" (Deuteronomy, 6:4-9; 11:13-21; Numbers 15:37-41). Primo Levi reworks some of its major ideas, making it possible to incorporate the demanding experience of the Holocaust into the Jewish religion.

Hilda Schiff
Author and Editor

Beth Shalom is a unique institution. As we know, it was founded by a Christian family ten years ago, and since then it has grown both in strength and stature. For me, what it stands for is its quiet and steadfast witness to the Jews of Europe in their darkest hour of suffering and annihilation. It is as though in their deeds they echo the words of the Russian poet Yevgeny Yevtushenko who, when he visited the ravine at Kiev after the war, where tens of thousands of Russian Jews were shot by the Nazis, identified with the victims to such an extent that he wrote in his famous poem "Babii Yar":

*"Here all things scream silently.... And I myself
am one massive, soundless scream...
I am each old man here shot dead. I am every
child here shot dead.
Nothing in me shall ever forget!"*

Those of us who have lived with the detailed knowledge of the Holocaust for so many years sometimes forget that the labyrinthine ways of Nazi evil are new and perhaps unbelievable to fresh generations of young people. Youngsters who are still at school or at college may not even be able to imagine being far away from home for any length of time, leave alone being dragged away from their parents, sent on a long train journey in utter squalor and, after being stripped naked, suffocated in an underground cellar with a poisonous substance formerly used only to kill rats. Isn't this just the stuff of nightmares, they might ask? Beth Shalom proves to them that it is not.

But, we may ask, should we burden our young people with such knowledge? Some educators say we should not, that it is too much for young people to take in and to bear. Beth Shalom does not subscribe to this point of view. It does not cover up, but on the contrary, through its publications as well as in other ways, it promotes knowledge and understanding of the meaning of the Holocaust. It demonstrates to us what it is to suffer, and what it is for the world to need redemption.

Moreover, thanks to Beth Shalom, young people might discover what it is to identify with those in greater trouble than they themselves. For example, in a poem by the well known Polish poet Jerzy Ficowski, to be found in *Holocaust Poetry*, an anthology of poems republished by Beth Shalom, they might read about the story of Dr. Korczak. This doctor who was in charge of a Jewish orphanage in Warsaw, voluntarily accompanied his group of 200 orphans when in 1942 they were deported by the occupying forces for the "crime" of being born Jewish. Dr. Korczak went with them not only to the gates of the death camp at Treblinka, but also right inside the gas chambers, where he too was killed. He could not find it in himself to leave them without at least one adult being present to comfort them, and to draw these abandoned children close to him in their most terrible hour. From Dr. Korczak we can learn what it is to show the deepest level of solidarity between one human being and another.

For my own part, I see these activities of Beth Shalom as life-enlarging activities in the sense that they help us to understand what the world is truly like, both the good and the bad, to "see life steadily and see it whole," as Matthew Arnold remarked. Above all, how else can we commemorate and pay homage to those countless individuals whose lives were destroyed and whose ashes were strewn beneath the many acres of the now beautiful meadows at Auschwitz, Treblinka, Maidanek and many other such killing fields?

In the Jewish tradition, there is a religious obligation enjoining us to remember the sorrows of our forebears. In Hebrew the word for this is *"Mitzvah"*, this obligation, and the blessing that accompanies it, is *"Zachor"* – Remember.

To fulfil this spiritual obligation, to remember, is Beth Shalom's mission. And its blessing.

music

The first music infused with the haunting dissonance of the Holocaust was written by composers themselves caught up in the events. From the haunting melodies laden with Terezin saturating the music of Pavel Haas and Gideon Klein to the parodies of Victor Ullman, composers attempted to confront their experiences through their music.

On the whole, though, composers did not write music about the Holocaust in which they were victims; but their non-victim Jewish and non-Jewish contemporaries did. Examples include Shostakovich's *Babi Yar Symphony* and his 8th String Quartet and Schoenberg's *A Survivor from Warsaw*. Many other pieces were written later in commemoration of the Holocaust by well known composers, such as Steve Reich's

Different Trains and Sylvia Boderova's *Terezin Requiem*.

The Holocaust Centre ensures that this anguished art is heard for the beauty of the music and as a memorial. It also encourages more recent artists grappling with depicting themes from the Holocaust in their work, through composition and performance at the Centre.

ke in performance at The Holocaust Centre

"The music of Kroke gave an insight into a whole culture. Ancient melodies, modern influences, a conversation between the parent and child, all aspects of day-by-day living, happy celebrations and sad events, were in the music. How good to leave The Holocaust Centre feeling the vibrancy of a living culture when you could have been easily overwhelmed by sadness in a place that remembers the Holocaust."

Rowan Cozens, Musician

"Kroke have greatly enjoyed the opportunity to participate in the work of The Holocaust Centre and have watched its development with interest and appreciation."

Jerzy Bawol, Kroke

Mark Wilson and Nick Allen
Solaris Quartet

The life of a professional musician can seem glamorous, exciting and full of new challenges. The reality, of course, is often very different: another town, another audience, the same old repertoire.

The Solaris Quartet, however, sees things differently. This is, in large part, due to promoting the music of composers caught up in the Holocaust. These works are of extraordinary power and of lasting musical value. They are compositions which deserve to be heard. The Holocaust Centre has provided a wonderful and appropriate location for Solaris to perform this valuable music and thus holds a special place in the quartet's affections.

Terezin is a garrison town north of Prague, originally built to house around 8,000 people. At the height of the Nazi genocide up to 50,000 people were crammed within its forbidding walls. It is extraordinary that

the composers Victor Ullmann, Pavel Haas, Hans Krasa and Gideon Klein, amongst others, could create such compelling works of art under these hellish circumstances.

Solaris was first invited to perform music from Terezin at The Holocaust Centre in 2002 and has enjoyed several return visits. These performances enable the quartet to meet several Holocaust survivors whose experiences supply invaluable insights into the terrible conditions in which the Terezin composers laboured.

The quartet is honoured to be counted as friends of the The Holocaust Centre. This is definitely not just another place to play, and the music of Terezin continues to shine as a beacon of hope from one of the darkest periods of our history.

Boris Feiner
Concert Pianist and Composer

Playing at The Holocaust Centre, Beth Shalom for its ninth anniversary was not only a very rare experience for me but also a great emotion. Being aware of the Holocaust and after serving for three years in the Israeli Defence Forces Army, I felt the need to contribute to the Centre by offering a concert of a special programme which could express the very long and most painful history of the Jewish people around the world.

I chose to play a classical repertoire consisting of works by Bach, Beethoven, Chopin, Granados, Stravinsky and my own composition. It was originally planned that every piece would carry its own character, but the whole concert would carry a line with a deep expression and meaning. The first sequence of Bach's Choral arranged by Petri, Beethoven's *Pastoral Sonata* and the last two *Ballades* of Chopin, then the interval, followed by Granados's *Ballade* from *Goyescas*, a work of my own and *The Firebird* by Stravinsky, arranged by Agosti, which had a very special effect on the audience, and through which I was able to establish a deep communication and share my own feelings. I felt strongly that everything I was trying to transmit was immediately understood and much appreciated. The atmosphere was so special that not even a single cough was heard during the whole concert of more than one and a half hours. I could really feel that my playing meant a lot to these people and that it was a unique experience, alight with energy and sensitivity for the audience and for me.

One day before the Victoria Vincent Memorial Concert, I went to the Centre in order to get familiar with its history and visit the memorial gardens. I was especially impressed by the great educational work that has been put into it and the great care of the place. I believe this is how the Centre makes its greatest contribution, and also in my particular field.

dramatic

arts

Shortly after the Centre opened, Holocaust survivors Victoria Vincent and Trude Levi realised through the Centre's publications that they had been liberated at the same bridge on the same day. The coincidence of their involvement in the Centre was followed by a meeting, which in turn was turned into a play. *Across the Bridge* was written and first performed at the Centre by Anna Cropper and Dalia Friedland.

Across the Bridge explores personal life stories and the issues of survival that have since emerged for the play's characters. It illustrates the type of dramatic representation that the Centre seeks to promote.

Dramatic performances have formed a regular part of the Centre's cultural calendar each year, with plays, commemorative sketches and readings.

323

arts

Jeffrey Cohen
Nottingham Friends of Austerlitz

The play, *The Austerlitz Scroll*, was performed by members of Nottingham Progressive Jewish Congregation (NPJC) at The Holocaust Centre. It tells the story of one people – and two communities. One was destroyed in Austerlitz-Slavkov and one lives in Nottingham. Two living, intertwining threads connect them – the story of a scroll and the story of Ruth Matejovska.

The NPJC has in its safekeeping a Torah scroll from the town of Austerlitz, also called Slavkov in Czech. It was one of over 1,500 scrolls confiscated by the Nazis, which were brought to London in 1964 and then distributed to synagogues throughout the world. Two members of the congregation, Neil and Sandra Pike, undertook detailed research to find out more about where the scroll came from. To their great fortune, they came into contact with Dr Erich Strach from Liverpool Eric left the Czech Republic in 1938. As a child, he visited Austerlitz regularly as his grandparents lived there. In 1990, Eric went back to Austerlitz and discovered there was a Jew still living there, Ruth Matejovska. Of about 135 Jews from Austerlitz and the surrounding areas who were transported to Terezin, she was one of only six who returned.

A group from the Nottingham Progressive Jewish Congregation, the Friends of Austerlitz, commissioned video testimonies for both Eric and Ruth to place on record their experiences before, during and after the Holocaust. The group then obtained an 'Awards for All' lottery grant to turn the video testimonies into a play, to tell the story of Ruth and her connection to Nottingham through the Torah scroll.

The Holocaust Centre was a perfect setting for the play. As David Lipman, Chairman of the Congregation, wrote the day after, "It was a privilege to be in the audience last night and to feel the power of the play. That an amateur cast can tell that story with such intensity, maintaining it for nearly an hour, without light relief, is its own tribute – to the commitment of the actors and to their ability."

The play was translated into Czech and on 5 June 2005 was performed by Austerlitz schoolchildren in the presence of the woman who inspired it – Ruth Matejovska.

Dalia Friedland
Actress, Israel

It all started in the house of the Israeli Ambassador to Great Britain, Moshe Raviv. Anna Cropper and I had performed a programme there about Jerusalem, city of the Jews, Christians and Moslems. Later, the Ambassador's wife told us that they had been invited to a new Holocaust Centre in the north of England, in the middle of nowhere. The Ambassador and his wife were extremely impressed.

The moment we saw the Centre, we knew the play must be connected with it, and especially what it stands for.

Our play, *Across The Bridge*, is based on a true story that happened at The Holocaust Centre shortly after it opened. In April 1996, two very special women, Victoria Ancona-Vincent and Trude Levi, met at the Centre and realized that they had both been on the same death march.

Victoria Ancona-Vincent, who passed away shortly after that meeting, and Trude Levi were both – and Trude still is – a very integral part of the Centre. Making their story into a play added one more brick to the activities of The Holocaust Centre, telling survivors' stories through drama, so that it should never happen again.

Trude Levi
Holocaust Survivor

I met Anna Cropper at the first anniversary of The Holocaust Centre. I had been a fan of Anna's in the 60s; she was a wonderful actress and hence when I met her, I was quite excited. The previous evening, they had performed *Ella's Story* at the Centre, the story of a survivor.

After the above play, Anna and Dalia had decided that they would like to write a story about two survivors meeting. My meeting with Victoria Vincent was the subject Dalia and Anna wanted for their play. The two actresses liaised with Victoria's husband and son and with me, and we became very involved in the writing of the play and seeing that the facts were all correct.

Across The Bridge was an instant success. The performances were all played to full houses and afterwards there was a discussion in which I took part every day.

At the first performance at the Centre, I was put in the front row facing Anna on the stage. It was a most odd experience seeing someone on the stage playing me: Trude Levi. Naturally I felt extremely honoured. Anna also said that she had never yet played a person who was sitting in front of her and she found it pretty daunting.

Over the years many people have approached me and asked why the play isn't being shown; they had heard about it but missed it and would love to see it.

Cathy Lesurf
Actress and Musician

"The line dividing good and evil cuts through the heart of every human being," to paraphrase Solzhenitsyn. This was the motif of *The Mobius Twist*; music, drama and memory woven together into one woman's story in which understanding the legacy of the Holocaust impacts on the modern world. It was my privilege to produce *The Mobius Twist* at The Holocaust Centre. My story also included British fascism and Bosnian refugees, the pernicious effect of personal ignorance and isolation and the tragedy of silence, for "What is not acknowledged cannot be healed" (Waldemar Ginsburg).

I did not arrive at this story through personal, family experience. The road ran through *Teeth Like Razors*, the lives and work of Brecht, Weil and Eisler, performed with Tanya Myers and Curt Glance. We performed this all over the UK, but at The Holocaust Centre, the audience taught me the true meaning of the work.

The road did not end with *The Mobius Twist*. I was invited to help shape and run the *Refuge* project, guiding students through the interview process with today's refugees, and adding to the Aegis archive by conducting in-depth interviews to camera through the film and photography of David Wilson. We were tapping away at that wall of personal ignorance and isolation, breaking the silence.

I have run a festival of music and dance every year since 2002. *The World in 1 County Festival* includes refugee artists and refugee children alongside mainstream entertainers including friends from The Holocaust Centre projects.

Jon Rumney
Actor

My first visit to The Holocaust Centre, Beth Shalom in 2001 coincided with performing at Nottingham Playhouse in *Ritual in Blood*. Set in 1255 Lincoln, the play dealt with the medieval English myth that Jews killed Christian children to use their blood in the making of the Passover matzo. In this particular case, a boy called Hugh fell from an apple tree in a Jew's garden and died of the injuries. In their greed to extract money from the Jews, the clergy and the state conspired to exploit the ignorance and prejudice of the Lincoln people by fanning the flame of the Blood Ritual myth. As a result, many Jews were murdered. The money taken from the Jews was used to help finance the building of Lincoln cathedral.

Some years ago, I took part in a play called *Ghetto* at the National Theatre. This play dealt with the destruction of the Vilnius ghetto by the Nazis.

What has all this to do with The Holocaust Centre?

During my visit, a group of schoolchildren were being shown round the memorial exhibition. Watching their faces, it was obvious that most of them had no knowledge of the Holocaust of 60 years ago, let alone the massacre of Jews in York and Lincoln in the 13th century.

Teaching the younger generation the terrible results of racial hatred and bigotry is essential to counter the prejudice and lies still being peddled today. Plays such as *Ritual in Blood* and *Ghetto* help to alert audiences to the dangers of racial hatred.

The Nottingham Youth Theatre interprets Greg Stanton's "Eight Stages of Genocide" through theatre, performed at The Holocaust Centre January, 2001

partnerships

"Barriers are removed, information imparted, education instilled."
Gerald Jacobs

the place of
partnership

During the ten years that the Centre has been open, there has been a significant development in Holocaust remembrance and education across the world. New centres have opened, scholarship has flourished, film, publishing and curriculum developments have been emerging in countries as far flung as South Africa, Japan and Argentina.

Partnership with organisations around the world has been an invaluable dimension of The Holocaust Centre's life and activity. Initially, having the support of Yad Vashem and the United States Holocaust Memorial Museum in setting up the Centre, as well as other Holocaust archives and institutions, was of great benefit in establishing the fundamentals of its standards.

Subsequently, The Holocaust Centre has been pleased to be able to share its experience with a number of partners, developing programmes, centres or policies for commemorating or teaching about the Holocaust. Members of The Holocaust Centre team have worked with colleagues in a number of countries, with whom common goals and aspirations are shared.

329

partnerships

cape town

holocaust centre

In 1999 South Africa's first Holocaust Centre opened in Cape Town. The driving force and director of the Centre, Myra Osrin, first visited The Holocaust Centre, Beth Shalom two years previously, in the early planning stages of the Cape Town Holocaust Centre project. At the time, we offered any support that would be helpful, having recently been through the long and arduous process of creating the Centre.

Over the next two years, a close partnership developed as we joined the Cape Town team. Many of the same principles that had worked well in the United Kingdom were applied to the Centre. However, there was a particularly demanding context in South Africa with the legacy of apartheid still hanging heavy over the country's recent past.

The thinking behind the Cape Town Holocaust Centre was to document the Holocaust with the historical integrity of events carefully protected, avoiding over-simplification or misapplication. The result was a museum which tells the story of the Holocaust and relates pertinent issues about the effects of divisive racism, in an appropriate way for young people who still remember growing up under the influence of apartheid.

331

partnerships

Myra Osrin
Director, Cape Town Holocaust Centre

In October 1996, on a visit to Israel, I read a feature article in the *Jerusalem Post* on the Beth Shalom Holocaust Centre, Europe's first Holocaust museum which had opened the previous September. Under a heading "The Power of One," the article revealed that the Centre had been set up by an individual using relatively meagre private funds.

I was intrigued and, on the way to the airport, made a quick five-minutes stop at Yad Vashem where the "individual" was attending an international conference – just enough time to seek out Stephen Smith and arrange a visit to The Holocaust Centre.

One month later, I made the one hour and twenty-minute train journey from London to Laxton, a journey which proved to be just the very first stage of a much longer journey, which not only changed my life and that of the small Cape Town Jewish community, but indeed was to make an impact on the wider South African society.

Experiencing The Holocaust Centre's small but impactful exhibition and Stephen's spontaneous enthusiastic offer of assistance led to the opening in August 1999 of the Cape Town Holocaust Centre, of which Stephen is our honorary consultant and esteemed trustee. The first and only such centre in Africa, the project has been successful far beyond initial expectations, playing a relevant role in the new democratic South Africa's transformation process. The Centre's education programmes are in ever-increasing demand from a very diverse spectrum of society, including high school and university students, police and correctional services, and religious and corporate groups.

The Cape Town Holocaust Centre is indebted to Stephen, James and Marina for their inspiration, assistance and most valued friendship. We are proud of our association with The Holocaust Centre, Beth Shalom, which since 1996 has continued to conceptualize and establish the extraordinary and important endeavours which this publication reflects – testimony to the "power of one" – an individual and a family.

Marlene Silbert
Education Director, Cape Town Holocaust Centre

As inspirational as The Holocaust Centre was in the establishment of our own Holocaust Centre in Cape Town, so too did it inspire and reinforce my personal belief that museums should be dynamic and meaningful educational institutions that are as much about our present and our future as about our past. Serious learning can – and should – take place at all museums and memorials and this can only be achieved through dedicated education programmes. The Holocaust Centre, Beth Shalom supplements, augments and supports formal education through the unique learning experiences it offers. It is a remarkable centre of learning where people, particularly young people, are encouraged to meet the challenges of the 21st century.

During my week-long visit to the Centre, I was privileged to observe the skilful way the Centre addressed the moral and ethical issues that arise out of Holocaust history, and how they related them to contemporary society. This resonated particularly strongly with me because of our own South African apartheid past, and my personal commitment to strive towards the creation of a society in which prejudice, racism, antisemitism, discrimination and marginalisation will not be tolerated. My experiences at the Centre impacted on the way I developed the education programmes at the Cape Town Holocaust Centre. These have now been widely acclaimed and I am immensely grateful for their support and for the valuable contribution the Smith family have made to the general functioning of the Cape Town Holocaust Centre. May they long continue with the extraordinary work they do.

Sniegoule Matoniene, Holocaust Commission, Lithuania

lithuania

During the Holocaust over 90 per cent of Lithuania's Jews were murdered. Most of them were executed by the *Einsatzgruppen* (killing squads) touring former Soviet territories with deadly effect. But a large number of Jews were also rounded up and shot by Lithuanian collaborators. The infamous white armbands of the Lithuanian Nationalists, who dragged Jews from their homes and village squares into the forests, haunts the history and memory of a country tossed back and forth between the most devastating political powers of the twentieth century.

Since regaining independence in 1991, Lithuania has had to rewrite its history from many perspectives and reorientate its identity. Among the many issues facing the country's historians is the issue of Lithuanian complicity with the Nazi regime. As part of this, a Presidential Historical Commission has been operating and new structures developed for national education and commemoration.

The Holocaust Centre was pleased to partner a significant grassroots initiative, the House of Memory, established by charity directors, Egle Pranckuniene and Marina Vildziuniene. The project, which organises teacher training seminars and produces educational resources and a range of activities for schools, is run entirely by Lithuanians for Lithuanians, and has had a significant impact on Lithuanian young people.

The Holocaust Centre remains involved with Lithuanian partners through the House of Memory and the International Commission for the Evaluation of the Crimes of the Nazi and Soviet Occupation Regimes in Lithuania.

335

partnerships

Egle Pranckuniene
Board Member, The House of Memory

Our friendship with The Holocaust Centre, Beth Shalom started in 1997 when Stephen Smith came to Lithuania for the first time. Since then, The Holocaust Centre is one of the main sources of inspiration for our activities in the field of Holocaust education and the commemoration of Jewish heritage in Lithuania. On a few occasions, different people and groups from Lithuania have visited the Centre, where they learned many important lessons, both personally and professionally.

One of the most memorable visits was in 1998 when a group of Lithuanian experts took part in the conference dedicated to the third anniversary of The Holocaust Centre. Stephen and James Smith have also visited Lithuania several times, meeting teachers, historians, Catholic priests, politicians and representatives of the Jewish community, and these meetings opened new horizons for many people in Lithuania.

Until 2000, we were a group of people of different professions with a common concern regarding education and commemoration of the Holocaust. All of us were doing something in our own field, but our efforts were quite chaotic and non-systematic. The Smith family encouraged and inspired us to establish an organization. This happened in March 2000. Since then, the House of Memory has been trying to facilitate awareness of the history of the Holocaust in Lithuania; to confront and expose manifestations of antisemitism, racism and xenophobia; to promote the building of bridges between the past and the future, and between peoples of differing national and cultural backgrounds, including among the young; and to create networks between organisations and individuals dealing with the Holocaust in Lithuania and other countries.

At the moment there are many organizations working in this field and our society is much more aware of the Holocaust, but nevertheless there are still many things to do. In cooperation with The Holocaust Centre, Beth Shalom, we organised two study visits for British groups to Lithuania and participated in an international project called "Faces of Victims". The main lesson we have learned from our partnership is that everything depends on individual people, their beliefs, attitudes, efforts and choices in life. We made our choice, encouraged all the way by The Holocaust Centre.

israel

Our journey toward the creation of The Holocaust Centre began at Yad Vashem. Having seen the memorial museum at Yad Vashem, we felt that there should be something similar in essence, if not in size, in the United Kingdom.

Yad Vashem was clearly the spiritual resting place of the Jews of Europe. Its dignity, its pain, its sense of purpose, all spoke about what needed to be said and done to convey similar meaning to wider audiences. During the creation of The Holocaust Centre, staff in the archives at Yad Vashem provided support in sourcing material for the permanent exhibition.

During the conceptualisation process of The Holocaust Centre, the team at Lohame Ha Getaot – The Ghetto Fighters' Kibbutz Holocaust Museum – provided insights to their museum and education programme, as well as providing important archival material to the Centre's museum team.

Partnership with both organisations continues through a variety of educational programmes, initiatives and publishing projects.

Raya Kalisman
Director of the Center for Humanistic Education, Israel

As an educational institution that has been in operation since 1995 at the Ghetto Fighters' Museum, the Center for Humanistic Education has developed a unique method for fostering a worldview based on the respect for diversity and a culture that helps people learn to live together. Study of the Holocaust and the processes that led to it serves as a point of departure for examination of our present with all its dangers, and of the existential need for moral alertness and tolerance towards others.

Our long-term connections with The Holocaust Centre, Beth Shalom, as well as generous support by UNESCO, gave us – educators from Rwanda and from Israel – an extraordinary opportunity to come together to learn and be immersed in the Center's humanistic core themes and practices in a seminar entitled "From Pain to Dialogue", 25 July-5 August 2005.

The participants from Rwanda came from the Kigali Institution of Education and from the Aegis Trust. We shared our educational beliefs and practices in struggling with what we perceive as one of the major threats to any society – the elimination of the "other" – individually and collectively. Both our groups are burdened with the painful heritage of that social illness.

The seminar was an exciting journey into educational challenges, which we, Israelis as well as Rwandans, face in our work, exploring the relevance of our experience for each other. We shared testimonies of surviving the Holocaust and the genocide in Rwanda. We dealt with issues like the significance of the Holocaust to the individual and to society, as well as the Jewish-Arab conflict and our educational belief that above and beyond diverse narratives, human fate bonds all men and women together.

Avner Shalev
Chairman of the Yad Vashem Directorate

In the last decade we have witnessed the creation of many Holocaust centres worldwide. The Holocaust Centre, Beth Shalom, however, stands out as a very special endeavour. It testifies to the dedication, commitment and talent of its founders.

Yad Vashem was established over 50 years ago in Jerusalem, the city symbolizing mankind's hope to mend the world through human deeds. Following their first visit to Yad Vashem in 1991, the Smith family undertook to grapple with this challenge in the deepest sense of the word, and to embark on a long and meaningful exploration of the cumbersome questions human society is facing in the post-Auschwitz era. In the ten years since its establishment, The Holocaust Centre has made a significant contribution to Holocaust remembrance and education. Asserting,

as Stephen puts it, that the Holocaust is not merely a Jewish matter, but concerns all people, The Holocaust Centre, Beth Shalom joined the ongoing international and intergenerational dialogue and became an important partner in many collaborative efforts in Europe and overseas.

In the past decade we have worked together in teacher-training programmes and the production of educational materials; we met and cooperated at various international conferences and organisations. As the living memorial to the destruction of the Jewish people established by the State of Israel on behalf of the Jewish people, Yad Vashem is proud to have played a role in the initiation of The Holocaust Centre, Beth Shalom. We are looking forward to deepening our cooperation in the future.

partnerships

sweden

In 1998 we were curious and pleased to be invited to a meeting in Stockholm at the initiative of the Prime Minister of Sweden, Göran Persson. At the meeting, the Prime Minister introduced a new project, The Living History Forum, which had been established to teach about the Holocaust and related issues. He also initiated a new international group, known as the International Task Force for Cooperation on Holocaust Education, Remembrance and Research.

In 2000 the Swedish Government hosted the first Stockholm Forum on the Holocaust. Along with fellow academics David Cesarani and Yehuda Bauer, Stephen Smith advised the Swedish Prime Minister's office on the creation and organisation of the Forum. The conference was attended by 50 governments, 22 heads of state and a substantial number of academics and educators.

Subsequent Stockholm Forum conferences have been held on the topics of "Racism and Xenophobia", "Reconciliation" and "Genocide Prevention". Since then, The Holocaust Centre has played an active role with both the Swedish Government and non-governmental partners in developing a number of initiatives.

341

partnerships

26–28 January 2000

The Stockholm International Forum on the Holocaust

A conference o
education, r

TASK FORCE FOR
INTERNATIONAL
COOPERATION ON
HOLOCAUST
EDUCATION
REMEMBRANCE
AND RESEARCH

Stockholm International Forum

Göran Persson
Prime Minister of Sweden

When we started the first governmental information project about the Holocaust in Sweden in 1997, the Beth Shalom Holocaust Memorial and Education Centre had been running for two years.

In The Holocaust Centre, Beth Shalom, and especially in its creators, Stephen and James Smith, we found important sources of knowledge and inspiration in our task.

The Swedish project, called Living History, was initiated as an attempt to reach out to young people in our own country with information about the Holocaust. It was a way to start a dialogue between generations about values, democracy and human dignity. It grew into a broad international cooperation, with the Task Force for International Cooperation on Holocaust Education, Remembrance and Research, and with a series of conferences named the Stockholm International Forum.

Stephen Smith has had an important role as academic adviser in our work with the four conferences in the Stockholm Forum series. He has attended all of them and contributed with his important knowledge and broad experiences. Focusing on anti-democratic movements today, the difficulties of reconciliation or the ways to prevent further genocide, Stephen Smith has been present, reminding us to use the past when shaping the future. Urging us never to forget the victims and their stories – may they have been in Bosnia, in Rwanda, or elsewhere in the world. Reminding us of the forgotten places of Jewish life that once existed, striving to keep history alive. Based on knowledge about the history of the Holocaust, the understanding of its consequences and evils, the Smith family is today a significant voice in every discussion on these issues. I wish to extend the deepest gratitude of the Swedish Government for this contribution.

Ten years after the opening of The Holocaust Centre, it is a leading partner in a vital and inspiring international cooperation between governments, universities and museums, between researchers, survivors' organizations, leading experts and others in the field.

I wish to convey my hope for many more successful years of important activities of The Holocaust Centre, Beth Shalom.

Christer Mattsson
The Living History Forum

Ever since Living History was initiated by the Swedish Prime Minister, The Holocaust Centre, Beth Shalom has served as a model for good practice in our field. The Centre is both an unusually down-to-earth and a visionary institute.

The unique combination of the vision that truly leads the work and the daily, practical struggle of getting the exhibition and seminars running, has led to an organisation that today, ten years later, stands on solid ground and dares to expand its commitment in what can be considered the only rational way – by taking on the challenge of contemporary genocides.

The employees and board members of Living History have frequently visited the Centre and we all returned with the sense that we should "*Just do it*". Together with the Centre, we share the fundamental understanding that there is no matter of more vital importance than our mission. No matter what other tremendous progresses mankind makes, our greatest challenge is to stop our will towards self-annihilation. The Holocaust Centre was always ready to assist us as we created our core Holocaust education and remembrance work, with numerous contacts, information, lectures and participation in the different Stockholm Forum conferences.

We look forward with pleasure to continuing this cooperation in the field of the Holocaust and other issues of contemporary urgency.

Anna-Karin Johansson
Deputy-Director, The Living History Forum, Sweden

The first time I visited The Holocaust Centre, Beth Shalom, the Living History project was still in its conceptual phase. Our visit to the Centre infused inspiration and energy into our efforts to raise awareness about the Holocaust and democracy issues in Sweden.

It has been fantastic to follow how a small dedicated team worked single-mindedly, with commitment and knowledge, to build up an institution that operates in many places throughout the world today.

The continuous dialogue between Beth Shalom and what has now become the Living History Forum has engendered many fruitful discussions about how our two organisations could work with the Holocaust as our starting-point, and relate this to other genocides and current issues in our respective countries.

In our international work, such as the Stockholm International Forum, Stephen Smith has been a faithful advisor who has generously shared his contacts, knowledge and ideas. In this way, he has contributed to a rapid development in this field all over the world over the past decade, never hesitating to bring up vital issues and taking a stand for the ideas he believes will lead to change. The work pursued by The Holocaust Centre is an example to us all.

force task

partnerships

As a result of the initiative of the Swedish Prime Minister, the Task Force for International Cooperation on Holocaust Education, Remembrance and Research was established in 1998. Initially four countries, the Task Force now consists of over 20 countries which meet as delegations twice a year to look at ongoing issues around the Holocaust, and how their respective governments are dealing with them.

This unique intergovernmental group brings together government officials, non-governmental groups and academic and educational experts under one roof. It assists with modest funding of projects, particularly in the former Communist countries of Central and Eastern Europe.

Since the inception of the Task Force, The Holocaust Centre has played an active role as a member of the UK delegation, led by the Foreign and Commonwealth Office. The Holocaust Centre remains committed to the important task of ensuring that good practice in the teaching of the Holocaust is shared as widely as possible.

Stephen Feinberg, Mark Weizman and Michelle Gross, members of the US Delegation to the International Task Force, Washington DC

Jerry Gotel, Gareth Ward and Trudy Gold, Director of the London Jewish Cultural Centre, at the International Task Force, Washington DC

Gareth Ward
UK Foreign Office Special Representative on Post-Holocaust issues

I first visited The Holocaust Centre, Beth Shalom on a bright Spring day in 2003. As I approached the tranquil setting in the Nottinghamshire countryside, I had mixed expectations. I already understood (or so I thought) how a well designed museum exhibition could spread awareness of what happened in the Holocaust, and how original sites, such as concentration camps, could engage emotions and create memories. Having recently taken on the role of Special Representative on post-Holocaust issues at the Foreign Office, I asked myself what role the Holocaust Centre would play.

I quickly found answers in the vibrancy and broad scope of the Centre. I was struck by the engagement of groups of schoolchildren as they interacted with the materials and responded to the teaching approach. The exhibition captured the human scale and inhuman dimensions of the Holocaust that can easily be lost in the wide sweep of the history of the Second World War. And then in the memorial garden, I was drawn involuntarily towards a quiet analysis of the lessons of right and wrong, and of the passing of time and the durability of memory.

The whole team at The Holocaust Centre combine a remarkable educational project with a site that is powerful in its own right. Stephen Smith also puts the Centre to work outside the UK, as part of the International Task Force on Holocaust Education, Remembrance and Research. The experience and knowledge gathered at The Holocaust Centre have been of use to many educationalists and museum curators from other parts of Europe and the world. I wish the Centre well as it continues to grow and reach new generations of young people with the essential story of the Holocaust.

Hannah Lessing
Secretary General of the Austrian National Fund for Victims of National Socialism

I am an unusual contributor to this book, as one of the few yet to visit the Centre. However, through my work, like many others, I have felt its far-reaching effects.

As the Secretary General of the National Fund of the Republic of Austria for victims of National Socialism and a member of the Austrian Delegation to the International Task Force. I have had the privilege to meet and work with the founders of the Centre regularly.

What has shone through is its integrity, along with professionalism, sensitivity, as well as a clear awareness of where Holocaust education and remembrance is going. Through many debates held at the Task Force at a high political level, I have seen The Holocaust Centre have consistent and considerable influence on Holocaust education and remembrance policy. It is clearly an organisation not afraid to lead from the front.

The National Fund also celebrates its tenth year in 2005, supporting Holocaust survivors through symbolic gesture payments, as well as projects for their personal and social needs.
The recognition and dignity The Holocaust Centre gives to survivors is cause for significant partnership. in coming years. I look forward to our organisations sharing the continued vision of ensuring the lives and voices of survivors continue to be heard.

aegis

"It will never happen again, we swear…" Song written by Rwandan schoolchildren

genocide

During the creation of The Holocaust Centre, two crises took place of huge international significance. One was in the Balkans, which resulted in the ethnic cleansing of Bosnian Muslims and the murder of in excess of 250,000 people. The other was the genocide in Rwanda, which resulted in more than 800,000 murders in the fastest act of genocide in history.

It was clear that 50 years after the Holocaust, international structures to prevent the incidence of genocide were sadly deficient. At the time, we decided that the Centre should play an active role in genocide prevention in the future.

In 2000 Aegis was established, operating from The Holocaust Centre. Aegis means 'protection'. Its aim was to work on preventative strategies in situations of potential or impending genocide. It was the desire of the Centre that protective measures be better understood and that international responses to genocide become more robust.

Aegis works alongside The Holocaust Centre, sharing the vision to ensure that people of all backgrounds learn from the Holocaust that genocide should become a thing of the past.

349

aegis

the place of prevention

The question is a demanding one.

How *do* you prevent genocide?

Mass killing, ethnic cleansing, state-sponsored crimes against humanity and genocide have been an ever-emerging trait of human behaviour and a blight on human history. It seems that the propensity for atrocity increases with each precedent that scars yet another populace and leaves its heavy legacy of painful memories.

We do know that genocide does not happen by chance. It is cold, it is calculated, it always takes time to emerge, it occurs over long periods of time, it is not inevitable and therefore is preventable. The difficult issue to resolve is how to understand the warning signs with sufficient clarity, interpreting them for what they are, and acting in a decisive and at times incisive way.

The gap between knowing that genocide is a possibility and the prevention of its occurrence is one which we are all far from resolving. International laws and conventions exist, but finding the political will to engage early is remarkably difficult to muster. It would seem still to be the case that the trigger point for political actors to engage is once women and children have been murdered in sufficient numbers for it to correspond to a textbook definition.

It is said that prevention is better than cure.

While current norms of political reaction remain the way they are, prevention is not even a remote possibility.

And there is no cure for genocide.

James M. Smith, Founder, Aegis

Roman Halter
Holocaust Survivor, Artist and Architect

Since the beginning of human history, mankind has always been killing one another – so much so that killing was thought to be a part of the natural human condition. But in addition to killing, humans go in for mass murder; the murder of a whole ethnic group is particular to humans only. Monkeys kill, but they do not go in for the deliberate and total murder of other groups. They do not commit *genocide*. It seems we humans are capable, when badly led or incited, of extreme ruthlessness and savagery and murder. The deliberate state-planned and state-implemented murder of European Jewry by the German Nazis in the 20th century, which is now known by the word "the Holocaust" was *genocide* on a massive scale, in which six million were murdered, amongst them roughly 1.5 million children.

There were other genocides which the rest of the world was unwilling to prevent. When genocide took place in Rwanda, peace-keeping forces which were there did nothing because their mandate was to keep peace and *not to prevent genocide*. What the world needs is a world force with the specific remit to act in places where genocide is about to occur. Just as we have fire brigades that stand by in case fire breaks out, so also the world needs a stand-by genocide prevention force with powers to act.

We also need "stations" – organisations like the Aegis Trust that make government, the public and the world aware of an impending danger of genocide, anywhere on this planet. We are all rich enough to afford its upkeep. We must also recognise that as humans, we are not only capable of murder but of great noble acts. In sane, peaceful and caring times, we should act by dipping into our pockets to ensure there are sufficient resources to prevent genocide from occurring anywhere on this earth.

Because prevention = action + $ & £

352

aegis

Patrick Mercer
OBE, MP, Shadow Minister for Homeland Security

I am enormously proud to have The Holocaust Centre, Beth Shalom and The Aegis Trust associated with my Constituency. In the last ten years they have continued to draw attention to one of the greatest blights on our society: genocide.

As a serving soldier I, sadly, saw genocide at first-hand during my time in the Balkans and later in East Timor. There can be no doubt that in far-flung places where the media and the authorities cannot penetrate, this sort of atrocity continues on a very regular basis.

The only way that we can counter this is by drawing people's attention to it. This is precisely why The Holocaust Centre and its continued success is so important. I wish everybody connected with this work every good fortune and hope that the next ten years are as successful as the last decade .

Photograph: ©Georgie Cohen

I think Aegis is a wonderful next step, or development, of the work that has already been done on Holocaust education and research through The Holocaust Centre. It is important because it not only builds on the useful work they have done on Holocaust education, but it renders it relevant for dangerous political or social situations today. What Aegis is trying to do is to prevent genocide.

Had there been a committed, energetic non-governmental organisation like Aegis in the 1930s, the whole history of the 20th century may have been completely different. We'll never know, but what we do know is that their active engagement with other governmental and non-governmental partners, their experience of working right across society has been demonstrated through The Holocaust Centre and I'm confident it will carry forward with Aegis.

James Kidner, Foreign and Commonwealth Office Head of Delegation,
Task Force for International Cooperation on Holocaust Education, Remembrance and Research

355

aegis

Barbara Harff

Professor of Political Science (retired)
US Naval Academy
Proventus Distinguished Visiting Professor
Strassler Center for Holocaust and Genocide Studies
Clark University, USA

As a genocide scholar for some 25 years, my interests have ranged from prevention (beginning in the 1980s) to identifying cases since WWII (from the mid-1980s), and then to comparative studies and systematic analysis of causes (from the mid-1990s). My current focus is identifying countries at high risk of future genocide and politicide, and designing strategies of prevention for specific emerging situations.

One of my scholarly friends, Yehuda Bauer, spoke to me some years ago of Stephen and James Smith, singing their praises and talking about how they had single-handedly built an outreach programme without parallel. I have visited Aegis and met the brothers at a number of professional and planning meetings, including the Genocide Prevention Conference convened by Aegis in Newark in January 2002. That conference brought together genocide scholars, survivors, policy makers and field experts. This is precisely the mix of people that is sorely needed to build connections among those who can work together to prevent future genocides. Aegis has done an astounding job in establishing a broad and influential network, from concerned citizens to scholars to those responsible for making and implementing policies of prevention.

The Stockholm Forum on the Prevention of Genocide, held in January 2004, was probably the most important international conference to date on this topic. It was the brainchild of Yehuda Bauer and Stephen Smith, with a small brains-trust of scholars and activists with whom I was privileged to participate. For me, this was the "mother of all conferences," a dream realized when more than 50 national delegations committed themselves to preventing future genocides. In addition, Aegis plays a central role in an informal advisory group to Juan Mendez, the UN Secretary-General's special advisor on genocide, whose office was announced at the Stockholm Forum.

Ted Robert Gurr

Distinguished University Professor
Founding Director, Minorities at Risk project
University of Maryland, USA

For four decades I have been analyzing deadly conflicts within states. My perspective has always been a global one, aimed at identifying the general causes of internal wars and state repression. In the mid-1980s I began the Minorities at Risk project which has since tracked some 300 politically significant ethnic, national and religious minorities. I and the many people who have contributed to the MAR project have regularly profiled their grievances, status, political actions and their impact on public policy. Barbara Harff's work on genocide raised one of the key questions of this work: What kinds of minorities, under what circumstances, are the prospective victims of state violence and the ultimate crime of genocide?

I first met James Smith in 2001 at Schloss Emlau in the Bavarian Alps, where we helped

culminated in the 2004 Stockholm Forum on the Prevention of Genocide. What impressed me then, and ever more so after the 2002 Genocide Prevention Conference convened by Aegis, was the organisation's commitment to memorializing the victims of all past genocides and politicides, from the Holocaust to Cambodia, Bosnia, Rwanda and beyond. The same breadth of vision and concern is evident in Aegis's recent efforts to generate political will in the UK and on the Continent for action to halt genocide in Darfur.

Aegis, with its founders and dedicated staff, are a major force in the gathering international movement to anticipate and prevent future genocides and mass political murders. They deserve full credit and support from the interlocking networks of scholars and activists who share their

From my observation of The Holocaust Centre, Beth Shalom and more frequent encounters with James and Stephen Smith, I believe the Centre has made a notable contribution in expanding knowledge about the Holocaust and making connections to other genocides, in a country in which this was acknowledged rather indirectly, if at all, prior to their efforts.

They have shown what dedicated individuals and a family can do on their own initiative, without reliance on existing academic or other institutions. Further, they have succeeded in changing the political landscape in the heart of the UK, despite starting from what might be seen as the rural periphery. The contributions of Aegis and The Holocaust Centre to Holocaust education and awareness of genocide in the United Kingdom seem to me to be pivotal – not only in the UK but in the international campaign to stop genocide.

Helen Fein
Executive Director, Institute for the Study of Genocide (New York City, NY)

Eric Markusen

Danish Institute for International Studies

James Smith and I were both in Kigali in November 2001 for a large, international conference organized by genocide survivors' organizations and the Rwandan Government. With a small group of conference participants, we visited the Gisozi genocide site, right in the heart of the city of Kigali. Approximately 250,000 people were slaughtered in the greater Kigali area alone. We were shown some large slabs of stone which covered mass graves, and looked into some mass graves that had been permanently covered; they were being gradually filled with caskets. We were shown a partially-built building that was to be the headquarters for the site. It was to include a display, classrooms and other facilities.

During that first visit to Rwanda, we were also shown the Murambi genocide site, not far from Butare, where hundreds of ghostly-white corpses of genocide victims are displayed for visitors.

For both of us, what we learned at the conference and saw at the genocide sites deeply affected our future work. I believe that James's experience at Gisozi and Murambi directly led to his passionate commitment to helping Rwandans recover from the genocide.

James, Stephen, Apollon and many other Aegis staff have made important contributions to remembrance, education and research about the Rwandan genocide. They helped the city of Kigali complete the

Gisozi Memorial Site in time for the official dedication by President Paul Kagame on 7 April 2004. Approximately 100,000 people visit the site annually, many of them Rwandans holding private memorial services at one of the mass graves. And they are working to develop and preserve the Murambi site. They have several other projects in Rwanda.

Beyond that, Aegis played a key role in persuading the Government of the United Kingdom to have the theme, "From the Holocaust to Rwanda: Lessons Learned, Lessons Still to Learn," on its third annual Holocaust Memorial Day.

Aegis has made many valuable contributions to the people of Rwanda and others who are concerned about the Rwandan genocide and all genocides.

Sculpture from The Kigali Memorial Centre

aegis

Jerry Fowler

**Staff Director, Committee on Conscience,
United States Holocaust Memorial Museum**

A central issue for anyone concerned with remembrance of the Holocaust is the connection between that memory and the persistent problem of genocide. Elie Wiesel and members of a Commission appointed by US President Jimmy Carter addressed this "perplexing and urgent" issue in 1979, when they recommended creation of a US national memorial to victims of the Holocaust. They were clear that the memorial had an obligation to address new threats of genocide. Indeed, failure to do so, they argued, "would violate the memory of the past".

Along with a tremendous surge of Holocaust remembrance and education in the 1990s, including especially the opening of The Holocaust Centre, Beth Shalom as the first Holocaust education centre in the United Kingdom, came grim evidence of the immensity of this challenge. World leaders uttered pious sentiments about the need to remember the Holocaust even as they

allowed genocide to proceed in the Balkans and Rwanda. It became clear that never forgetting the Holocaust did not by itself result in fulfilling the oft-betrayed promise of "never again". Truly honouring the memory of the past required more.

The emergence of Aegis out of The Holocaust Centre, therefore, was both natural and necessary. The Centre's fundamental mission of Holocaust remembrance and education needed the complement of an institution that could actively honour Holocaust memory by promoting the prevention of modern genocide on a broad array of fronts: academic, educational and political.

The Holocaust was a watershed event in human existence, one that resulted in the beginnings of a worldwide consensus that "genocide" is an international crime that all humanity should strive to prevent, suppress and punish. But deepening that consensus to the point where we have a world without genocide will be a generations-long struggle. There is a vital role in the vanguard of that struggle for Aegis, The Holocaust Centre and all of us committed to honouring victims of the Holocaust.

Dick Geary
Professor of Modern History at the University of Nottingham

When I took up the Chair of Modern History at the University of Nottingham, I was astonished but delighted to discover the existence of a Holocaust Memorial Centre in rural Nottinghamshire. My first visit with a group of students in the mid-1990s impressed me greatly. In particular I was struck by two things: first, the way in which the opening section of the permanent exhibition located the Nazi Holocaust within the context of centuries of Jewish persecution throughout Europe; and second, by the testimony of a Jewish Lithuanian survivor, who was at pains to point out the persecution that his co-religionists had experienced in Lithuania even before the arrival of the German death squads in 1941.

Without denying the uniqueness of the Jewish Holocaust (the intentional and often mechanised extermination of six million Jews by the Nazi regime), it seems to me to be equally important to place the 'Final Solution' in the context of other genocides, cases of ethnic cleansing and social exclusion on the grounds of race; for only in this way will the present generation learn the lessons of cultural and racial intolerance. Fortunately, the collaboration of the Centre with Aegis promises to do precisely this, as Aegis is concerned with past and contemporary genocides and examines the thorny question of genocide prevention. I hope this area of activity will continue to expand and also concern itself with the social exclusion, forced migration and death of millions of Africans through the institution of slavery.

Refugee, Kosovo, 1999

"First of all what can I say about The Holocaust Centre? Absolutely fantastic!... I strongly believe that an event such as the Holocaust should be taught to every generation, despite their race, colour and culture... And the real question is: Are we really doing enough as a nation to prevent such things, knowing in recent years the vicious cruelty and massive ethnic cleansing in the former Yugoslavia and in Rwanda?"

Dubahar, age 18, Small Heath School

all party parliamentary group

On 19 July 2005, MPs and members of the House of Lords came together to inaugurate the Genocide Prevention All Party Parliamentary Group (APPG). Made up of over 120 UK parliamentarians, it is already one of the biggest cross party groups in Parliament. It is chaired by the former International Development Secretary of State, the Rt. Hon. Clare Short MP (Labour), with John Bercow MP (Conservative) and Lord Anthony Lester QC (Liberal Democrat) as vice chairs.

The Genocide Prevention APPG will form the backbone of the Aegis Trust policy work. We provide research and administration to the group, and working with the chair and vice chairs, we will help decide the issues that the parliamentarians will examine.

The group's purpose is simple: to ensure that the United Kingdom does all it can to prevent genocides and crimes against humanity. It will do this by increasing the flow of independent information and analysis to UK parliamentarians about genocides and crimes against humanity. It will also support parliamentarians so as to increase the effectiveness of their scrutiny of government and promote understanding of the importance of long-term approaches to genocide prevention.

Genocide prevention has never been comprehensively examined by policy-makers, even after the tragedies of Rwanda and Bosnia. The Genocide Prevention APPG will change this. Long-term solutions are ultimately required if genocides are to be prevented. Intervention, crisis management and humanitarian assistance are complex issues, which will only be addressed through serious and sustained work. This group will provide the platform for that work.

Through the APPG group, we aim to support individuals like Juan Mendez, the Special Advisor on Genocide Prevention to the UN Secretary-General, and institutions like the International Criminal Court. It is also hoped that the Genocide Prevention APPG, the first of its kind, will encourage parliamentarians from other countries to set up similar committees.

The group will help to lead the debate on genocide prevention and raise it up the policy agenda. Whether dealing with an ongoing crisis or working to prevent genocides in the future, the Genocide Prevention APPG will give a strong and sustained voice to our work.

361

aegis

"Everybody says 'Never Again' - after the Holocaust and Srebrenica and Rwanda. But it keeps happening again and again - in Darfur, in Eastern Congo and to many other groups. We must do more to understand causes and take preventative action. Aegis has taken the lead in genocide prevention. I hope the launch of the All Party Group in Parliament will increase the effectiveness of this work."

Clare Short, MP

Short, Chair of All Party Parliamentary Group on Genocide Prevention with John Bercow, Vice Chair

Photograph: ©Geoff Pugh

societies ^{aegis}

Aegis Societies for universities were first conceived in summer 2004. Their aim is to raise awareness of genocide and the work of Aegis, and to support the campaigns of Aegis. It is hoped that in the future the societies may form a substantial grassroots political base for Aegis, adding support and weight to the campaigns against genocide. Aegis Societies will arrange speaker events, attend rallies, write articles and letters, create poster campaigns, use concerts and other events for campaign purposes, and build lasting coalitions with other student societies to support Aegis' campaigns.

Students are an important group to reach for two reasons. Firstly, they are future politicians, lawyers and entrepreneurs at an impressionable age, and working with them may reap benefits in the future. Secondly, they are broadly more receptive than the general public to discussion of the issues that Aegis is tackling. Students at university are better equipped than those at secondary-school age to understand the complex situations on which Aegis is campaigning, and able to grasp the fundamental importance of political pressure and political will in the work that Aegis is doing. The aim for Aegis Societies is to capture the potential that students have to form a grassroots support base for Aegis, to work and carry lessons learned from the past into their future careers.

The inaugural Aegis Society, based at Oxford University, was created in Spring Term 2005 by Jonathan Bower, who had spent a highly rewarding gap year with Aegis in 2003-4. James Smith and Kemal Pervanic, survivor of Omarska concentration camp, spoke at the inaugural event, entitled "Protect Darfur: Response to a Genocide". This promising start was attended by over 100 students and was very well received. The Society continued the momentum, submitting articles, designing a poster campaign, turning a concert attended by 200 people into an Aegis campaign event. Members also attended the "Protect Darfur" rally in London on 15 May 2005, as well as joining the Aegis contingent in smaller numbers at the "Make Poverty History" rally in Edinburgh in July.

Through a press release in summer 2005 and the logistical support of the National Union of Students, the Society was able to motivate groups at other universities to mark a day of solidarity for the survivors of Darfur's genocide. The Aegis Society stall at Freshers' Fair was privileged by the presence of a survivor from Darfur, creating a memorable impression on incoming students. In Autumn Term 2005, new Aegis Societies were founded at Cambridge University and Kingston University, London.

363

aegis

International Criminal Tribunal for Rwanda

The International Criminal Tribunal for Rwanda (ICTR) began formal proceedings in November 1995. Based in Arusha, Tanzania, after four years of work, twenty-eight indictments were issued and only seven accused convicted. Two thousand cases have been disposed.

The ICTR is judging the main architects of the Rwandan genocide, but the bulk of the prosecution is left to the Rwandan national legal system. Rwanda passed a law specifically for the punishment of genocide in 1996. Despite the immense difficulties, the foundation is being laid to build trust and reconciliation.

Kigali, 30 December 1996 Silas Munyagishali, former deputy prosecutor in Kigali, and Theodomir Rutirubuwa, former local administrator in court in Kigali, accused of masterminding genocide.

Gacaca

Gacaca, meaning 'Justice o[...]
modem mechanisms in lower [...]
caseload.

Local tribunals inspired by a traditio[...]
resolution have been introduced; the[...]
whenever the need arises, and seek to [...]
reconciliation which is acceptable and s[...]

Gacaca was developed for settling commun[...]
transgressions, not for judging genocidaires.[...]
adapt to deal with such huge crimes.

After 1994, the [...]
justice above all e[...]
the Hutu want dem[...]
above all else. The m[...]
fears dem[...]
The majority fears [...]
The mino[...]
democracy is a[...]
finishing an u[...]

Family Story

[...]rne Kabuhizi. In mid May 1994
[...]nths pregnant and due to give
[...] couple were not found.
[...]shes, where they had
[...] the unborn foetus,
[...] to shield herself

There are one hundred and twenty thousand Hutu in prison in Rwanda in appalling circumstances. At the present rate, it will take between two to four hundred years to try all detainees.

R W A N D A

darfur
protect .

We recognise several phases to genocidal violence. In the primary phase, there is a build-up of exclusionary ideology, the emergence of propaganda, the development of violent methodologies. Then comes the crisis or secondary phase, where murder and widespread genocidal violence become the norm. Then there is the aftermath, the tertiary phase, where the consequences for individuals and society are deepfelt for several generations.

In the primary phase, it is necessary to predict, to provide opportunities for reform, for education, democracy and diplomacy. It is important to take a long-term view and to work structurally towards prevention.

In the tertiary phase, it is important to rebuild societies, to support survivors, ensure the experience is acknowledged, and education and remembrance developed in a constructive way.

In the secondary phase, it is important that action is taken quickly, decisively and without unnecessary prevarication. It is during times of crisis that the campaigns team at Aegis act to ensure that issues of importance are raised up the political agenda and state actors engaged as thoroughly as possible.

The 'Protect Darfur' Campaign run by Aegis is an example of crisis campaigning, where a combination of expert reports, websites, news items, parliamentary alliances and non-governmental cooperation have resulted in raising significant public profile in a timely way.

365

aegis

John Fransman
Holocaust Survivor

Over the years I have come to know the Smith family well and come to respect their deep faith and commitment. I have seen their endeavours to help heal the scars of Jewish survivors and give us dignity, and their efforts to educate and eradicate the ancient antisemitic prejudices of our Christian neighbours, which in Europe led to the Holocaust. I have seen how they took concerted action and harnessed local Midlands support to bring desperately needed medicines and clothing to the refugee survivors of the Kosovo and Srebrenica massacres in former Yugoslavia. And again, I saw how they involved themselves in the aftermath of the Rwandan genocide of Hutus by Tutsis by helping to create meaningful memorials and education centres that will help to bring reconciliation and healing to the survivor victims.

More recently, they have developed Aegis, a think-tank engaged in studying how to become cognitive of the signs that precede potential genocides, with the intent of setting in motion political action to prevent genocides being carried out. Quite properly, Aegis has taken on as a first task the Darfur Campaign to save a threatened minority population from its own Sudanese Government, not too dissimilar from the Rwanda experience.

It has been impressive to see how a determined, humane organisation can be so effective in helping to heal this world, by not only speaking effectively but by also translating those words into actions. It is not easy to stand back, only to watch and not be affected. That is why so many people who visit The Holocaust Centre are infected and spurred into a response to do something!

When the World Federation of Jewish Child Survivors of the Holocaust (WFJCSH), to which the Child Survivor Association of Great Britain is affiliated, composed a letter concerning the problems of the people in Darfur and asked the various affiliated Chapters to send it to President Bush and to their local representatives, as Chairman of our Association, I was only too pleased to send it with my covering letter to both Prime Minister Blair and Foreign Minister Straw. I was most disappointed with the replies I eventually received from the Foreign and Commonwealth Office and felt it appropriate to inform Aegis of the correspondence.

When I was invited to the House of Commons by Clare Short to the All Party Genocide Prevention Group campaign, I was happy to add my voice as a Holocaust survivor in particular. Holocaust survivors are very wary of comparisons with genocides and even minor tragedies that are commonly described as such, and we guard our "Holocaust" jealously as a unique event.

Nevertheless, there are comparisons and parallels to the events unfolding in Darfur that are worth noting, such as the prevalence of bystanders who took no action at a conference in Evian in 1938 and who take no action now, and by so doing condoned the expulsion, pillage, rape and murder of Jews in Nazi Germany and Europe and now are condoning the Sudanese Government's involvement in the expulsion, pillage, rape and murder of a minority African people within its own larger Muslim Arab population, both Christian and Muslim.

Then and now, there is a mistaken belief in superior racial characteristics and again a call for *Lebensraum*. Once more there are the bystanders; they are the other governments in Africa, in Europe and Asia, Russia, China, the Americas and the United Nations Security Council in particular. If the Sudanese Government is allowed to succeed in destroying these people, what will stop the Iranians from attempting to do the same to Israel, to annihilate my Jewish home, my escape route from an inhospitable Europe?

For these reasons, the activity of Aegis, and my own belief in Judaism which leads me to seek justice, to support the weak, even my self-interest, all contribute to my support for the 'Protect Darfur' Campaign.

"Aegis has absolutely been of great value to me as a survivor from Darfur and asylum-seeker in the UK. It has helped to protect and support me and is doing good work in interviewing survivors to get proper information about what is happening in Darfur. Through its work and 'Protect Darfur' campaign, it is encouraging people to be aware of the reality of the genocide in Darfur. I would like to thank Aegis for this very important work."

Anwar Bakar, Darfuri Survivor

"History will not forget your humanity for Darfur."

Hassan Angrib, Darfuri Survivor

368

aegis

Fysal Hussein Omar
Survivor from Darfur

I would like to thank all those involved in the campaign against genocide, particularly Aegis and the 'Protect Darfur' campaign, because a lot of people are beginning to understand exactly what is happening in Darfur through your programme.

There is no doubt that the painful memory of the millions of victims of genocide in the Holocaust and Rwanda will live with us forever. For many years to come, we will continue to unearth the remains of children, women and men hacked to death in one of the most frenzied, planned and organized massacres ever witnessed by the world.

Yet genocide has been revisited in the past two years. Still sore and raw in our memories, the genocide of Rwanda has given way to that of Darfur. The same crimes, the same atrocities and the same disregard for human lives. In the name of greed, hatred and spite, the Janjaweed, the Sudanese Government-armed militias – very much the equivalent of the Interahamwe and Impuzamugambi of Rwanda – have killed, looted, burnt and raped their neighbours. Like vultures, they have cleansed villages of their people and destroyed the dreams of entire communities.

The early warning signs were very much present in Darfur. For more than three decades, indigenous Africans – Fur, Massaleet and Zaghawa to name but a few – were at the mercy of successive ruthless regimes, military as well as so-called democratically elected governments. Ruling

by the gun and with the gun, they imposed a religious-ethnic-sectarian ideology on the country. Their proxy killers, Moajhideen in the south and Janjaweed in Darfur.

African leaders do not want to disarm other state leaders regardless of Darfur's second genocidal campaign. The first campaign was against the Christian and animist people of south and central Sudan, with most of the deaths occurring over a decade beginning in the early '90s and in 2002. It was indeed "genocide in slow motion". Instead of disarming the Janjaweed, the Sudanese Government is providing them with military uniforms and integrating them into its regular forces and into the much-hated Popular Defence Forces. They have now been posted in and around Nyala, capital of Southern Darfur, preventing the return of refugees. They are attacking internally displaced people and preventing them from returning to their homes. They are occupying the farmland and villages of farmers they chased away earlier, and refusing to allow them to retake possession of what remains of their homes.

Nowadays people are saying that Darfur has got better. But there is nothing left for the Janjaweed to burn. And the killing still goes on.

Massive thanks on behalf of Darfuris.

"I have just seen the film you made and am chilled, so moved and infuriated by the notion that we should waste time arguing about semantics in the face of such a catastrophe. Congratulations – its simplicity is devastating."

Carrie Supple, Author of *From Prejudice to Genocide*

Captain Brian Steidle

US Marine Corps (fmr)

In September 2004, I was invited to serve in Darfur as an unarmed military observer and US representative with the African Union. I was armed only with a pen and my reports were my ammunition. Our mission was to report back on the violations of the ceasefire agreement, such as an attack on villages, troop movements and military operations. While conducting these investigations, we observed villages of up to 20,000 inhabitants burned to the ground, hundreds of thousands of displaced civilians and the results of violent atrocities including the rape of women, the torture of men and the murder of children.

My conscience would no longer allow me to stand by without taking further action, and I became convinced that I could be more effective by bringing the story of what I witnessed to the world. I am now working with my sister, Gretchen Steidle Wallace, founder of Global Grassroots, in stopping the violence.

Three of the most important points that I implore the international community to consider include:

(1) the atrocities resulting in millions displaced and hundreds of thousands killed are ongoing today and must be addressed urgently before thousands more die;

(2) these crimes against humanity result from a government-sponsored military operation that is systematically eliminating the black African population from all of Darfur;

(3) this conflict can be resolved through weapons sanctions, a no-fly zone throughout Darfur and greater international support for an expanded mandate for the African Union.

Every day we saw villages burned to the ground with nothing left but ash frames. In my team's area of operation, which was South Darfur, I estimate nearly 75 per cent of the villages had been decimated as of the beginning of February. We witnessed scores of dead bodies providing evidence of torture – arms bound, males castrated, children beaten to death, people's body parts removed and execution-style deaths. We would interview women who had been gang raped – I remember receiving a report that cited around 70 rapes in internally displaced persons camps over a period of a few days.

Women and children bear the greatest burden of this conflict. The IDP camps are filled with families that have lost their fathers. Women are forced to seek firewood and water daily with the almost certain risk of rape. Should men be available to venture out of the IDP camps, they face the risk of castration and murder. So the families decide that rape is the lesser evil. Children have not been spared in the violent attacks, and many end up missing and have never been seen again. When they finally are able to return home and rebuild, many women may have to support themselves alone. Many rape victims are ostracized and others face unwanted pregnancies and an even greater burden of care.

I believe this conflict can be resolved through international pressure and international support of the African Union. More specifically, I believe weapons sanctions and a no-fly zone throughout Darfur are critical. I have witnessed the effectiveness of the African Union and believe they can stop the conflict with more support from the "West."

The AU can secure and protect all villages in Darfur with the right support.

People at the grassroots level worldwide have the power individually to help stop the killing. It is critical for individuals to write their government leaders and ask them to take action. Speak out and tell others of the atrocities. For the first time, we might be able to stop genocide in the making. Organizations such as Aegis are at the forefront in this struggle to raise awareness and assist the people in Darfur.

Now it is your turn.

We cannot fail the men, women and children of Darfur.

Charles Keidan
The Pears Foundation

The Pears Foundation has supported Aegis Trust's campaign to "Protect Darfur" since its inception in April 2005.

Aegis tasked itself with highlighting atrocities committed by the Janjaweed militia in the Darfur region of Western Sudan, with the apparent complicity of the Sudanese Government. The UN system had failed to respond adequately and, by early 2005, the issue had become all but invisible.

The aim of the "Protect Darfur" campaign was therefore clear: to generate media and political attention, demanding robust action to stop the murder, rape and displacement of the men, women and children of Darfur. The Aegis team is hard-working and focused, and with good reason: they know that many African lives in the villages of Darfur are at stake.

We have seen the commitment of Aegis at first hand – from the cross-party launch in Parliament to the demonstration outside Downing Street and the Sudanese Embassy, to the "Make Poverty History" rally in Edinburgh. Aegis knows that "Genocide makes poverty" and they also know that crimes against humanity have continued for too long, in too many places, over the last 60 years. The Pears Foundation supports Aegis because, like them, we do not want to give up or stand by. We want to contribute to stopping these abuses now and in the future.

aegis

"Action must be taken now to end this atrocity of genocide in Darfur. Inaction is killing people just as much as the Janjaweed militias."

Amy Rinkle

Revd. S. J. Ridley
Barnard Castle School, Durham

This really is an incredibly valuable day for our Year 9s and they come away understanding much more fully the nature of prejudice and the roots of genocide. Thank you, too, for keeping the issue contemporary with your short video on Darfur... We are trying to find a fruitful angle... to get Darfur more into the school consciousness.

Above photographs ©Brian Steidle

Dr David Magrill
Former President, Nottingham Hebrew Congregation

The foot-dragging over Darfur is an international disgrace. The slaughter was clearly predictable and was eloquently predicted, and yet neither the UN nor any democratic Western government has produced an effective measure to combat it. Not even a convincing condemnation! How many more genocides are we going to have to witness?

"If this was happening to my family, I would want others to do what they can to help. I want the UK Government to intervene through all means to protect the innocent in Darfur."

Dave Thompson

"What if it was you? Wouldn't you want help?"

Camilla Barker

374

aegis

kosovo

appeal

It was Easter weekend 1999. The crisis was in full throttle in Kosovo. Refugees were spilling over the borders into Macedonia and Albania. It was not clear what was happening in Kosovo. Were the troops of Milosevic 'merely' driving people out, or were more serious events occurring? Would the whole region be turned into a bloodbath? These were questions which were not sufficiently clear. With a track record which included Sarajevo and Srebrenica, it did not look good.

We telephoned the aid agencies to see if there was anything we could do. There was no answer. It was Good Friday. The answering machines suggested we call back on Tuesday.

That weekend we launched the first Aegis campaign, to raise awareness in our region about what was happening in Kosovo, and to engage local people in making their voices and concerns heard.

Over several weeks a concerted radio and television campaign was created, along with the establishment of a warehouse for material aid. Over 50 articulated lorry-loads of material and food aid were sent to the region. Hundreds of volunteers gave time to assist; hundreds of thousands of people were engaged in understanding that their voice does make a difference.

James Smith worked with the International Medical Corps in Albania as a doctor, assisting with repatriation. Members of the Aegis team worked with Caritas and other aid agencies in supporting refugees in Stenkovac, Macedonia, during and after the crisis.

aegis

"It is remarkable to me that the people of the East Midlands have achieved so much in a short time."

David Grubb, Executive Director, Children's Aid Direct

"Before I forget, I want you to have this."

A woman donating the coat she was wearing after emptying her car boot

Shirley Shaw
MBE, Kosovo Appeal Volunteer

It was Easter Saturday evening, 3rd April 1999, when a surprise call came from Stephen Smith, saying that he had become involved with the desperate situtaion in Kosovo. He was setting up a collection, packing and delivery point at his Wellsprings factory to send urgent supplies to the poor, homeless and desperate people in Kosovo.

Stephen asked me if I could help in any way, to collect medical supplies, blankets, clothes or toys etc. It was a daunting task as everyone seemed to be away for Easter weekend.

However, with a little help from my friends, I arranged a local collection point and with the marvellous generosity of organisations like the Rotary Clubs, we soon got several loads of essential items.

When I went over to Stephen's factory, it was absolutely incredible - it was like a film set. A huge undertaking, a hive of industry - Yasmin and Stephen's friends, colleagues and workers were all coordinated and were beavering away sorting and packing; and there was hardly time to talk! Then the

lorries were expertly packed and sent on their way for the long, torturous journey to Kosovo. This activity went on for days and days...

It was the most unique experience for us all.

Vernon Coaker
Member of Parliament

The Holocaust Centre, Beth Shalom seeks to remind us today of the continuing importance of the universal values of mutual respect and tolerance. Its strength, however, is not only to remind us of the past when these values were under vicious attack, but of the need for us to remain vigilant today. As always, democracy and tolerance for all, irrespective of race or religion, are values which need to be guarded by us all.

Kosovo, a part of Europe just two hours' flight from London, witnessed a brutal programme of ethnic cleansing just seven years ago by Serbs of ethnic Albanians. Men, women and children were slaughtered and driven out of their homes simply because of their ethnic background.

I saw it in Kosovo and it inspired me to speak out again in defence of freedom. For most, however, it is The Holocaust Centre which is the reminder and the inspiration, providing not only practical help but demanding that we all stand up for what is right. The victims of all genocides deserve no less and to those who suffered in Kosovo each individual can only say, "Never again".

The horrors displayed there are shouting at us all to act now.

aegis

Elizabeth Jaeschke de Buenrostro

San Diego, California

In May 1999, I went into Albania as a volunteer field coordinator working for International Medical Corps (IMC). Quite frankly, my job was to keep our people there, who were suffering from compassion fatigue, sane. Basically, I was an all-purpose problem-solver during a time when the war in Kosovo was concluding and repatriation was just beginning.

Ground zero was complete chaos. The general feeling was of a mad, restless anxiety with everything in ruins. One of the most horrific problems was that our volunteer doctors and nurses were overwhelmed by need and utterly without equipment. Imagine having to perform surgery literally using knives and forks. The emotional impact was powerful and devastating. On top of that, all of us were working round the clock, Russians, Romanians, the English, Irish, Arabs, Kurds, Africans, Americans and Albanians – we all had different ways of seeing the world, the conflict and handling the oppressive heat. Doctors were wrestling with war even in the operating rooms. Believe it or not, all that kept whatever order there was in the area were the mafias, slave-traders and gun-runners.

In the midst of this madness came Dr James Smith from England. He was like an angel, my bit of sanity. He was the first volunteer I'd met who not only wasn't afraid of the usual swarming of the local gypsy kids; he borrowed money to get them ice cream and utterly charmed them. That alone set him apart. So it wasn't any surprise to me that he came up with the idea of Aegis.

Alban, a refugee, told me once, "Having 'refugee' on your back is a heavy burden that he will carry for the rest of his life. As refugees, we have lost everything – our families, our homes, our dignity. And now you're one of us; forever it will be written on your back as well, because you've come into this chaos with us, into the mud, to help us rebuild." James learned that, too. And so that's what the awakening of Aegis is all about. It's not just responding to war in our hearts but with our actions. It's working hard to educate people so that it never occurs in the first place.

Certainly, it's difficult to read about genocide and its aftermath, but when you look into a brother's eyes and witness the terror, or listen to little children crying all through the night, it changes you forever. Certainly rebuilding work is crucial, but all the more powerful is creating the conditions in which it's unnecessary because the genocide was prevented.

This is the power of Aegis.

zimbabwe

"We should not mix sport and politics."

When the International Cricket Council and the English Cricket Board were reluctant to withdraw the planned World Cup cricket matches in Harare in 2003, it seemed that a very clear political statement was being made. The welfare, the well-being and the lives of many millions of people were less important than a sporting fixture.

In 1936, there was no genocide in Nazi Germany. There was a racist, ideologically driven, brutal regime, which had clearly spelled out its supremacist ideals and was acting upon them. Yet many countries convened in Berlin for the Olympic Games and continued their sporting fixtures. The rest of the world thought it was keeping sport and politics apart. The Nazis certainly did not.

When we say that our role is to apply what we have learned from history, it seems necessary to follow through in practice. The Aegis campaign team took the threat of exclusion seriously in Zimbabwe because to be a bystander to violence and atrocity is ultimately to be complicit in its outcomes.

379

aegis

"A year ago, I introduced Aegis to Elias Mudzuri, then MDC Mayor of Harare. At short notice, Aegis stepped in to contribute emergency funding to Mudzuri to enable him to visit New York and raise Zimbabwe's crisis with key figures there. Without the money, Mudzuri could not have made the journey. He was the first Zimbabwean politician to visit the UN for this purpose. A year on, the UN has an envoy on the ground in Zimbabwe, in some measure thanks to this first step."

David Banks, Coordinator for the All Party Parliamentary Group on Zimbabwe

30 January 2003: cross-party support in Parliament for Aegis' Zimbabwe campaign. Left to right: Dr James Smith, Director, Aegis Trust; Lord Laird of Artigarvan (Ulster Unionist); Lord Hoyle of Warrington (Labour); Rt Hon Michael Ancram MP QC, Shadow Foreign Secretary (Conservative); Michael Moore MP, Foreign Affairs spokesperson (Liberal Democrat).

balkans

Eight weeks before The Holocaust Centre
opened, in July 1995, a genocidal massacre
took place in Srebrenica, Bosnia Herzegovina.
Violent ethnic cleansing, murder, torture and
incarceration had been occurring on a
worrying scale for three years. Casualty
figures were rising daily.

Kemal Pervanic

Author of *The Killing Days: My Journey Through The Bosnian War*

Life is a creation that reaches beyond human bounds. It's a gift we should all celebrate, yet it is the case that only we humans violate this basic cornerstone of everything that is. And in this violation we are cruellest to each other.

The Holocaust Memorial Centre is a unique place in the British Isles where survivors of different genocides are regularly invited to remind a variety of audiences of human suffering, and of the fragility of the state we called peace.

As a survivor of the Bosnian genocide, the Centre regularly provides me with an opportunity to share my experiences of incarceration and brutality in two Serb-run concentration camps, Omarska and Manjaca, in north-western Bosnia. My experiences are nothing special. In the darkest hours of my incarceration I reminded myself of this fact. I predicted that one day when I was free I would witness the same brutality employed against others in another corner of this small world. Tragically, I was right.

Genocide isn't particular to societies weighed down by ancient hatreds or ethnic tensions. Genocide begins when blame is concentrated on a particular group for a society's misfortunes. And genocide proceeds when that blame is used to justify the progressive denial of human rights to these "outsiders amongst us". Is this familiar? Yes. It is familiar because the potential for genocide lies in any society, rich or poor, regardless of location, history, race or language. This is why the Centre, in creating a space for genocide survivors like myself to speak, allows us to alert audiences that genocide is perpetrated not by monsters but by ordinary people. Genocide thrives off ignorance. And the Centre has played a crucial role in challenging such ignorance. So that alongside "Never Again", will echo "Never Again Can We Claim Not To Know."

rwanda

Rwanda has long been close to our hearts and on our troubled conscience.

By April 1994 we were well on our way to completing The Holocaust Centre as a warning from history. We did not realise how imminently that warning should be heeded, this time not in Europe, not for Jews.

Broadcasts about bloodshed in Rwanda took weeks to catch our attention – it was portrayed as yet another African civil war. Without the familiar symbols of cattle trucks and barbed wire, we did not imagine that genocide was taking place. At the time we did not understand that genocide does not happen the same way twice.

A million people were murdered during three months, largely by machete, shooting, drowning in the river or by grenades thrown into crowded locked buildings. This time we could not pass judgement on another generation for failing to stop it. We watched genocide live on television.

Seven years later, we received a fax from the Rwandan Minister of Culture, François Ngarambe, asking us to work with him on a memorial and education exhibition. He later told us: "We need you here in Rwanda because genocide was not part of our history until recently. In Europe, however, you have much experience of this and have developed ways to remember and learn from it."

Survivors from Rwanda, the President of the Widows Association AVEGA, Ancilla Mukabaruga, and the head of the National Unity and Reconciliation Commission, Aloisea Inyumba, visited The Holocaust Centre and urged us to work with them to apply our experience here in Rwanda.

Their requests demanded humility on our part. What worked in Europe might not work in Africa. We were at the bottom of a steep learning curve again.

James M. Smith
Founder and Chief Executive

Eight hundred corpses on tables in a school. A faded red dress on a little girl; someone's daughter, still and nameless for seven years. United Nations ground sheets fluttered over the windows. In life they could not save the victims; in death, they offer shelter from the elements.

Nothing could have prepared me for schools like Murambi, or places like Nyange where a priest ordered his church to be bulldozed with his Tutsi congregants inside, or Nyanza where thousands were slaughtered when the United Nations troops with whom they had sheltered pulled out of Rwanda.

"People want to forget and if we do not remind everyone what happened, it may all happen again," said one survivor who guards Nyarama church, where bones remain, slowly rotting. Some feared that leaving human remains on church or school floors made the memory of the genocide banal, but others insisted it was necessary.

Only a small number of genocide victims were exposed to public view, but they make a powerful statement. As physical and human evidence of mass murder, they are an inescapable truth, invoking anger and grief in all of us who were not there. How, we may ask, do those who witnessed this cope with their memories and loss?

In November 2001, Yael Danieli, an eminent Israeli psychologist, persuaded me to attend the "Life after Death" conference she organised in Rwanda with the survivors' umbrella association *Ibuka*, which means "remember". I prepared a paper on memorials and education, then discarded it. It was void of meaning in the face of survivors whose wounded hearts were still wondering why they were chosen for total destruction and why the world merely watched while it happened. They did not need so-called experts to talk to them. They were the experts, in so far as anyone understood anything about that senseless barbarity.

The next two years we spent listening, talking and involving ourselves in the dilemmas and struggles around the memory of the genocide. "What do you need before you will give the remains of your relatives a dignified burial?" I asked. "Dignity," one survivor replied. "They were abandoned, raped and slaughtered. The only possible worse indignity will be if they are buried, then forgotten."

Stephen Smith recorded our observations in the short film *Secrets of a Thousand Hills*. One message was clear: survivors needed someone to listen to them and desperately wanted their story to be told. They felt sidelined, left to pick up the shreds of their hurting lives on their own.

Some people *did* care and that is why agencies such as the UK Department for International Development under Clare Short committed much aid and development to Rwanda, aiming to build the governance required to stabilise the country.

On the grand scale, survivors did not ask for much, but the important work of many foreign organisations was skewed against them. It started immediately when the aid agencies and journalists poured across the border to the refugee camps, feeding and filming those who fled Rwanda after the genocide, including many who were

complicit in murder. Human rights organisations, with the exception of African Rights, focussed more on defending the rights of perpetrators and less on the material and social loss of survivors.

"The Government has a fund for survivors," I was told by one European organisation. "We do not want the rest of the population to be jealous if we benefit the victims of genocide." Intellectual debates among expatriates revolved around who should be considered a victim, who a survivor. Meanwhile, in their presence, the widows who contracted AIDS after being raped, often by the men who killed their husbands, were not given medication until a decade later. By then, most had died a slow death, just as the rapists had predicted.

386

aegis

I was deeply concerned that if by the tenth anniversary of the genocide in 2004, the international community had made no effort to visibly show that we care about the genocide and its victims, many Rwandans would feel an insult had been added to great injury. If the sites of genocide were all decaying and neglected, it would also be hugely embarrassing for foreign dignitaries arriving in Rwanda to beat their breasts and cry "Never Again".

The Mayor of Kigali, Théoneste Mutsindashyaka, and the new Minister of Culture, Robert Bayigamba, visited The Holocaust Centre in the UK and we signed a memorandum of understanding between Aegis and the Kigali City Council, which led to the creation of the Kigali Memorial Centre. At the time it was known as 'Gisozi' after the district in the capital city which had became the burial site of the region's dead.

Around a quarter of a million victims are buried at the site, and people are still being exhumed from mass graves around Kigali City eleven years later and taken there for burial.

Why should we invest so much in memory of the genocide? Traumatic events like genocide impact on people's national identity. If left to its own devices or manipulated, collective memory can fester. It needs to be managed and shaped.

Second and third generation Holocaust survivors often inherited fear and mistrust. In a country where perpetrators and survivors must build their nation together, memory may polarise communities and lead to fragmentation and risk of further violence.

Failure to openly address the genocide then and to foster responsibility for the failure to prevent it may undermine long-term unity and reconciliation. All the investment in development may unravel a generation later. Democracy will not be trusted if the genocide and its lessons are swept under the carpet "for the sake of the future".

While important for survivors, memorials may also divide society by accusing the majority 'Hutus' of being untrustworthy killers. We expressed the danger of this collective blame to the first Minister of Culture we met, François Ngarambe. In the absence of a formal policy for the genocide sites and memorials, he gave us our only and somewhat profound brief: "In creating memorials, make sure they don't accuse the children of perpetrators, but rather, they must accuse the ideology that led to genocide." This remains the brief, a constant challenge to fulfil at these sites.

The memorials have significance for three main groups:

- For survivors: because their experiences need to be acknowledged. They provide a dignified memory for those who perished.

- For the international community: because we need reminding about our responsibility to protect those under threat of genocide.

- For children in Rwanda: because addressing the genocide and educating about individual responsibility promotes stable democratization. It is one key to developing communities free from fear and mistrust.

To build a nation after its very fabric and people have been torn apart is a daunting task. Our Rwandan colleagues, partners and friends have inspired us by their determination and strength in such adversity.

*"The completion of Kigali Memorial Centre and Murambi in 2004,
was not the end of our task, but the beginning of a struggle for truth
and justice that will last for generations."*

James M. Smith

James Smith, founder of Aegis, identified
in 2001 that developing a meaningful
memorial and education programme in
Rwanda was essential. He directed the
Aegis Rwanda projects which included the
establishment of the Kigali Memorial
Centre, the Murambi Memorial Centre and
now the *Gacaca* Audio-Visual
Documentation Programme.

François-Xavier Ngarambe
President of *Ibuka*, Rwanda

In 2004, on the eve of the tenth commemoration of the genocide of the Tutsi in 1994, I remember Stephen and James Smith stressing in all the meetings we had together that the Kigali memorial should "belong" to genocide survivors.

Indeed, from the early stage of designing the project, right up to its completion and inauguration, genocide survivors were consulted and informed. We were asked to give our opinion, our comments at all the important stages of evolution of the project.

On 7 April 2004, when the entire human community commemorated the genocide, the opening and most important ceremony in Rwanda was organised at the Kigali Memorial site. In the name of the rest of the population, 350 people (250 genocide survivors and 100 official representatives from all over the world), buried the remains of some victims, paid respect to all victims, and visited the newly opened and really impressive memorial.

Very recently, I realised how the memorial plays a key role in "life after death" when I was called by a very anxious genocide survivor, who said, "I know there is a plan to organise a visit to the memorial for some genocide perpetrators, who have supposedly 'confessed' their crimes. In the name of my fellow survivors, I beg you, please ask the management of the memorial to stop this very shocking initiative." I checked and found the information was correct. I then consulted

some genocide survivors, the leadership of *Ibuka* and Kigali City Council authorities. All agreed that the initiative was really misplaced and the visit should be cancelled, which was done immediately.

This incident gave me a chance to know exactly what the opinion of the survivors was about the memorial and Aegis. One of them, who knows the exact role of Aegis Trust and The Holocaust Centre, told me, "Thanks to our friends from the UK – God bless them – we have our private place that nobody can profane. We will never accept that genocide perpetrators come to dirty it. When we feel lonely and sad, when we have the feeling that things are falling apart around us, we go to Kigali Memorial Centre and we talk to our loved ones. We communicate with victims of all genocides, and this really gives us peace and comfort."

No one can express better than that widow (who lost all her family members) the gratitude of all genocide survivors to James, Stephen, Aegis and The Holocaust Centre, Beth Shalom's members and personnel. They contributed in a very significant manner to the efforts to preserve the memory of the genocide, rehabilitating the dignity of the victims and offering space for reflection and understanding genocide in order to prevent it from happening again.

In the name of all genocide survivors and their friends, let me simply say: *Thank you so much for your valuable present and God bless you all.*

James Smith is a highly perceptive yet deeply modest man, who is helping us all to put the essential building blocks in place to rebuild our nation and realise a vision of the future in which Rwanda will be free of the curse of ethnic hatred.

François Ngarambe, President, *Ibuka*

390

aegis

Théoneste Mutsindashyaka
Mayor, Kigali City Council

In Rwanda, only in 100 days in 1994, about one million Tutsi and some moderate Hutu were systematically slaughtered. That genocide prompted conditions in which there was only place for death, despair and mistrust among people rather than life, hope and trust. Aegis, the Government of Rwanda and the Kigali City Council worked together to give hope to the future of Rwandans and survivors in particular. It conceived, shaped and furnished the Gisozi Memorial Centre which provides a place for survivors to remember their lost loved ones in dignity, seeing some of them there at least in remains of bones.

Aegis also did work to make the Centre educational for old and especially new generations. The Centre also reflects on and reminds the international community that the genocide in Rwanda was preventable.

Aegis did a commendable job in a short time, but its lesson of genocide prevention will last forever.

Kigali Memorial Centre

"As a Rwandan I feel this is a very important step that Aegis Trust has supported - the documentation of survivors' horrors, their anguish and their hopes for the future, as well as the frustrations with life of the very people that lived through the genocide. It is not only important for this generation but for future generations to learn and avoid similar paths."

Rosemary Museminali,
Ambassador of Rwanda in the UK

Apollon Kabahizi
Country Manager, Aegis Rwanda

I was born on 18 April 1972 in Kigali, Rwanda. As a result of the conflict and genocidal ideology that had dominated Rwandan politics for many years, I journeyed the four corners of the globe. Finally, I came to discover The Holocaust Centre, Beth Shalom through the launch of Aegis. It has served both as a model and an inspiration to me. The Holocaust Centre and its sister organisation Aegis have brought untold benefit to the field of genocide remembrance in Rwanda – and through that, to the future of my country.

Some 60 years ago, the cry was "Never Again", but that failed miserably and more innocent victims – including my parents, brother and sister, friends and over 70 of my extended relatives – have paid the price once again. And I was not the only victim of that failure – thousands of orphans, widows and other people have to live with the consequences of this mess.

When I returned to Rwanda working for The Holocaust Centre, I was not looking for pity in any way. I had experienced what had happened eight years before and was rather looking for ways to build a better future in which my children – the future generation – could live free from fear of genocide.

The last four years working for Aegis have been an inspiration and an important step in the rebuilding the country needs in order to come to terms with the past. We cannot pretend the genocide of 1994 did not happen; it will continue to impact on the future of Rwanda. Its memory has the potential to divide and destabilise Rwandan society. Ignoring the genocide and survivors is equally unhelpful to the process of reconciliation and nation-building.

Through its work with Aegis and other partners in the creation of Kigali Memorial Centre and Murambi Genocide Prevention Centre, through projects working closely with survivors, educationalists, academics and policy makers, The Holocaust Centre has provided the blueprint and demonstrated how Rwandans can overcome the challenge facing the country. It shows how a society can be built free from the threat of dangerous divisive ideology in order to dissipate the threat of future tensions. In my view, genocide education in Rwanda, using the Centre as a model, must be delivered to every stratum of society and, critically, must be reflected in Rwandan Government policy.

A very discreet, highly perceptive, yet deeply modest place, The Holocaust Centre is of great value to me as a place of reflection, inspiration and a developing learning environment. The insights and experience I have gained there about creating memorials and managing projects in Rwanda have given me and the rest of the staff a level of understanding of the needs of survivors that I have rarely seen displayed by other organisations. In addition to this, the Centre has rapidly come to understand the nuances of Rwanda's challenges without attempting to push solutions that would be appropriate in Europe, but unworkable in Rwanda.

Through the Smith family and its staff, the Centre has demonstrated a remarkable ability, time and time again, to cut across Rwanda's complicated post-genocide politics, to remind us all of the vital cause for which we are working. It has proved essential to the process of channelling so many good intentions into effective practical action, and for the survivors, it brings inspiration and encouragement in the place of despair.

aegis

Beatha Uwazaninka-Smith
Survivor Team Member, Aegis

I used to wonder what would happen to us.

I never had the chance to bury my immediate family as most of them were thrown in the river and ended up in Lake Victoria. Those who were in the city, like my Uncle Gashugi and his family, were nowhere to be found after liberation. The last I saw them was on the first day of the genocide when I fled from Uncle's house while my cousins were being killed with machetes. Of eight of us, only I survived the next hundred days. I had no idea where the remains of their bodies ended up. Perhaps if they were found, they were taken and buried at Gisozi.

I tried not to be a survivor. During the day I pretended it was not on my mind. I learned Swahili and English to try and find a new identity, to escape the memory of those bad times. But at night the past always returns.

Up until ten years after the genocide took place in Rwanda in 1994, survivors – including myself – had no hope and nowhere we could say, "This is our place." Foreign researchers, students, tourists, visitors, journalists, aid agencies and politicians heard our stories and yet we never saw anything come of it. Perhaps in their own countries they took something from it. Maybe they used it to support aid and development. But we rarely saw anything. I thought it better that we survivors keep quiet for the benefit of the future. People did not like us to "keep on talking about our bones". People suggested it would get in the way of reconciliation. So we kept our nightmares to ourselves. That was the sacrifice we made.

I met James Smith in 2001 when he was setting up the Aegis office in Kigali. He was waiting for the proprietor of the office equipment shop next to the one where I was working. I asked him what office he was setting up. He told me about Aegis and the Holocaust Memorial he and his brother Stephen had created in England. When he told me about what he was doing in Rwanda, I was dismissive. I did not see how talking about the past could be helpful. I was wrong. I had no idea what precious and great things were going to be created in my lovely country, for the sake of my people who I had no chance to be with since the genocide. For what Aegis has done, I cannot find any way to explain how I feel. I am so grateful; there is no way I can repay.

I am now married to James and have seen the work of Aegis and The Holocaust Centre from the inside out. I have learned a great deal about the Holocaust and spent a lot of time with Holocaust survivors, hearing their stories and sharing personally with them. I now work at The Holocaust Centre, talking to visitors and showing them around. I sometimes tell my own story of survival in Rwanda, too.

In Rwanda, thanks to long hours and sleepless nights, the vision that James outlined to me outside the shop three years ago is now a reality. We now have a place where we can remember our loved ones and cry without shame or regret, and where we can feel that at least there is rest for some of our family and friends. I don't feel we need to keep our past deep inside us any more. Kigali Memorial Centre is a place that makes me proud today. We have the respect and confidence to be just who we are. We can now hope for the future as a new generation will learn from our misery. I hope people all around the world will learn too, and stop this happening to others.

Franco K. Kanimba
Country Coordinator, Aegis Rwanda

"This place... I know, is a place of both great pain and suffering but also a place of epiphany; because Rwandans have suffered a great deal, but it's very important that you and others... help people to remember, and to learn from that, and to understand how we need to try to stop genocide in the future."

Robert Zoellick, US Deputy Secretary of State

The history of Rwanda's post-independence period has shown that education failed to promote universal positive values such as justice, peace, human rights, democracy, respect of life, respect of the individual and public property, patriotism, dignity, moral integrity and honesty.

At different periods of our history, one can name killings that did happen: 1959, 1961, 1973, 1990-1994 and the apocalypse itself in April 1994. It appears that three generations were corrupted by the ideology of genocide, the first in 1959, the second in 1973 and the third in the early 90s. The consecration of this ideology united the older generation of 1959 and the younger generations to reach towards the "Final Solution", as we know that even old people were involved in the genocide. Persecution, torture and killing of Tutsis was considered an act of bravery, therefore erecting a culture of impunity in three generations. The failure of education is also shown by the fact that in schools and even at the National University of Rwanda, teachers killed their students.

The problems of Rwanda are wide, diverse and complex, requiring an equally diverse but integrated future leadership approach through the education of young people, which will finally help to prevent genocide happening again and allow reconciliation to take place.

The challenge facing Rwanda today is how to build a society free from the threat of such dangerous ideology. This needs to be approached on a number of levels by every member of Rwandan society right up to government policy. Today, young people must face their past, learn from its mistakes and turn towards the future.

It is a fact that memory ignored is more likely to lead to unintended outcomes. Therefore, it is essential that a historical memory is cultivated that promotes rather than undermines democratic values. However, the memory and the reason for it must be defined: what to remember and why? It is a starting-point for reconciliation; remorse at what extent, knowing who to reconcile with and why?

Rwanda is an unprecedented case with a particular context in which to implement an Educational Programme. This is because elsewhere young people are dealing with facts and events mainly faced by their parents in the past, and they are called upon to draw their future based on the "past". The "past" in the Rwandan context is to be understood differently. For many of them, it is not about their parents' experience in the past; it is about their "past" which is still "present" in their minds. And for others, it is about what they heard about a history that is theirs.

Memorials such as the Kigali Memorial Centre help to keep the memory alive. It tells the Rwandan story and the most important fact is that it is the Rwandan history told by Rwandans themselves. Through its exhibition, it challenges prejudice and discrimination, and provides lessons which can have a positive impact in the everyday life of Rwandans.

For many, it teaches about their own experiences in the past and enlightens their ability now to make choices, and for young people to make decisions in the near future based on their convictions and beliefs for the country. It is about rebuilding trust in humanity.

Memorials allow the open discussion of the legacy of the past in order to prevent negative consequences for future generations. Conversely, they enable us to learn together about the painful events of the past in a non-threatening environment. Rwandans, and especially children, can rebuild their trust in one another. It strengthens their desire to share a beautiful future, and their understanding about preventing the repeat of such an atrocity is increased. Our experience has shown us that the Memorial, principally the Kigali Memorial Centre, provokes talks, group discussions and brainstorming among pupils visiting the Centre.

The above shows that in the long run, memorials contribute towards generating collective reflection in building hope and trust, and therefore play a big role in reconciliation. It is a question of reconciling with our past and with ourselves, and reshaping our collective conscience.

Yves Kamuronsi

Genocide Survivor, Team Member, Aegis Rwanda

When Aegis started creating the Kigali Memorial Centre, my job was to scan genocide victims' pictures and any documents relating to the Rwandan genocide or history.

With the ongoing work, my first days were not easy all. It was very hard for me to believe that all the pictures I was scanning belonged to thousands of innocent people who were killed only because of who they were! It was not easy... not easy at all to believe that none of the people in those more than 1,000 pictures was alive.

In addition to those difficulties, it was also hard for some of the victim's family – brother, sister or any other family member – to give out the victim's picture to be scanned. They wouldn't give it because they didn't understand the purpose and the reason why we were asking for those pictures. However, some of those who did allow us to use the pictures would stand next to the scanner until the work was

done – because most of the time they only had one photo of the victim.

Working at Kigali Memorial Centre gives me a very deep perspective about the Rwandan genocide. Certainly, this is because I was too young to understand in more detail when it happened. But while scanning, especially some important documents like newspapers published before and during the genocide, I was able to understand. By then I could realise what bad times our parents went through. I could imagine what it was like before I came to work at the Kigali Memorial Centre.

In time, when the Kigali Memorial Centre opened, my scanning job became easier and I was happy to realise how important it is for a country to have a place that shows its history... especially for survivors. It was also good to realise that people could finally understand the importance of putting the picture of their beloved in the

Centre. On the other hand, I remember that survivors used to call me in the middle of night, asking me to scan a picture for them because they were coming for a burial the following day and wanted the victim's picture to be seen inside the Memorial when they visited after the burial ceremony.

Personally, Kigali Memorial Centre is part of my life as it contributes to my better understanding of events that occurred in the past. I also think that it's the key for a brighter future – knowing the past and preventing the future – for Rwandan society. It's a place that lets the international community and the entire world know that what happened should never happen again in this country, or anywhere else in the world.

The Kigali Memorial Centre is a place that I keep in my heart wherever I go.

Henriette Mutegwaraba

Genocide Survivor, Guide, Kigali Memorial Centre

I have worked as a guide at the Gisozi National Genocide Memorial site since it opened in 2004. All my family, except my sister and me, were killed in the genocide of 1994.

Most tourists who visit Rwanda come to see the gorillas, but many also visit our site. Quite a few become emotional when they see what the genocide meant for the people of Rwanda. Our national tragedy is a lot less well known than the Holocaust. The majority of our foreign visitors express surprise and shock at the numbers of people who were slain, the speed with which it happened and the very close relationships that often existed between murderers and victims.

We also receive many Rwandans. For them the experience is different. All of us are more or less aware of what happened and

when. So for my countrymen there is less of a journey of discovery, but perhaps a more intense emotional experience. Some even become traumatised as they relive the events of 1994. Some see for the first time how events they witnessed locally were repeated across the country. This, too, can be quite a shock.

For the guides working in this emotionally charged atmosphere, it is a very draining experience. We try and help those who have been affected by their visit to the Museum and inevitably we become affected by their sadness and our own memories.

Generally, visitors, both Rwandan and foreign, are extremely complimentary about how the origins and events of the genocide are portrayed. But they rarely leave us with a smile on their faces.

"Last month we had a very extraordinary meeting. The members of Parliament from the Great Lakes Regions and the Horn of Africa were here and we took them to Gisozi site, which to us was very educational and 'wrote' the genocide in pictures. Some people think ten years after is a long time, but when they visit the sites which have contributed to it, it brings the genocide into memory again; it makes it real and it makes it fresh."

Aloisea Inyumba, Senator, Rwandan Government

400

aegis

President Paul Kagame visiting the Kigali Memorial Centre prior to its opening in April 2004

Ardyn Halter

Artist

In 1994 I was in Rwanda with Aegis to install the two stained glass windows I was commissioned to design and make on the themes *Descent to Genocide* and *The Way Forward* for the National Genocide Memorial at Kigali Memorial Centre.

It is now early morning in Poznan and later today my father, Roman, my sister Aloma and I will drive with a film crew to his native village of Chodecz, where only four people out of the Jewish population of 800 survived the *Shoah*. Then we will continue the half-hour drive to Chelmno where my father's mother, half-sister, two of his first cousins and many more of his second cousins were murdered.

Before travelling to Rwanda in 2004, I did not think that being there, meeting survivors, or seeing killers recently released from prison, a mere ten years after the genocide was perpetrated, would affect the way I see or think about the *Shoah*. It has.

The humanism of my upbringing makes me want to believe that education about genocide, in the right way and at formative moments in a person's life, can change individuals and societies. I would like to believe that education can set a person on a different tangent, nudge him or her in a way that later in life he or she will react, think, respond differently from what might be seen as an inevitable, bestial course of behaviour. Would that such education might steer the individual against neutrality, indifference to the plight of others, steer them to the good against their worst instincts, make them conscious of tolerance, of our prejudices, alert us to our attitudes to strangers in our midst.

I am not sure that this is possible. But I fervently believe that there is no alternative than to try. The Holocaust Centre, Beth Shalom and Aegis have taken on this task. It is impossible to gauge the impact of their

work. Time alone will reveal this – or perhaps not – for the greatest success of the important task undertaken by the Smith family will be if their work, the messages conveyed are internalised year after year, generation by generation, if knowledge and understanding permeate societies and – *nothing* happens. That would be their greatest success.

Their energy and vision has already been communicated to and has affected hundreds of thousands of people in the UK, in Rwanda and further afield.

If a visitor to the Kigali Memorial Centre finds that seeing, or later remembering, the two stained glass windows, or even colours of part of one, helps him or her to think about the place, to focus their own experience, to consider what people are capable of doing to their fellow human beings, then my small part in the work will have been worthwhile.

Jon Silverman
Writer and Broadcaster

On a January day in 2004, I sat in a room in the uncompleted Genocide Memorial Centre at Gisozi, Kigali. There must have been nearly 100 Rwandese in the room. They were about to conduct a census – of the dead rather than the living. These "data collectors" listened to two young white men, Stephen and James Smith, inspire them with the importance of their mission, which was to record the names and family histories of all those who had been slaughtered. "If I take away your name, who are you?" asked Stephen.

The following day, Stephen drove me to Murambi, not too far from the Burundi border, where the Aegis Trust was striving to preserve the memory of a killing frenzy in which 40,000 people were killed in 48 hours. On this tranquil hilltop, I renewed my acquaintance with Emmanuel Mulangira,

whose wife and five children died there. I interviewed Emmanuel for the BBC. Even journalists can sometimes feel like voyeurs at sites of mass murder, but the work of the Smiths in Rwanda, cemented by James's marriage to Beatha, has imbued all those who come into contact with it with a sense of shared purpose. That is a rare legacy.

I have reported from Rwanda on three occasions since 2001. When I think of that country, I think not only of the bleached skulls at Murambi and the pink-shirted *genocidaires* in prison, but the impressive figure of Apollon Kabahizi, the Aegis Trust's in-country manager. A survivor, yes; a Tutsi, yes, but a man working to construct a new future from a rancid past. The Trust, too, looks to the future and not just to the past.

403

aegis

Fergal Keane
OBE, Writer and Broadcaster

As a witness to genocide, I am convinced that placing the narrative of suffering into the institutional memory of the world is vital. We need to know the facts, the stories of survivors, the failures and omissions of those who had the power to take action but failed, the responsibility of the killers at a local and national level. All of these things – these vital strands of the story of suffering – are what the Aegis Trust is helping to embed in our collective consciousness and in our individual consciences. For years they have patiently and with great sensitivity placed the memories of survivors before the world. Just as important, they have worked to make sure the Rwandan genocide is seen in the context of a world history already stained with the horror of ethnic violence. For this Aegis Trust deserves our warm thanks and support.

Gerald Caplan
Author of OAU Report, *Rwanda: The Preventable Genocide*

Rwanda was abandoned or betrayed by the world's actors before, during and for ten years after the genocide. Suddenly, in the year since the 10th anniversary, Rwanda is everywhere, iconic, a symbol of humankind at its most despicable. Darfur has become "another Rwanda", not least because it too is being abandoned and betrayed. At the macro-level, the film *Hotel Rwanda* is probably most responsible for Rwanda's penetration of mainstream culture. At the ground level, at every turn, in Rwanda itself as in the UK, Beth Shalom's Holocaust Centre has kept the torch of memory burning.

My personal debt to the Centre is considerable. I was invited, as a genocide neophyte, an outsider, to an intimate workshop with 55 internationally-known genocide experts – that's a good chunk of the world's total – and was welcomed into a world where I felt (probably perversely) at home. Those links have been indispensable to my own modest genocide prevention work ever since, and I cherish them.

In Rwanda, the 10th anniversary found its focus at Kigali Memorial Centre, the national memorial site built by the Centre. It's hard to imagine exactly how the commemoration would have unfolded in the absence of that structure, as it's hard now to imagine Kigali without it. It's the way both Rwandans and *muzungu* learn the harsh truths of Rwandan history over the past century, and – who knows? – maybe its very presence will lighten the burdens of reconciliation. Or maybe that's just the kind of optimism that the Centre generates, a necessary commodity as they and we turn to the next tragic crisis.

Ancilla Mukarubuga
Genocide Survivor

This short presentation shows why and how memorial sites contribute to education and reconciliation focussing on young people. It would not be so easy to understand if I, as a survivor myself, had not visited The Holocaust Centre in 2000, when I was President of *Avega*, The Rwanda genocide widows' association.

Why a memorial site?

I take my first thought from Holocaust Centre founder Stephen Smith, who said, *"Not everyone has the privilege of dignified death, but there is an obligation on those who remain to maintain a dignified place of memorial. Cemeteries should be places of respect and memory."*

Memorial sites are signs of respect and dignity to those who have been killed in the Holocaust or in genocide. They are a symbol of the atrocities done in different genocides, but also tools of education, healing and reconciliation, and somehow a way of setting up strategies for a better future for young people. For survivors who have the right to claim compensation and rehabilitation, psychosocial programmes, social justice, they are a symbol of recognition.

Memorial sites and young people

In the case of Rwanda, memorial sites are under the Ministry in charge of Youth, Culture and Sports; well positioned indeed! Genocide was the result of strong discriminatory programmes and involved mostly young, active people and a high proportion of the population. To correct and carry out good strategies, young people have the opportunity to understand genocide, its causes and consequences, as well as to propose prevention strategies.

Memorial sites and education

Memorial sites are a very rich school to learn and condemn the past, to understand the present and plan for the future. They are a space for young people to know the origins of a genocide, all the actors and other people directly or indirectly involved – religious people, politicians, teachers, lecturers, the role of the international community and the United Nations.

The Holocaust Centre, Beth Shalom, Kigali Memorial Centre, Murambi, Bisesero, Nyamata, Nyarubuye and so on, are signs that each genocide is specific and does not benefit anybody.

Memorial sites, healing and reconciliation

Reconciliation is a process in which healing comes first; it involves two sides. It comes from real mourning and a personal development where the victim accepts what is lost and decides to cope with the new life. Young people are empathetic; they are the ones who influence changes in behaviour, and then forgiveness and reconciliation are possible. They constitute a major force for social rehabilitation, civic and peace-building programmes.

Let us all contribute to the preservation of the memorial and learn how to prevent genocide for a safe world for future generations, a world where people do accept each other. Let us all make a real and true call for "Never Again".

Thank you!

"Every time I come to this place I meet my people. Therefore it is where we belong as well. For me I am home with my family."

Perpétue Rwihimba

Esther Mujawayo Keiner
Genocide Survivor, Rwanda

September 2005, ten years for The Holocaust Centre, Beth Shalom, eleven years after the genocide of the Tutsis in Rwanda.

When I survived the 1994 genocide without a machete, with all my three daughters, it was a miracle, a miracle which didn't occur for many of my friends within *Avega* who have lost not only their husbands, but also all their children, and most of the time were dying of AIDS, contracted during the rape they underwent during the genocide. I decided to break the silence and speak

wherever I can be heard, to let the world know that it should have prevented that genocide before it happened; it should have stopped it while happening, and it should not be forgotten in order for it not to happen again.

It was during such a campaign that I heard about The Holocaust Centre and Aegis, and the work they were doing in keeping memories in order to educate the world. When I visited the Centre, I dreamt that we could do something similar for Rwanda.

The dream became a reality. I visited Kigali Memorial Centre last year. The memory is there. No one can deny it any longer. The victims are remembered in dignity. The betrayal of the world is recognised.

Educating the generations to come is vital. Perhaps I can dream of a better world for my children? What Aegis is doing in Rwanda is just a piece of the whole work needing to be done in Rwanda, but it is a masterpiece. Thank you and congratulations.

murambi

At least 40,000 people were murdered in this school on a hilltop in Gikongoro province, south Rwanda. It is now the Murambi Genocide Memorial where Aegis Trust is working with Dr Celestin Kanimba, the director of the National Museum of Rwanda.

Funded by the Dutch, British and German Governments, it is one of seven genocide sites recognized to be of national significance by the Government of Rwanda, who have also earmarked Murambi as a regional Genocide Prevention Centre.

education

programme

The most important function of the genocide memorial sites in Rwanda is the education of young people. The future of Rwanda is in their hands and they need to be equipped to deal with the difficult task of rebuilding.

For the young people of Rwanda, dealing with genocide may be necessary, but it is not easy. Children of survivors, perpetrators and of those who returned from exile have somehow to learn together. Emotions are intense and while this should not be confused with trauma, the turmoil in their hearts and minds needs to be handled carefully.

Trauma also needs to be monitored in pupils, staff and survivors.

Aegis works with the National Curriculum Development Committee headed by John Rutayisire and with the Kigali Institute of Education to examine how best the genocide memorial centres and work of

Aegis can support and shape the national education objectives and be implemented nationally.

Many of the adults in Rwanda, particularly the majority population who were there at the time of genocide, feel that teaching and remembering about the genocide may accuse them of complicity and create collective guilt. They do not have a strong urge to face the past. The right space at the right time needs to be found for this kind of learning about sensitive issues.

As in The Holocaust Centre in the UK, creative educational work is a good medium both to reinforce the knowledge and understanding and to convey values and attitudes. In Rwanda there is a significant additional role that can be played by theatre and music. By expressing the lessons they are learning in music and dance, children perform to the wider community and their parents.

409

aegis

Mashiriki group performing at a school in Gikongoro as part of the Aegis outreach project from the Murambi genocide memorial, July 2005

Song written and sung by schoolchildren at the genocide site in Murambi

*No don't worry, No don't worry
It will never happen again we
swear
They started a long time ago
And divided us*

We could not believe it

*No don't worry, No don't worry
It will never happen again we
swear
When they realised that was
not enough
They said that your children
don't come from the same
womb
They come from somewhere
else
You will find out*

*No don't worry, No don't worry
It will never happen again we
swear.*

"From today's visit I have seen how the genocide started and those who started it.
They started by dividing society. As a lesson from that we must consider ourselves as one person, be it the Hutu, the Tutsi or the Twa. We are all the same people. There is no difference between us."

Schoolchild after visit to Kigali Memorial Centre

"I have learnt not to follow rumours.
That should stop divisionalism. That is what I have gained."

"People of my age should come and see what happened. They will see how bad it is. Therefore they will choose to do good."

"The message I can give them is to try to come and visit by themselves and see the history of Rwanda. They should come and see what took place during the genocide and get to know what can be learnt from that memorial site."

Schoolchildren after visit to Kigali Memorial Centre

Photograph from Children's Exhibition in Kigali Memorial Centre:

Francine Murenzi
Age: 12
Favourite sport - swimming
Favourite food - eggs and chips
Favourite drink - milk and tropical Fanta
Best friend - her elder sister, Claudette
Cause of death - hacked by machete

"I am thankful for the way you continually give yourself in order to help orphans and widows. And most of all, I wanted you to know that I am doing much better today thanks to the medication you gave me. The good you did to me has given me back hope that I can continue living, and even if I died today, I am confident that Patrick [my son] will be fine as long as God continues to protect you.

Thank you so much! It has been said that out of the overflow of the heart the mouth speaks; so is your heart shown by your deeds. May God bless you."

Anne-Marie, widow and HIV-positive rape victim of Rwanda's 1994 genocide

412

aegis

special
guests

The Kigali Memorial Centre is part of the protocol for official visits to Rwanda. It also plays a significant role in introducing special visitors to the country to the history and consequences of the genocide.

Recent visitors have included Laura Bush, Bill Clinton, Cherie Blair, Thabo Mbeki, The King of Swaziland, Laurent Gbagbo (President, Côte d'Ivoire), Guy Verhofstadt (Prime Minister, Belgium), Pierre Prosper (US Ambassador, War Crimes Issues), among others.

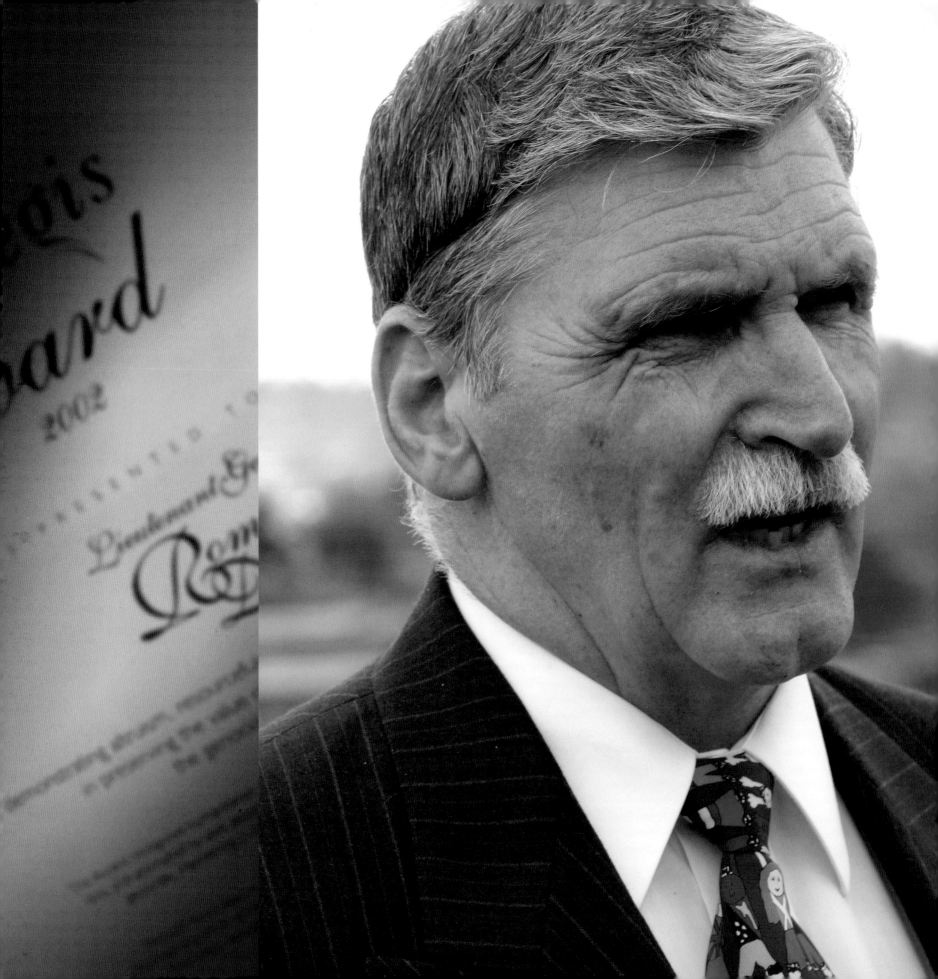

Aegis Award:
Acceptance Speech

Lt. Gen. Romeo A. Dallaire

UN Commander

I am humbled, because it is very difficult for a field commander to accept recognition for a mission that ultimately failed. The mission did not achieve its aim. I was not successful in convincing the international community, my superiors, as to the catastrophic scenario that was playing out before, nor was I ever able to convince them that once the genocide had commenced, that it was appropriate to take risks and to accept casualties in order to stymie a flood of destruction, slaughter and brutalisation of a people in its own country.

In less than 100 days over five million people were affected by this civil war and genocide, either displaced internally, made refugees, injured or killed. Over 300,000 children were killed in less than 100 days. Too many were killed by other children, brandishing weapons, absolutely totally indoctrinated by a doctrine of hate, of difference, of 'those not like us', and the risks of 'those not like us' continuing to live among us. That was strong enough to mobilise youths so impressionable, and already so disenfranchised from their country because of the over-population, to take up light weapons, small arms and machetes and with

a few drugs, maybe a few dollars or crate of beer provided daily, go through the country and day after day chop up adults, children, rip out of the womb children that still hadn't had the chance to be born.

I am, however, enormously grateful for this opportunity to keep the Rwandan genocide in the focus of the international community, that is now so wrapped up in a whole new generation of complex conflict.

The Rwandan genocide was not a blip in history. The Rwandan genocide and the reactions to it were an expression of the immaturity of the human race to be able to recognise that every human is human; that some are not more human than others; that every human deserves the support, help, opportunity over however many decades, and deserves those rights in order to progress and to advance as full-fledged members of humanity...

"The Aegis Trust which Dr James Smith operates with his brother is a rallying place for those wanting to go beyond the well trodden roads of conventional genocide prevention,... advancing the study and the practical resolution of conflicts."

Romeo Dallaire, UN Commander in Rwanda, 2004

Patrick Mercer, Romeo Dallaire and Peter Hain at the Aegis Award ceremony, January 2001

in our back yard

"I'm sorry to be here…"   Benjamin W. Vergara-Carvallo

rights and wrongs
human

Not all acts of human rights abuse are genocidal.

All genocides abuse human rights.

Understanding how we play a responsible role in encouraging human rights and combating human wrongs is an integral part of teaching about the Holocaust.

The Nazis began their genocidal campaign by a purposeful erosion of human rights. The introduction of race legislation, the imposition of banning decrees, forced expulsion from employment, financial sanctions and exclusion from society all undermined the rights of the Jews as individuals and as a community.

The result of these early abuses was the attempted emigration of thousands of Jews, trying to flee the intolerable circumstances of degradation, impending poverty, persecution and fear. 'The Jews' were the asylum-seekers of the 1930s. Their cold reception, in many cases their rejection, added one more layer of human indignity to the anguish they had already experienced.

Through the programmes at the Centre, and particularly through its commitment to Citizenship education, the issues facing vulnerable communities in Britain today are explored. It is a responsibility of the Centre to ensure that these values are upheld within our society.

419

in our back yard

David Luwum came to Britain as an asylum seeker from Uganda, fleeing Idi Amin's regime. He now lives and works in Nottingham.

refuge

In 2000 debate around so-called "bogus asylum-seekers" was rife. Tabloid newspapers were sweeping in their condemnation of government policy and the attitude toward asylum-seekers was one of degrading, isolating hostility.

421

in our back yard

The Holocaust Centre embarked upon a project to introduce young people to the issues faced by refugees and asylum-seekers. "Refuge", as the project was entitled, engaged ten schools in Nottinghamshire, each of which was teamed up with a refugee or asylum-seeker. The oldest refugee, Lisa Vincent, was 80 years old and had come with the *Kindertransports*. The youngest, Jetmir Geta, was 16 and had come from Kosovo.

In each case the refugee spent several months meeting with pupils, sharing testimony, sharing personal experiences, outings, home visits and social events. They spent time in small groups and time at The Holocaust Centre.

The result was an education pack, "Refuge", which contains refugee testimony, pupil responses, resources for classroom use and many hours of video materials.

"Refuge" has become a model peer-education programme and is now replicated in many regions of the country.

"Refuge was an interesting project. It was a good idea to do it so that everyone can understand the background of refugees and why they come to the UK."

Jetmir Geta, Refugee

Benjamin W. Vergara-Carvallo
Refugee

"I'm sorry to be here..."

I remember those were the first words I spoke at the launching of the Refuge Project. At the end of the meeting I was already committed to the project.

How valuable and gratifying it is for a refugee to meet the young people of the country, moreover in an environment that was to their liking. Being accustomed to requests for the "bloodiest bit" of life under human rights abusers, in my case Pinochet's dictatorship in Chile, I was pleasantly surprised to see that, once again, the children are really our teachers. Their interest and commitment pointed to the roots of the refugee's issue, and how knowledgeable they are, can be and became.

It is looking through those prisms that the value of The Holocaust Centre acquires its true value.

The interaction there of so many sections of society, projects and programme does produce the result that motivates me to be of any assistance I can to them, as I can contribute to my field of interest through and with them.

I believe that *"children are born to be happy."* Having had conversations with them, at the Centre and in schools, gives me the strength to continue holding that belief. I wish that they never see and suffer the pain of torture and exile.

It will be *one* and *all* of them who will sustain the respect of the dignity and the rights of every individual of every race, religion and colour in this country – my country of adoption – and the world.

Thank you for contributing to my desire, my dream and my vision.

422

in our back yard

"I'm really glad I've been involved in it. It has widened my outlook. I feel a closeness to Jetmir. I admire him greatly for what he has gone through. It has made the children realise it is a real thing... to actually meet someone. It is something that has gone to their hearts."

Jenny Bryant, Assistant Head,
Brunts Comprehensive School

> *"This carefully researched resource is a valuable support to teachers in this very important field."*

Tony Breslin, Chief Executive, Citizenship Foundation

423

in our back yard

> *"The Refuge Project films are excellent, very good to engage class interest and stimulate discussion. In the right school, it could be fantastic with all those cross-curricular links and clear outcomes."*

Ailish d'Arcy, Teacher,
West Bridgford Comprehensive School

Dr. Nadja Smailagic
Researcher, Research & Development Dept., Nottinghamshire Healthcare Trust

My connection with The Holocaust Centre, Beth Shalom began in 2001 and has developed through my involvement in the Refuge Project and further activities.

The proposal for the Refuge Project I had received, and discussion with my friends Cathy Lesurf and David Wilson who were currently working on that project, inspired me to discover more about it. I was invited to pay a visit to The Holocaust Centre to meet Marina, Stephen and James Smith, its founders. The friendly and respectful atmosphere enabled me to connect with the place and the people. I felt that I was acknowledged not only as a refugee from former Yugoslavia and a Bosnian survivor, but also, and most importantly, as a human being.

Through the experience of my daughter, Sanela, as a refugee school pupil in Great Britain, I understood how important it would be to change perceptions and raise awareness of issues related to the refugees and asylum-seekers amongst schoolchildren within British society. I considered the

opportunity of developing the resource for Citizenship by school pupils extremely valuable. Belief in change and positive outcomes of the project encouraged me to share my experience with young people.

I am a regular speaker at Refuge Project seminars for teachers, and occasionally I visit the schools and meet schoolchildren.

The Holocaust Centre and its team are honorary members of the Refugee & Asylum Seeker Managed Innovation Network, funded by the Research & Development Department, Nottinghamshire Healthcare Trust. There is a huge potential in working collaboratively on further research projects with respect to Refuge and educational awareness for local and regional schools.

Lucy Russell

Lecturer, Goldsmith's College, London

The Refuge Project pack, produced by the Aegis Trust, provides an alternative and more in-depth presentation of the experience of refugees. The pack challenges students' preconceptions through the personal stories of individual refugees and asylum-seekers. The resource is based on Nottinghamshire's Refuge Project, in which students at schools in the county had the opportunity to meet and learn about refugees and asylum-seekers. What began as a community and citizenship programme has resulted in a resource which can be used by teachers across the curriculum...

This is an approach that many history teachers use to teach about the Holocaust, the aim being to get beyond the statistics (and newspaper headlines) and show students that refugees are real people. Do we talk enough about empathy in history these days? This is the aim here: how would you feel? How would you cope? How would you like to be welcomed to Britain?... This is really useful material for history teachers intent on bringing citizenship into their subject.

Times Education Supplement, 1 October 2004

"When I met Simon I was really shocked… It just changes things for you. I was surprised how small-minded I was before – things that seem bad for me were really small in comparison to what people have to go through... Before you judge people, make sure you take time to sit and listen to them and find out what they are about."

Heather, age 17

Susanna Hrustic, a Gypsy refugee from Bosnia-Herzegovina, now living in Nottinghamshire

"My attitude has changed.
It's made me realise above all else
that when you see refugees, they
are not just faces on the TV or 6
o'clock news, or whatever.
They are people with real
problems and real issues and
they want to talk about them..."

Ian, age 15

"I think that if more people learn
what I have learnt, then there will
be less suffering in the world, less
war, people should understand
each other."

Michael, age 14

travellers gypsies and

There is a substantial Gypsy community in Nottinghamshire. There is misunderstanding, hostility and the perpetuation of stereotypes about Roma lifestyle, tradition and behaviour.

At The Holocaust Centre, we have a commitment to ensuring that the hostility is challenged and the ignorance informed at both a community and leadership level within our area.

During the Holocaust, the Roma and Sinti communities lost unknown numbers of their community. Their children were experimented upon in Auschwitz, large numbers were gassed and burned. Still today, not enough is known about Nazi policy toward Gypsy communities or the fate of many lost communities. We do know that the policy differed to that for the Jews. We also know it was genocide.

A recent conference about Gypsies and Travellers at the Centre illustrates the type of community work the Centre is involved in at a local level. We want to ensure that the issues of prejudice in our own back yard are engaged with clarity and good leadership.

427

in our back yard

Rodney Bickerstaffe
Former General Secretary of UNISON

We remember Roma victims of the Holocaust along with the Jews, homosexuals, the disabled and trade unionists, and the many others sent to their death, lest we forget! There is a real danger for the future if we forget some of the important lessons that should be learnt from the Holocaust.

Who would have thought we would have seen in this country a national newspaper run a campaign against Gypsies and Travellers called "Stamp on the Camps". Since the tabloid campaign on Travellers started, there has been an increase in racist incidents towards Travellers, according to the Commission for Racial Equality. This includes an arson attack against a Gypsy camp in Lanarkshire and evidence of Traveller children staying away from school because of the stress and fear of the current atmosphere.

The Roma and Travellers generally, I think, have been very, very badly treated over the centuries, not least in the 20th and 21st centuries.

Should people not have the right to their own plot of land on this huge and beautiful planet of ours? I think they should.

"Thank you for a wonderful and inspiring conference."

Martin Collins, Director of the Irish Traveller Movement in Britain

"I have an amazing sense of empowerment – feeling more able to positively work against the racism that many of the young people I am working with experience daily."

Lise Lavelle, CNXnotts

Trude Levi
Holocaust Survivor

As a result of the Holocaust, I became stateless. To be stateless means to be an asylum-seeker and regarded by many as a pariah. Therefore I have great sympathy with today's asylum-seekers. I know what it feels like to be unwelcome, not to have a work permit and be obliged to work illegally. It is necessary to eat and have a roof over one's head. I know what it feels like to be hungry and to feel really cold.

It took me 13 years to become a British citizen with full civil rights. I was 33 years old when I was permitted to vote for the first time, something that everyone born in a democratic country has the right to. I cherish my right to vote, to be permitted to take part, however slightly, in decisions about how the place where I have made my home should be run...

I do think it is important that people realise the harm done by generalisations: that we should not speak about the Germans, the Irish, the Gypsies, the English, or the Hottentots... I firmly believe that every so often we do need to put ourselves in the minorities' shoes and seriously consider how we would feel if we were being treated in the way we treat them. I hope that those who listen to me will think about what they have heard. About the fact that we were all born by accident in the culture, civilisation and religion, or with the colour we have, and that therefore we must learn about, appreciate and respect the cultures of others; that although we are all individuals, each of us is morally responsible for how we behave towards our fellow human beings.

ten years ahead

"What better place to reflect on the chaos and inhumanity in the world?"   Stephen Adutt

plans for the future

The Holocaust Centre is constrained by space.

In June 2005, half of the school visit requests were turned down because of lack of capacity. The Centre needs a new auditorium, a learning centre, a gallery on contemporary genocide, library and research facilities, in addition to parking and amenities.

Plans have been drawn up for the development of the Centre in the coming years.

This development is essential to reach the audiences who want to listen, to struggle and to engage in the challenge that the Centre presents.

It is essential to make the vision of preservation, protection and prevention a more likely reality.

433

ten years ahead

ten years ahead

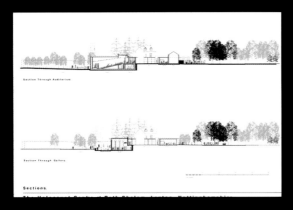

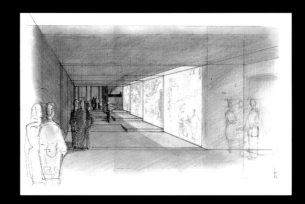

Stephen Adutt

Architect, Professor Emeritus, University of Brighton

Visitors to The Holocaust Centre, Beth Shalom are moved. All remark on the uniqueness which they experience. Why is this so? Perhaps because of a contrast. The realities of shattered worlds, of massive incomprehensible cruelty and barbarism 'out there' are brought back to us 'here' via lectures, exhibits and multimedia facilities, but are brought not to a museum in a city nor to any bustling urban scene, rather to an ordinary farmhouse lying in the most rural of English surroundings, in rolling farmland cultivated continuously for centuries, calm, steady, sturdy and safe. What better place to reflect on the chaos and inhumanity in the world? What better place to try to understand, to visualise better societies, to influence change for the better?

It is intended that a new Centre should respond to two challenges.

Place: How should we respect a very rural place, a ridge and gentle hillside of farmland with its particular local traditional building history? How can one build considerably more accommodation yet not overwhelm the scale of the existing? How do we ensure the existing remains special?

New Life: Balancing the new life with continuity of purpose. Will the accommodation needed for more purposeful functioning upset the unique character of The Holocaust Centre? How do we ensure growth, without losing character?

An architectural Feasibility Study has been carried out to test the challenges of Place and New Life within the Trust's wish to provide:

The enhancement of the existing Holocaust Exhibition, retained in its present location and with lift access;

A new gallery on themes of worldwide genocide and intolerance;

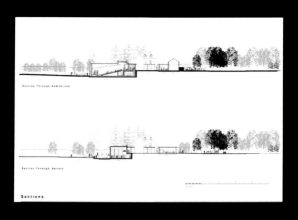

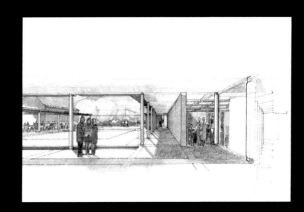

A new auditorium

A new cafeteria and kitchen serving up
to 150 people at one time;

A new entrance hall, with reception and
temporary exhibition space, all linked to
a bookshop and reading area;

A new administrative workspace;

The existing Memorial Hall again
becoming a quiet place for remembrance.

It is my belief that in the next ten years the
very special character of the Centre, its
serenity, its beauty, its dignity can be
preserved, and at the same time, a
stronger, larger, more functional space
developed to allow more people to
experience what hundreds of thousands of
visitors have experienced in the last ten
years.

ten years ahead

the place of peace

"I always find it a haven of peace..." Hana Eardley

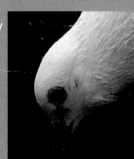

Gerald Jacobs
Assistant and Literary Editor of the *Jewish Chronicle*

For Jews, The Holocaust Centre, Beth Shalom affords an invaluable perspective. Away from the events it commemorates; away from the main centres of population; away, even, from Jewish stewardship, it has provided both balm and inspiration.

That it has been established by a Christian family – and grown in strength and reputation over its first decade – is itself a step towards its founders' desire for what is called in Hebrew, *tikkun*: healing.

Stephen Smith has described the motivation for the establishment of the Centre as a painful recognition of the responsibility of Christian Europe for antisemitism, for setting up the climate in which casual, bestial cruelty could flourish. "The rejection of Judaism, and of Jews, was necessary for Christianity's sense of identity," Stephen suggests. "Where," he and his brother James asked themselves, "was the European response to this European crime?"

Indeed, many Jews, and not just *Shoah* survivors, have a built-in wariness of Christians, and not just Nazis. Beth Shalom has addressed this openly and sensitively. It has become a place where barriers are removed, information imparted, education instilled.

The Centre has a healthy attitude to survivors, treating them as ordinary people whose extraordinary experiences can be conveyed to other ordinary people – especially the young – who, as a result, are likely to pause before stepping on the path to destruction. In its verdant setting, it offers an oasis of serenity, an atmosphere in which the Jew can realise that he or she should breathe freely alongside all other individuals of all other nations.

True *tikkun* has resonance. It goes deep. And Beth Shalom and Aegis tackle the roots of prejudice, the sources of ignorance, in order not merely to renounce hatred and excoriate genocide, but actively to seek their prevention in the future.

"An incredible amount has been achieved which seemed quite impossible ten short years ago. Holocaust awareness is now very much in the public domain, thanks largely to the efforts of the Centre. Good luck for the next ten years."

Thea and Heinz Skyte, Kindertransport Survivor and Refugee

"When I heard about the proposed Holocaust Centre in Laxton, I was deeply moved. I am so grateful for the tremendous work the Smith family has done to preserve the memory of the Holocaust."

Margret Grundmann, Holocaust Survivor

Aubrey Newman

**Emeritus Professor and Founding
Director of the Stanley Burton
Centre for Holocaust Studies,
University of Leicester; Teaching
Team, Holocaust Centre**

The strengths of The Holocaust Centre, Beth
Shalom are also potentially its weaknesses.

As survivors become fewer and fewer, who
will be left to bear witness and to lend their
personal credence and testimony fur future
generations?

Will books and videos be enough?

Will those continuing the work of the Centre
be able to ensure that testimonies at second
hand have the same impact that they had
originally?

This is the challenge.

*"The Holocaust Centre, Beth Shalom is
something very special to me. I call it
my second home and admire the work
of the Smith family. My support for
the Centre is very important to me.
Having no surviving relatives, I regard
the entire Smith family as part of my
family. After the first ten years, may
the Centre continue for many years to
come and through education help to
prevent another Holocaust."*

Bernard Grunberg, Holocaust Survivor

442

the place of peace

Gillian Walnes
Executive Director, The Anne Frank Trust UK

The Holocaust Centre, Beth Shalom has been linked to the Anne Frank work since the inception of the Centre in 1995.

In 1997, at the beginning of the national tour of the exhibition "Anne Frank – History for Today," The Holocaust Centre helped initiate the visit of the exhibit to the West Midlands town of Walsall and introduced us to Dr Deirdre Burke and her students, who took a major part in the event.

In October last year (2004), "A History for Today" was on show at Southwell Minster near Newark, just down the road from the Centre. Of course The Holocaust Centre's team, by then somewhat expanded, were very much involved in the event.

In the intervening years, my path has crossed many times with both Stephen and James Smith at various events and meetings of mutual interest. I would like to mention an aspect of working with Stephen and James that many of the contributors may overlook to mention when evaluating the remarkable achievements of the Smith family. And that is humour. We laugh together often.

Aegis and The Anne Frank Trust, of course, share the same aims and vision of a world rid of the curse of racial hatred. Stephen and James Smith seem to understand that the converse of evil is goodness, and the converse of misery and suffering is not the perhaps unattainable concept of happiness, but appreciating and enjoying the moment.

I suppose I could, and maybe should, cite the educational outcomes of our shared Holocaust education work through statistics and curriculum links, (somewhat like a report to funders). Statistics are not necessary. There's no question of The Holocaust Centre's tangible success in this arena and I salute you for this.

Please allow me the opportunity of saying thank you, Stephen and James – you are such a pleasure to be with. Thanks for the gossip and the fun over ten years.

Maybe that's also a lesson for humanity and a remembrance of the ordinariness of lives lost.

Hubert Locke

**Professor and Dean Emeritus,
the Graduate School of Public Affairs,
University of Washington**

For a decade, The Holocaust Centre, Beth Shalom has uniquely carried out two urgent tasks. It has been a place of commemoration – reminding all who come within its precincts, and countless others who are reached by its messages, of the obligation not to forget the calamity that befell the millions of Jews and others who perished at the hands of the Nazis. It has also been, with equal fervour, a place of conscience – dedicated to the proposition that such a calamity should never reoccur and that every effort must be made toward that end.

These twin tasks will continue to be of the utmost importance in the years ahead. As the voices of those who were victims of the Holocaust are stilled, their witness, preserved at places like The Holocaust Centre, will become even more compelling and momentous. And as the world

struggles to rid itself of the plague of genocide, the task of raising and nurturing generations of young people who are reminded of its horrors and intolerant of its persistence will continue to be an urgent necessity.

To watch the work of the Centre grow and evolve over the past decade, and to have an opportunity to have a small part in its efforts, has been, for me, a special privilege. I join with countless others in saluting what, by any estimate, is one of the outstanding institutions of our time.

Stephen Twigg

Director, Special Projects for the Aegis Trust, Former Minister of Education (2002/5)

When I lost my seat at the General Election in May, one of the first letters I received was from James Smith, asking if I wanted to do some work with The Holocaust Centre, Beth Shalom and the Aegis Trust.

I remember my first visit to the Centre as both a deeply moving experience and an inspiration. The Centre is the practical embodiment of Holocaust education in particular and Citizenship education more generally. The Centre's education programme has given a remarkable opportunity to thousands of secondary-age students over the past decade.

Recently I visited Rwanda and saw the work of the Aegis Trust there in remembering and learning from the genocide of 1994; the Nazi Holocaust features in that programme just as Rwanda features in Beth Shalom's. "Never again" is the slogan of today's Rwandan youth; the same powerful sentiment that echoed across Europe in 1945.

The voices of survivors are at the heart of the education programme. The interaction of survivors and visitors has perhaps more impact than anything else we do. Children are seldom afraid to ask direct questions and survivors' answers provide the sort of education that should be accessible to all.

The next major challenge comes with the construction of the Primary Learning Centre at Beth Shalom, extending education about the Holocaust to younger children. The plans are ambitious and timely; the new Centre will enhance the impact and profile of Beth Shalom.

We live in difficult and challenging times where the need for good education about the Holocaust, genocide and other mass atrocities is greater than ever. The work of the Aegis Trust and Beth Shalom is a beacon of light and hope.

"The beauty, peace and tranquillity is like a tonic when visiting Beth Shalom. Also, the empathy and understanding one receives from Stephen Smith and his family is greatly appreciated."

Trudy Murray, Kindertransport Survivor

the next
ten years

The vision of The Holocaust Centre and Aegis is to see a world where genocide is diminished, where no one is killed or even suffers discrimination because of who or what they are.

To fulfil this over the next ten years, we must continue to do much more of the effective work we already do.

But it is not nearly enough. We can be certain that over the next decade people will be marginalised, excluded, dehumanised and become scapegoats in societies all around the world, including our own.

We should understand that genocide is not extreme conflict; it is extreme exclusion, so we need to challenge exclusion and promote inclusion at all times.

A vulnerable group somewhere, without a voice, will soon be targeted for total destruction. We must be a voice for them.

But a voice is not enough – they must have protection, until they can be included properly in their own society again.

In summary we will strengthen Aegis to undertake:

- Protection of those at risk in a genocidal crisis, through campaigning and policy work;

- Prevention of genocide through tackling root causes and through education;

- Preservation of memory of genocide to inform and inspire the first two.

The next ten years must first secure the work of The Holocaust Centre and Aegis. Then we must embrace the challenges that human nature in the twenty-first century has given us.

The task is not a small one.

We set out to create a place that would be a Beth Shalom, *a place of peace, in memory of the victims of the Holocaust.*

We also hoped that in some small way the work of the Centre would encourage more people to think about what they are able to do to create a world that is a little less violent.

It remains our solemn duty to remember the victims of the Holocaust. Ten years on, it is only the beginning of the responsibility to remember and respect lives wasted on the altar of National Socialism's genocidal tirade against the Jews.

And ten years on, we feel we have failed. There has been yet more unrest, yet more violence, yet more exclusionary ideology, yet more genocide.

But, as this book has shown, we are not alone, because there are many of us committed to the cause, to work together, to share together.

In such a hopeless world.

That is our only hope.

449

the place of peace

"Congratulations to Marina, Eddie, Stephen and James on the 10th anniversary of their opening of Beth Shalom. This is a remarkable institution, providing a unique opportunity for teachers and their classes to learn about the Holocaust. We wish the Smith family a future as remarkable and as successful as the 10 years past."

Lili Stern-Pohlmann and Peter Janson-Smith

donors

with thanks...

"You realise that one person can make a difference." Sophie, age 14

452

donors

Many people contribute to the Centre in all sorts of ways.

We would particularly like to acknowledge the financial contribution of those individuals who have donated to us in our tenth year, either through the *Witness* book project or other ongoing aspects of our work in the UK and abroad.

Your support is sincerely appreciated.

Friends of Beth Shalom

Hilary and Cyril Dennis MBE
Graham Edwards
Flodrive Holdings Limited
Michael Gross
Morven and Michael Heller
The Lapid Trust
Joanna Millan
The Pears Foundation
Dame Simone Prendergast
The Sigrid Rausing Charitable Fund
Danny Rivlin
Leslie and Sheila Silver
Marcus and Gunilla Storch
Ann and David Susman

Witness Project Donors

Aimwell Charitable Trust
Mr and Mrs N. Adamson
Alfred and Isabel Bader
Beaverbrooks the Jewellers
Joanne Black and Nick Young
The Black Family
Sir Victor Blank
B'nai B'rith Leo Baeck (London)
The Boarer Family
Arnold Burton
Diane and Henry Charles
Lewis Chester of Pentagon Capital Management
Sir Trevor Chinn CVO
Richard and Denise Clements
Smader and David Cohen
Stanley Cohen Charitable Trust
The Community Security Trust
Sidney and Elizabeth Corob
Maurice and Susan Cresswell
Paul, Judy, Nicole and Jack Dewinter
Lloyd and Sarah Dorfman
Nathalie and Joe Dwek
Earls Court and Olympia Limited
Leonard Eppel CBE and Mrs Barbara Eppel
Joseph Esfandi
Mr and Mrs E. S. Fattal
Sheila and Stafford Fertleman
Martin Finegold
Dr and Mrs O. Fleming
Hedy and Felix Franks

Jackie and Michael Gee
Bernard Grunberg
Pinchas and Dorothy Gutter
The Harrington Charitable Trust
Gilad Hayeem
Alan and Sabine Howard
Brenda and Jane Justice
The Kagan Family
Michael and Ilse Katz Foundation
Sylvia and Brian Kerner
The Kirschel Foundation
The Kyte Charitable Trust
Chantelle Lee
Shamea Lee
Lindsay and David Levin
Lord Levy
Alicza and Steven Lewis
Ellen Litman MBE and Family
The Lowy Mitchell Foundation
Daniel Mendoza
The Mintz Family Foundation
Carolyn and Mark Mishon
Bob and Gerry Norton
Geoffrey and Sharon Ognall and Family
Maurice and Katy Ostro
Elizabeth and Daniel Peltz
The Phillips Family Charitable Trust
The Posen Foundation
Gregory Price and John Bower
The Prinold Family

453

donors

Rachel Charitable Trust

The Rapp Family Foundation

Adam and Jo Richardson

Julian Richer

Steve and Christine Robinson and Family

Stuart Roden

Joshua and Michelle Rowe

Mr and Mrs N. Rowley

S and U Investments

Mr and Mrs S Sharpe and Mr and Mrs M Robinson

Billy and Barbara Sharron

The Shear Family

Michael and Melanie Sherwood
Charitable Foundation

The Solomon Family Charitable Trust

The DYNA and FALA Weinstock Charitable Trust

Rosalyn and Nicholas Springer

Ann Susman Charitable Trust

The Wigoder Family Foundation

Mr and Mrs Ian Wilson

Poju Zabludowicz

Laura and Stephen Zimmerman

With additional thanks to

Pam Adamson

Stuart, Joy, Susanna and Jonathan Bower

Hannah Chapman

Louise Langford

John Chillag

Mr and Mrs Hirschfeld

Bernd Koschland

Lesley Lesiuk

Lottie Levy

Jenny Low

Craig, Joan, Hayley and Chris Mercer

Gerald and Christine Morgan

The Newell Family

Rudi Oppenheimer

Kevin and Diane Page

Alan and Sue Rockley and Family

Harold Rose

Shaare Hayim Ladies Guild Family

Mr and Mrs Frank D. Spiegel

Cyril Stein

Sternberg Charitable Trust

Edward and Jean Symmons and Family

Vi Tomlins

Mr and Mrs Underwood

Katheryn Wesley

Wendy and Alan Whitworth

Aegis International Supporters

Belgian Government

Casey Wasserman Foundation

Comic Relief

*Deutsche Gesellschaft für Technische
Zusammenarbeit*

Ivory Coast Government

Netherlands Government

Swedish International Development Agency

UK Department for International Development

William Jefferson Clinton Foundation

454

donors